Writers in Residence

Answer Key

Volume 1

Apprentice

by Debra Bell, PhD

Hannah Eagleson, PhD

Apologia Educational Ministries, Inc.

WRITERS IN RESIDENCE ANSWER KEY, VOLUME 1

Published by
Apologia Educational Ministries
1106 Meridian Plaza, Suite 220/340
Anderson, Indiana 46016
www.apologia.com

Manufactured in the USA
First Printing: October 2015

ISBN: 978-1-940110-71-4

Cover Design: Doug Powell
Book Design: Holly Grundon

Printed by Bang Printing, Brainerd, MN

Apologia is a trademark of Apologia Educational Ministries, Inc.,
and is registered in the U.S. Patent and Trademark Office.

When I Was Young in the Mountains by Cynthia Rylant
From WHEN I WAS YOUNG IN THE MOUNTAINS by Cynthia Rylant,
copyright © 1982 by Cynthia Rylant, text. Used by permission of Dutton Children's
Books, a division of Penguin Group (USA) LLC.

Boy: Tales of Childhood by Roald Dahl
From MORE ABOUT BOY: TALES OF CHILDHOOD © 2009 by Roald Dahl.
Reprinted by permission of Farrar, Straus, and Giroux, LLC. All Rights Reserved.
Permission to reprint in Canada secured from David Higham Literary Agency.

A Girl from Yamhill by Beverly Cleary
COPYRIGHT © 1988 BY BEVERLY CLEARY.
Used by permission of HarperCollins Publishers.

The Abracadabra Kid by Sid Fleischman
Copyright © 1996 by Sid Fleischman. Used with the permission of Greenwillow Books.
Used by permission of HarperCollins Publishers.

"All-Ball" by Mary Pope Osborne
From "All-Ball," copyright © 1996 by Mary Pope Osborne.
Originally appeared in *When I Was Your Age,* Volume 1 (Candlewick Press).
Used by permission of Brandt & Hochman Literary Agents, Inc. All rights reserved.

Contents

Note: No answer key is required for modules 21 and 22.

How to use This Answer Key

Writers in Residence
TAKES THE PAIN OUT OF
Teaching Kids to Write!

This Answer Key is your road map to using *Writers in Residence*, Volume 1. You will find all the tools you need to do the following:

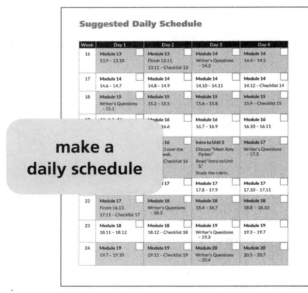

make a daily schedule

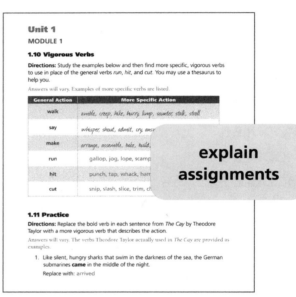

explain assignments

keep track of progress

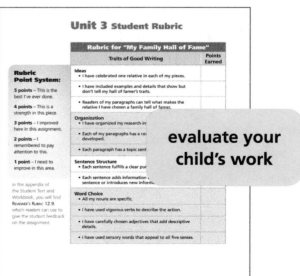

evaluate your child's work

Answers

This Answer Key contains answers or sample answers for the following student activities from the Student Text and Workbook:

- activities where one correct answer is required
- activities where answers may vary, but a set range of answers is acceptable
- activities where the student is asked to give examples

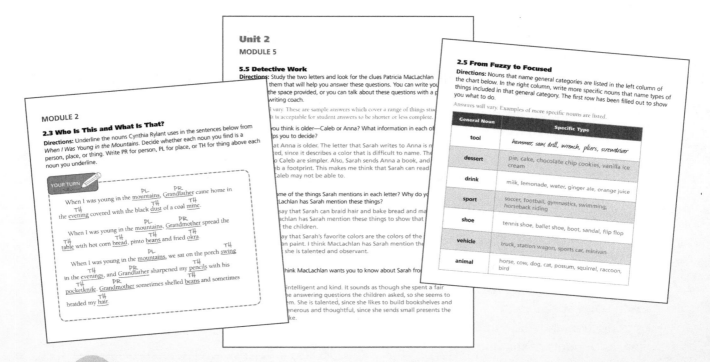

The Answer Key does not provide suggested answers for open-ended or creative writing assignments. In most of those instances, you will find a student sample in the Student Text and Workbook that you can use to guide your feedback and evaluation of the student's work.

Student samples are found in the Student Text and Workbook.

Writers in Residence
TAKES THE MYSTERY OUT OF EVALUATING
What Your Kids Write!

Rubrics

Use the rubric at the beginning of each unit in the Student Text and Workbook to direct your child's attention to the requirements of each writing assignment.

> A rubric is a special checklist for evaluating and grading writing or other projects.

Rubrics for both the student and readers are specifically designed to match each unit's writing assignment.

The student rubric for each unit appears in the introduction and again in the last module of the unit in the Student Text and Workbook. Student rubrics are reproduced for your reference on pages 84–93 of this Answer Key.

The rubric is organized using the six traits of good writing. See pages xxii and xl–xli of the Student Text and Workbook for more information about the six traits writing model.

Rubric Point System:

5 points – This is the best I've ever done.

4 points – This is a strength in this piece.

3 points – I improved here in this assignment.

2 points – I remembered to pay attention to this.

1 point – I need to improve in this area.

Rubric for "When I Was Young"	
Traits of Good Writing	**Points Earned**
Ideas • I wrote about just one place.	
• My memories are specific and vivid.	
Organization • My sentences are in chronological or topical order.	
• I like the way the order of my sentences makes pictures in my mind.	
• My readers like the way I have organized my sentences.	
Word Choice • All my nouns are as specific as they can be.	
• I have used vigorous verbs to describe the action.	
Conventions • I have capitalized all the proper nouns and the first word of each sentence.	
• I have remembered to put a period at the end of each sentence.	
• I have checked to make sure all my words are spelled correctly.	
Total	

Unit 1: 50 points possible

Bulleted points tell students the specific characteristics of each trait to include in the assignment.

Rubric for "The History of Me"

Traits of Good Writing	Points Earned
Ideas	
• I have chosen a title that creates interest.	4
• I have a repeated idea or theme in my life history.	3
• I have focused on events from my life that are surprising, humorous, or dramatic.	4
• I have included clues that give my readers a vivid sense of time and place.	3
• I have developed my cast of characters.	3
Organization	
• I have a beginning, middle, and end.	4
• My opening hooks my readers.	5
• I build suspense and create uncertainty.	3
• I develop one event in detail to build to a climax.	3
• In the end, I resolve the tension and answer all my readers' questions.	3
• I close the circle with my conclusion.	4
Sentence Structure	
• Each sentence fulfills a clear purpose in the paragraph.	4
• Each sentence adds information about the preceding sentence or introduces new information.	3
• I have used transitional words and phrases to connect my ideas.	3
• I have used prepositional phrases to build better sentences.	3
Word Choice	
• All my nouns are specific.	5
• I have used vigorous verbs to describe the action.	5
• I have carefully chosen adjectives that add descriptive details.	3
• I have used adverbs to connect my ideas.	3
• I have used adverbs to answer questions about the action.	3
Voice	
• I have added dialogue to important moments in my autobiography.	5
• I have included an internal monologue in several places to show my readers what I thought and felt.	3
• I have added emotion to my writing.	4
Conventions	
• I have followed the rules for capitalization carefully.	5
• I have punctuated the end of each sentence correctly.	5
• I have indented to show where a new paragraph begins.	5
• I have checked to make sure all my words are spelled correctly.	4
Total	**102**

Rubric Point System:

5 points – This is the best I've ever done.

4 points – This is a strength in this piece.

3 points – I improved here in this assignment.

2 points – I remembered to pay attention to this.

1 point – I need to improve in this area.

Scoring

The five-point rubric scoring system emphasizes "progress, not perfection" as the goal.

The student rubric helps students learn how to evaluate their own writing and track their progress. Students discuss the strengths and weaknesses of each piece with a parent, teacher, or writing coach before deciding how many points they should receive.

The rubrics for later units expand as new traits are introduced and previously taught traits and skills are reinforced and practiced.

A reviewer's version of each rubric is provided in the appendix of the Student Text and Workbook. Parents, teachers, and other readers can use this rubric to give the student feedback on each completed writing assignment. (Only the points earned on the student's rubric, however, are gridded in on the Apprentice Log.)

Students may grid in their total points on the Apprentice Log in the appendix of the Student Text and Workbook.

Checklists

Use the checklist at the end of each module in the Student Text and Workbook to direct your child's attention to every task that must be completed in the module.

Checklist for Module 4

Directions: When you have completed a task, make a ✔ in the "Done" column. Ask a parent, teacher, or writing coach to award you points for each task using the checklist point system. Grid in the points you have earned on the APPRENTICE LOG in the appendix.

Checklist Point System:

1–6 points may be awarded by a parent, teacher, or writing coach for each task completed. Here are the recommended guidelines:

6 – exemplary in quality *and* effort

5 – exemplary in either quality *or* effort

4 – acceptable in quality *and* effort

3 – acceptable in either quality *or* effort

2 – needs improvement in quality *and* effort

1 – incomplete

Tasks	Done ✔	Points Earned
4.3 Let's Start at the Very Beginning • Write what all the sentences have in common.		
4.4 Find the Subject • Circle the subject of each sentence.		
4.5 Find the Predicate • Underline the entire predicate of each sentence.		
• Double underline the simple predicate of each sentence.		
4.6 Is the Thought Complete? • Capitalize the first word and put a period at the end of each group of words that forms a complete sentence.		
4.7 Compound Subjects • Complete the sentences using the compound subjects provided.		
• Write two original sentences with compound subjects.		
4.8 Compound Predicates • Complete the sentences using the compound predicates provided.		
• Underline the complete predicate and mark each verb with a "v." above it.		
4.9 Review • Draw a line connecting each grammar term to its example.		
4.10 Mastery Test • Write sentences that fit the patterns requested.		

Student Copies

The checklist at the end of each module in the Student Text and Workbook helps students to stay on track and to complete all assignments.

Parent Copies

You will find the student checklists reproduced on pages 94–144 of this Answer Key. Use these checklists to track progress and evaluate student work.

Scoring System

After students complete each assignment in the module, a parent, teacher, or writing coach should use the six-point scoring system to award points based upon their effort and quality of work. Students may grid in the points they are awarded on the Apprentice Log in the appendix of the Student Text and Workbook.

Student Tasks

The checklist includes every task the student must complete in the module.

Guidelines for Evaluation

A guiding principle of the Writers in Residence series is "progress, not perfection." With this in mind, begin any evaluation of your child's work by considering his or her age and experience. Your feedback and the points you may award should always be based upon a comparison of *this* work with your child's prior work. Use the point systems for both the rubrics and checklists to set a standard for the student to reach toward.

Praise + Targeted Feedback = Progress

For maximum benefit, any evaluation of the student's work should be accompanied by targeted feedback. Targeted feedback is specific and concrete. For example, you might say, "The verb *rambled* in this sentence is very strong. I can picture the action precisely. Can you think of a verb to replace *said* in the next sentence that is just as precise?"

Praise—such as "This is excellent!" or "You've worked very hard, and I am so pleased"—is important, but this is not feedback. Praise is a source of encouragement—a gift we should give generously to our children. However, praise in the absence of targeted feedback doesn't help kids improve; it only helps them to keep putting forth effort. You will notice that the checklist point system is based upon *quality* and *effort*. Parents, teachers, and writing coaches help students reach both of these goals with the powerful combination of praise and targeted feedback—and that produces progress.

Talk about It, Talk about It, Talk about It

So how should you proceed when a student's answer is wrong or wide of the mark? Simply talk about it—a lot. Ask questions, draw the student out, and try to get to the bottom of his or her erroneous thinking or lack of appropriate effort. Use the assignments in WIR as discussion starters. If students know you will devote time to talk with *them* as you evaluate the quality and effort of their work, they will put more time into the task in the first place. Where parents, teachers, and writing coaches commit their time shows students what is most important. So distribute your time wisely.

Tell me more about why you chose this answer.

I got my idea from this page.

Unit 1

MODULE 1

1.10 Vigorous Verbs

Directions: Study the examples below and then find more specific, vigorous verbs to use in place of the general verbs *run*, *hit*, and *cut*. You may use a thesaurus to help you.

Answers will vary. Examples of more specific verbs are listed.

General Action	More Specific Action
walk	amble, creep, hike, hurry, limp, saunter, stalk, stroll
say	whisper, shout, admit, cry, answer, agree, stutter, scream
make	arrange, assemble, bake, build, create, invent, sew, shape
run	gallop, jog, lope, scamper, sprint, scuttle
hit	punch, tap, whack, hammer, cuff, slap
cut	snip, slash, slice, trim, chop

1.11 Practice

Directions: Replace the bold verb in each sentence from *The Cay* by Theodore Taylor with a more vigorous verb that describes the action. (The verbs that are bold here in the Answer Key are red in the Student Text and Workbook.)

Answers will vary. The verbs Theodore Taylor actually used in *The Cay* are provided as examples (following "Replace with").

1. Like silent, hungry sharks that swim in the darkness of the sea, the German submarines **came** in the middle of the night.

   Replace with: arrived

2. One German sub was even **seen** off Willemstad at dawn.

   Replace with: sighted

3. I **went** down to the old fort with Henrik van Boven, my Dutch friend who was also eleven.

   Replace with: stole away

4. I **had been** there many times with Henrik and other boys when we were a few years younger.

   Replace with: played

5. They once **attacked** the island, I knew, long ago.

   Replace with: stormed

6. They **sent** us away, telling us to go home.

   Replace with: chased

7. An army officer **got** out of his truck and told us all to leave the Queen Emma bridge.

   Replace with: climbed

8. He **said**, "Don't you know they could shoot a torpedo up here and kill you all?"

   Replace with: growled

9. We suddenly became frightened and **went** home to the Scharloo section where we lived.

   Replace with: ran

10. My mother got very upset. She **took** my shoulder and shook it.

    Replace with: grabbed

MODULE 2

2.3 Who Is This and What Is That?

Directions: Underline the nouns Cynthia Rylant uses in the sentences below from *When I Was Young in the Mountains*. Decide whether each noun you find is a person, place, or thing. Write PR for person, PL for place, or TH for thing above each noun you underline.

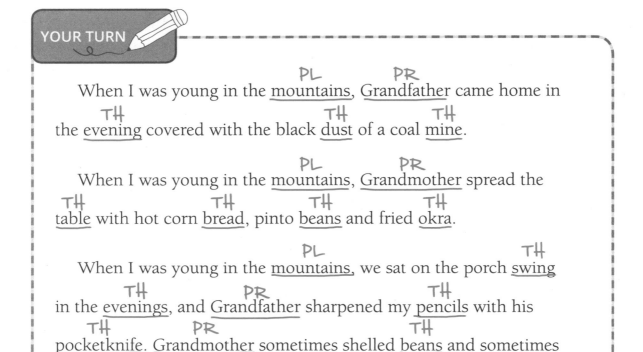

YOUR TURN

When I was young in the mountains [PL], Grandfather [PR] came home in the evening [TH] covered with the black dust [TH] of a coal mine [TH].

When I was young in the mountains [PL], Grandmother [PR] spread the table [TH] with hot corn bread [TH], pinto beans [TH] and fried okra [TH].

When I was young in the mountains [PL], we sat on the porch swing [TH] in the evenings [TH], and Grandfather [PR] sharpened my pencils [TH] with his pocketknife [TH]. Grandmother [PR] sometimes shelled beans [TH] and sometimes braided my hair [TH].

Note: In line 1, the word *home* functions as an adverb. If a student marks this as a noun, use the opportunity to explain that many words can function as more than one part of speech. See page 303 in the Student Text and Workbook.

2.5 From Fuzzy to Focused

Directions: Nouns that name general categories are listed in the left column of the chart below. In the right column, write more specific nouns that name types of things included in that general category. The first row has been filled out to show you what to do.

Answers will vary. Examples of more specific nouns are listed.

General Noun	Specific Type
tool	hammer, saw, drill, wrench, pliers, screwdriver
dessert	pie, cake, chocolate chip cookies, vanilla ice cream
drink	milk, lemonade, water, ginger ale, orange juice
sport	soccer, football, gymnastics, swimming, horseback riding
shoe	tennis shoe, ballet shoe, boot, sandal, flip flop
vehicle	truck, station wagon, sports car, minivan
animal	horse, cow, dog, cat, possum, squirrel, raccoon, bird

2.11 Practice

Directions: Draw three lines under the first letter of each word in the following paragraph that should be capitalized. (The first sentence has been done for you.) Look for proper nouns and common nouns used as personal names. Look for the word *my* to help you recognize the difference between a common noun and a common noun being used as a personal name.

YOUR TURN

The chronicles of narnia is a series of children's books by c. s. lewis. My favorite copies are illustrated by pauline baynes. My father first read these books to me at bedtime before I could read. Sometimes my sisters and I even went to bed early just so dad would start reading the next chapter sooner. For hours katie, kristen, and I pretended to be lucy, susan, and peter fighting against aslan's foes. We made plato, our dog, play mr. tumnus, but he often wandered away right when the battle was getting started. Sometimes mom let us finish our schoolwork early just so we could return to playing "narnia." My mother said she was glad we would rather use our imaginations than watch television.

Directions: Write two sentences that include both common nouns and proper nouns.

Answers will vary. Sample sentences are provided.

YOUR TURN

George Washington rode horses named Blueskin and Nelson during the war. After the war ended, the horses lived out the rest of their days in the stables of Mount Vernon.

MODULE 3

3.4 Time after Time

Directions: Practice putting events in chronological order with this activity. Read the story. Then number the parts of the story with numbers 1–7 in the order in which they occurred. Number 1 should be the first thing that happens in the story, and number 7 should be the last thing.

Numbers	Parts of the Story
7	went to work
4	walked dog
1	alarm buzzed
3	dog barked
5	began to rain
6	picked up umbrella
2	woke up

3.12 Unit Review

Directions: You may write out your answers to the questions below in the space provided, or you can talk about these questions with a parent, teacher, or writing coach. You can also look over all the information in the modules you have completed to help you decide on your answers. Use the unit review to help you master the writing tips and tricks you learned about in these modules.

1. Name one place you have learned about where writers can get ideas for their stories. (1 point)
    Writers get ideas from their childhood memories.

2. Name the kind of verbs writers use to make their sentences specific and vivid. (1 point)
    Writers make their sentences specific and vivid by using vigorous verbs.

3. Give three examples of verbs you can use to replace the underlined verb in the following sentence to make the sentence more specific and vivid:
    Callum <u>hit</u> the ball. (3 points)
    Answers will vary. Examples are provided below.
    whacked, bunted, slugged

4. In this unit you learned about types of nouns. Give an example of each type below. (4 points)
    Answers will vary. Examples are provided below.
    common: cat, raincoat, calculator, policeman
    proper: Queen Elizabeth II, Jenny, Mr. Davis, Big Bird
    general: animal, plant, planet
    specific: golden retriever, geranium, Jupiter

5. Name the type of noun that must be capitalized. Why? (2 points)
    Proper nouns must be capitalized.
    Proper nouns must be capitalized because they name a particular person, place, or thing.

6. List ten nouns that should be capitalized. (10 points)

    Answers will vary. In particular, students learned in 2.9 that personal names are capitalized.

    Examples: Darth Vader, President Washington, Mark Twain, Lucy, Rover, Mom, Dad

7. Review the vocabulary words you learned in **1.12 WALK THIS WAY.** Write four favorite action verbs that you can use instead of *walk*. (4 points)

    Answers will vary, but should include any four from this list:
    amble, creep, dodge, hobble, meander, prance, saunter, stagger, stalk, stride, scurry, or trudge

8. Name one way writers can organize their ideas to create a clear picture in readers' minds. (1 point)

    Students should name either chronological order or topical order.

9. What tips and tricks did you learn in this unit that you want to remember to use in the future? (3 points)

    Answers will vary.

10. What is your favorite memory sentence you crafted in this unit? Why is it your favorite? (1 point)

    Answers will vary.

MODULE 4

4.4 Find the Subject

Directions: Circle the simple subject of each sentence below. To find the subject of a sentence, ask yourself, "Who or what is this sentence about?" (Sentences are from *The Best Christmas Pageant Ever* by Barbara Robinson.)

YOUR TURN

1. The (Herdmans) were absolutely the worst kids in the history of the world. (page 1)

2. (They) lived over a garage at the bottom of Sproul Hill. (page 4)

3. (Imogene) shrugged. (page 9)

4. (Mother) didn't expect to have anything to do with the Christmas pageant. (page 15)

5. Our Christmas (pageant) isn't what you'd call four-star entertainment. (page 17)

6. (Charlie) is a shepherd this year. (page 15)

7. (Mother) just stared at them. (page 31)

8. (Leroy) was Melchior. (page 55)

9. The first pageant (rehearsal) was about as much fun as a three-hour ride on the school bus. (page 38)

10. (I) was amazed. (page 49)

4.5 Find the Predicate

Directions: Underline the complete predicate of each sentence on the next page. To find the predicate of a sentence, first find the subject by asking, "Who or what is this sentence about?" Then ask, "What am I being told about the subject?" Underline your answer to the second question. Then double-underline the simple predicate (the main verb). The first one has been completed for you.

YOUR TURN

1. The Herdmans <u>were absolutely the worst kids in the history of the world</u>.

2. They <u>lived over a garage at the bottom of Sproul Hill</u>.

3. Imogene <u>shrugged</u>.

4. Reverend Hopkins <u>looked unhappy</u>. (page 69)

5. Mrs. Armstrong <u>called two more times that week</u>.

6. Charlie <u>is a shepherd this year</u>.

7. Mother <u>just stared at them</u>.

8. Leroy <u>was Melchior</u>.

9. The first pageant rehearsal <u>was about as much fun as a three-hour ride on the school bus</u>.

10. Ralph <u>whacked Imogene on the back</u>. (page 63)

4.6 Is the Thought Complete?

Directions: Decide if each group of words is a complete sentence. If so, capitalize the first word and put a period at the end.

YOUR TURN

1. the high school football game

2. $\overset{A}{a}$ calico cat hid in the bushes.

3. over the river and through the woods

4. $\overset{T}{the}$ angels appeared before the shepherds.

5. raced down the hill

4.7 Compound Subjects

Directions: Create complete sentences using the compound subjects provided.

Answers will vary. Examples are provided below.

1. Hansel and Gretel went home.
2. The drum corps, marching band, and drill team practiced every day.
3. A piece of string and a paper bag can save your life.
4. The owl and the pussycat went sailing.
5. Grandfather's car and truck are both red.

4.8 Compound Predicates

Directions: Complete the sentences on the next page by choosing a subject for each. Use the compound predicate provided. Also, underline the complete predicate and mark each verb with a "v." above it. Remember to capitalize the first word of the sentence and put a period at the end of it.

Answers will vary. Examples are provided below.

1. make stir-fry or bake lasagna

   My grandma will **make** stir-fry or **bake** lasagna for dinner.

2. caught crawfish and fished for trout

   My sister **caught** crawfish and **fished** for trout.

3. can gather firewood or help to pitch the tent

   My brother can **gather** firewood or **help** to pitch the tent.

4. hit the wall and rolled down the driveway

   The Frisbee **hit** the wall and **rolled** down the driveway.

5. waltzed across the stage and bowed grandly to the audience

   The conductor **waltzed** across the stage and **bowed** grandly to the audience.

4.9 Review

Directions: Draw a line connecting each grammar term to the underlined example that it names.

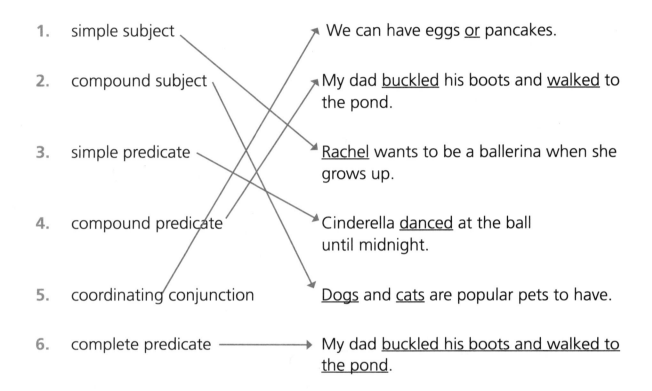

1. simple subject   We can have eggs <u>or</u> pancakes.

2. compound subject   My dad <u>buckled</u> his boots and <u>walked</u> to the pond.

3. simple predicate   <u>Rachel</u> wants to be a ballerina when she grows up.

4. compound predicate   Cinderella <u>danced</u> at the ball until midnight.

5. coordinating conjunction   <u>Dogs</u> and <u>cats</u> are popular pets to have.

6. complete predicate   My dad <u>buckled his boots and walked to the pond</u>.

4.10 Mastery Test

Directions: Create sentences that follow the patterns requested. Make each sentence about you with a superpower or about your archenemy.

Answers will vary. Examples are provided below.

1. Write a sentence with a simple subject and a simple predicate.
    Pirate Jack shrugged.

2. Write a sentence with a compound subject and a single verb in the predicate.
    Pirate Jack and his parrot shrugged.

3. Write a sentence with a single noun in the subject and a compound predicate.
    Pirate Jack sighed and shrugged.

4. Write a sentence with a compound subject and a compound predicate.
    Captain Amazing and Pirate Jack turned and charged.

Unit 2

MODULE 5

5.5 Detective Work

Directions: Study the two letters and look for the clues Patricia MacLachlan included in them that will help you answer these questions. You can write your answers in the space provided, or you can talk about these questions with a parent, teacher, or writing coach.

Answers will vary. These are sample answers which cover a range of things students may notice. It is acceptable for student answers to be shorter or less complete.

1. Who do you think is older—Caleb or Anna? What information in each of the letters helps you to decide?

   I think that Anna is older. The letter that Sarah writes to Anna is more complicated, since it describes a color that is difficult to name. The answers to Caleb are simpler. Also, Sarah sends Anna a book, and she sends Caleb a footprint. This makes me think that Sarah can read already and that Caleb may not be able to.

2. What are some of the things Sarah mentions in each letter? Why do you think Patricia MacLachlan has Sarah mention these things?

   The letters say that Sarah can braid hair and bake bread and make stew. I think MacLachlan has Sarah mention these things to show that Sarah can take care of the children.

   The letters say that Sarah's favorite colors are the colors of the sea and that Sarah can paint. I think MacLachlan has Sarah mention these things to show that she is talented and observant.

3. What do you think MacLachlan wants you to know about Sarah from reading her letters?

   Sarah sounds intelligent and kind. It sounds as though she spent a fair amount of time answering questions the children asked, so she seems to care about them. She is talented, since she likes to build bookshelves and paint. She is generous and thoughtful, since she sends small presents the children may like.

4. Why do you think MacLachlan decided to have Sarah write different letters to each child?

This shows that Sarah is interested in each child as an individual and pays attention to each one in ways that are best for that child. It also allows MacLachlan to show different aspects of Sarah's character, which might have been harder in just one letter.

5. From the clues in each letter, how would you describe Sarah? What kind of personality do you think she might have?

I think Sarah is lively and intelligent, as well as kind and thoughtful.

5.7 Vocabulary: I Am What I Am

Directions: Look up the definition for each character trait listed below. Write the definition on the lines provided. Then give an example of a person you know or a character from a book, a movie, or the Bible who exhibits this trait. The first one has been done for you.

Answers will vary. Sample answers are provided.

1. **attentive:** (adj.) paying close attention to; observant; thoughtful of others
   Example: The prophet Samuel was attentive to God's commands.

2. **bold:** (adj.) brave or courageous
   Example: My brother is a bold lifeguard who dove into the water to rescue a drowning girl.

3. **determined:** (adj.) firm in one's purpose, decided
   Example: Gandalf was determined in his refusal to take the one Ring.

4. **finicky:** (adj.) fussy or hard to please
   Example: My baby sister is a finicky eater.

5. **glamorous:** (adj.) flashy, dazzling, exciting
   Example: In the book *Jacob Have I Loved*, Sara Louise is jealous of her glamorous twin, Caroline.

6. **impatient:** (adj.) restless, unwilling to wait, easily annoyed
   Example: Sarah was impatient about God's promise to her.

7. **industrious:** (adj.) hardworking, productive, diligent
   Example: My dad is a very industrious businessman.

8. **inventive:** (adj.) imaginative, good at coming up with ideas or making new things, clever
   Example: Sherlock Holmes is an inventive detective who always solves the crime in a new and surprising way.

9. **prim:** (adj.) stiff and proper
   Example: Miss Beadle is the prim schoolmarm in Laura Ingalls Wilder's books about life in Walnut Grove, Minnesota.

10. **sincere:** (adj.) honest, coming from a person's genuine feelings
    Example: John was a sincere and beloved disciple of Christ.

11. **sly:** (adj.) mischievous; clever in a tricky and sometimes dishonest way
    Example Gollum is a sly character in The Lord of the Rings.

12. **timid:** (adj.) shy or afraid
    Example: The Cowardly Lion in *The Wizard of Oz* is timid at the beginning of the story, but by the end he is courageous.

5.8 Show but Don't Tell

Directions: Study these sentences from the letters that Patricia MacLachlan has her character, Sarah, write. Then decide which character traits on the chart in **5.6** Adjectives Describe Characters best describe what Sarah might be like from the clues in each sentence.

Answers may vary. Sample answers are provided.

1. Yes, I can braid hair and I can make stew and bake bread, though I prefer to build bookshelves and paint.
   Character trait: able, active

2. I am enclosing a book of sea birds so you will see what William and I see every day.
   Character trait: generous, intelligent, thoughtful, studious, sweet

3. My cat's name is Seal because she is gray like the seals that swim offshore in Maine.
   Character trait: inventive, attentive

4. Yes, I can keep a fire going at night.
   Character trait: able, industrious, dependable

5. I do not know if I snore. Seal has never told me.
   Character trait: witty

5.10 Here We Go on a Noun Hunt . . . Again!

Directions: Go back to the letters in **5.4 EXPERT MODEL**.

- Circle every person, place, and thing Sarah mentions in her letters.
  See pages 27 and 28 of this Answer Key.

- Think of some of the people, places, and things where you live that you might want to write about in your letters to your future family.

- Use the chart below to list some of the nouns you find in Sarah's letters and some of the nouns in your life.
  The chart below includes sample nouns from Sarah's letters. Students may choose different ones.

- Remember, writers use specific nouns to make their stories vivid and interesting. Be as specific about the people, places, and things you care about as Sarah has been in her letters.

People, Places, and Things			
	Nouns: People	Nouns: Places	Nouns: Things
Sarah's letters	Caleb, William, Sarah	Maine, Sarah's house, the children's house	the sea, bookshelves, fire
My life	Answers will vary.	Answers will vary.	Answers will vary.

EXPERT MODEL

Dear (Anna),

Yes, I can braid (hair) and I can make (stew) and bake (bread), though I prefer to build (bookshelves) and paint.

My favorite (colors) are the (colors) of the (sea), blue and gray and green, depending on the (weather). My (brother) (William) is a (fisherman), and he tells me that when he is in the (middle) of a fog-bound (sea) the (water) is a (color) for which there is no (name). He catches (flounder) and sea (bass) and (bluefish). Sometimes he sees (whales). And (birds), too, of course. I am enclosing a (book) of sea (birds) so you will see what (William) and I see every (day).

Very truly yours,

(Sarah Elisabeth Wheaton)

Dear Caleb,

My cat's name is Seal because she is gray like the seals that swim offshore in Maine. She is glad that Lottie and Nick send their greetings. She likes dogs most of the time. She says their footprints are much larger than hers (which she is enclosing in return).

Your house sounds lovely, even though it is far out in the country with no close neighbors. My house is tall and the shingles are gray because of the salt from the sea. There are roses nearby.

Yes, I do like small rooms sometimes. Yes, I can keep a fire going at night. I do not know if I snore. Seal has never told me.

Very truly yours,

Sarah Elisabeth

MODULE 6

6.5 Capitalize Place Names

Directions: Circle all the capital letters in Tom's letter to Huck in **6.4 PARTS OF A PERSONAL LETTER**. Why do you think these words are capitalized? Write down three possible rules for capitalizing words that may apply.

235 Church Street

St. Petersburg, MO

October 5, 1876

Dear Huck,

I know I've got it easy in some ways, compared to you—home-cooked dinners and things of that sort. But I'm tired of all that, Huck. I'm tired of Aunt Polly being unkind to me, trying to force me to drink that nasty Pain-Killer and then getting cross when I fed it to the cat. And I'm tired of old Becky Thatcher too, not even noticing my best handsprings. She called me a "show-off." Can you believe it? Well, I'm sure I don't care anyway.

This is the thing—I'm ready to start a new life, a life of piracy. That's right—I want to be free and easy, like you are. Joe Harper's in too. His mother

just whipped him for drinking some cream he knew nothing about! So that's three of us, and I reckon that's the perfect number.

Meet us at Jackson's Island, will you? It is three miles south of town. You know the one. There's a log raft there we can capture, and I'll bring food. Come around midnight and don't forget to be quiet about it. The last thing we need is any grown-ups poking their noses into our pirating business. A pirate's life is for me, I'm sure of it . . . getting up when we want in the morning and doing as we please.

Yours truly,

Tom Sawyer

P.S. Bring your fishing pole.

Answers will vary. Sample answers are given below.

1. Personal names are proper nouns, so they are capitalized.

2. Place names are also proper nouns and should be capitalized.

3. The first word of a sentence should be capitalized.

6.7 Practice

Directions: Draw three lines under the first letter of every word in the following sentences that should be capitalized. These sentences are from *A Kid's Guide to Washington, D.C.* by Diane C. Clark

1. can you locate washington, d.c., on a map of the united states? it's that diamond-shaped dot on the east coast bordered by maryland on the north and virginia on the south. (page 9) (11 capital letters are missing.)

2. it doesn't look like much, does it? compare it with the size of california or texas. washington even makes rhode island look huge. yet this sixty-nine-square-mile area is the capital of the country, the headquarters of the federal government, and the home of embassies that represent countries all over the world. (page 9) (8 capital letters are missing.)

3. more than 170 countries have embassies in washington. many of them line a section of massachusetts avenue known as embassy row. (page 10) (7 capital letters are missing.)

4. in 1912, the city of tokyo, japan, gave three thousand cherry trees, or *sakura*, to the united states. that's where washington's cherry blossoms originate. (page 12) (7 capital letters are missing.)

5. but, do you know what "d.c." stands for? it means district of columbia, named for christopher columbus. (page 12) (8 capital letters are missing.)

6. more than thirty-three million people fly into one of the area's three airports each year. the closest is ronald reagan washington national airport, just fifteen minutes from the white house and across the potomac river, which separates washington from virginia. (page 14) (13 capital letters are missing.)

7. try to grab a window seat, because as you land you'll get a great view of the capitol, the washington monument, and the lincoln and jefferson memorials. (page 14) (6 capital letters are missing.)

8. driving from the north brings you through baltimore, maryland, a major east coast port city. several miles to the east is the chesapeake bay—an arm of water jutting in from the atlantic ocean. (page16) (10 capital letters are missing.)

6.8 Punctuate!

Directions: In the chart below, draw a supersize version of the punctuation mark next to its name.

Punctuation Marks	
period	•
question mark	?
exclamation point	!
comma	,
semicolon	;
colon	:
dash	—
apostrophe	'
hyphen	-
quotation marks	" "
parentheses	( )
ellipses	• • •

6.9 Commas in a Personal Letter

Directions: Draw a box around every comma you find in the example of a personal letter in **6.4 PARTS OF A PERSONAL LETTER**. Why do you think a comma is used in each place?

235 Church Street

St. Petersburg, MO

October 5, 1876

Dear Huck,

I know I've got it easy in some ways, compared to you—home-cooked dinners and things of that sort. But I'm tired of all that, Huck. I'm tired of Aunt Polly being unkind to me, trying to force me to drink that nasty Pain-Killer and then getting cross when I fed it to the cat. And I'm tired of old Becky Thatcher too, not even noticing my best handsprings. She called me a "show-off." Can you believe it? Well, I'm sure I don't care anyway.

This is the thing—I'm ready to start a new life, a life of piracy. That's right—I want to be free and easy, like you are. Joe Harper's in too. His mother

just whipped him for drinking some cream he knew nothing about! So that's three of us, and I reckon that's the perfect number.

Meet us at Jackson's Island, will you? It is three miles south of town. You know the one. There's a log raft there we can capture, and I'll bring food. Come around midnight and don't forget to be quiet about it. The last thing we need is any grown-ups poking their noses into our pirating business. A pirate's life is for me, I'm sure of it . . . getting up when we want in the morning and doing as we please.

Yours truly,

Tom Sawyer

P.S. Bring your fishing pole.

Answers will vary. Examples are provided below.

A comma is used in a personal letter to separate the city and state in an address, to separate the day and the year in a date, after the salutation, and after the closing.

MODULE 7

7.10 Unit Review

Directions: You may write your answers to the questions below in the space provided, or you can talk about these questions with a parent, teacher, or writing coach. You can also look over all the information in the modules you have completed to help you decide upon your answers. Use the unit review to help you master the writing tips and tricks you learned about in these modules.

1. In unit 1 you learned that writers get ideas from their memories. In this unit you learned about another source of ideas writers often use. Name it. (1 point)

   Writers also get ideas from their imaginations.

2. Name one strategy you can use to generate ideas for your stories. (1 point)

   Answers will vary. Sample answers are provided, but students only need to list one answer.

   Imagine a situation and then ask yourself questions about it.

   Set a timer for 60 seconds and imagine something. Then ask yourself questions about what you imagined.

   Read examples of other writers' work to get a sense of the kind of details you might like to include in your own.

3. Name some of the tips and tricks writers use to make sure their readers stay interested in the stories they write. (1 point for each tip, maximum of 5 points).

   Answers will vary. Sample answers are provided, but students only need to list five answers to receive maximum points.

   Use specific nouns.

   Use vigorous verbs.

   Test out your writing with your readers to see if they like it.

   Use questions to discover what your readers find most interesting.

   Use questions to review your own writing.

   Be sure you've remembered to "show but not tell."

4. Name the part of speech we use to describe a person or a character in a story. (1 point)

Adjectives are used to describe people or characters.

5. Explain what it means to show but not tell a character's traits when you write a story. (2 points)

Answers will vary. A sample answer is given below.

Rather than using general words to tell a reader what a character is like, you use specific details and examples to convey the person's traits.

6. Name all the parts you should include in a personal letter. (5 points)

The parts of a personal letter are heading, salutation, body, closing, and signature.

7. List all the places in a personal letter that a comma is required. (3 points)

A comma is required in the address in the heading. (Example: St. Petersburg, MO)

A comma is required after the date in the heading. (Example: October 5, 1876)

A comma is required after the salutation. (Example: Dear Huck,)

A comma is required after the closing. (Example: Yours truly,)

8. In this unit you learned about ten types of proper nouns you should capitalize. Give an example of each type. (10 points)

Students should list the ten types of proper nouns mentioned below with an example of each. However, the examples may vary.

planets and heavenly bodies (Earth, Mars, Sun, Milky Way)

continents (North America, Australia, Asia, Europe, Antarctica)

countries (the United States, England, Chile)

states (Oregon, Arizona, Florida, New York, South Dakota)

cities (Albany, Portland, Tulsa)

streets, roads, and highways (Pennsylvania Avenue, Sunset Boulevard, Wall Street, Route 66)

bodies of water (Hudson Bay, Pacific Ocean, Lake Erie, Mississippi River)

mountains (Rocky Mountains, the Alps, Pike's Peak)

buildings and monuments (Pentagon, Empire State Building, Eiffel Tower, Statue of Liberty)

recognized geographic regions (East Coast, Pacific Northwest, Great Lakes, the Great Plains)

9. Explain how readers can help you improve your writing. (1 point)
   Answers will vary. A sample answer is given below.

   Readers can give feedback that will help me make my writing more interesting and clear. Readers can let me know if they understand what I am trying to "show but not tell" about my characters. They also help me to know if other readers will want to keep reading.

10. Which of the letters that you wrote in this unit do you like the best? Why? (1 point)
    Answers will vary.

MODULE 8

8.1 Review Your Progress

Directions: In module 4, you visited the Writer's Workshop for the first time. Before you learn the new information in this module, review what you already know about sentence parts.

1. subject, predicate

2. who, what

3. subject

4. verb

5. compound

6. compound

8.5 Answer the Question

Directions: Add a word or group of words to the following sentences to answer the questions.

Answers will vary. Sample answers are provided.

1. *Where* did she sing?
   She sang in the shower.

2. *When* did she sing?
   She sang at 6 a.m.

3. *How* did he score?
   He scored magnificently.

4. *What* did he score?
   He scored a goal just before the game ended.

5. *Why* did the dog attack?
   The dog attacked because someone threatened its master.

6. *Whom* did the dog attack?
   The dog attacked the villain.

8.6 More Than One Question

Directions: Write new sentences by adding information to the subject and simple predicate that answers the questions.

Answers will vary. Sample answers are provided.

1. *Where* did she sing? (Give a two-part answer that uses a coordinating conjunction.)
   She sang in the shower and at Carnegie Hall.

2. *When* did she sing? (Give a two-part answer that uses a coordinating conjunction.)
   She sang in the morning and the evening.

3. *How* and *when* did he score?
   He scored magnificently during the final minute.

4. *Where, when,* and *what* did he score?
   He scored a touchdown during the Super Bowl on Sunday night.

5. *When* and *why* did the dog attack?
   The dog attacked yesterday because she was protecting her puppies.

6. *Whom* and *where* did the dog attack?
   The dog attacked Mr. Smith near the library.

8.9 Link Up

Directions: Build four sentences by choosing a subject from column 1, a linking verb from column 2, and a complement from column 3.

Answers will vary. Sample answers are provided.

I was our secret weapon.

The frog is the spy.

My orchard smelled rotten.

The Incredible Hulk seemed magical.

8.10 Work Zone

Directions: Create sentences using the building blocks specified below the line. The first one is completed for you. Remember to capitalize the first word of each sentence and put a period at the end.

Answers will vary. Sample answers are provided.

1. Cash Denton performed at the Kimmel Center in November.
   subject + action verb + where + when

2. The boy hit the ball quickly.
   subject + action verb + what + how

3. Jenny was captain last spring.
   subject + linking verb + complement (renames) + when

4. Andy and Meg sang and danced with their brothers and sisters.
   compound subject + compound predicate + with whom (two-part answer linked by a conjunction)

5. The ice cream and the cookies were fresh and delicious.
   compound subject + linking verb + compound complement (describes)

6. Bilbo ran out of the cave and into the bushes to escape the goblins.
   subject + action verb + where + why

7. The basketball player dribbled and passed the ball.
    subject + compound predicate + what

8. The zebra ran.
    subject + predicate

9. Mom smiled at the butterfly.
    subject + predicate + (your choice)

10. The cat and dog ran and climbed with the boy into the mountains in the spring, moving quickly to avoid the flooding.
    compound subject + compound predicate + with whom + where + when + how + why

Unit 3

MODULE 9

9.3 Expert Model

Directions: Study these two paragraphs closely. Notice how much you learn about Roald Dahl's father in two brief paragraphs. Do you see the vigorous verbs and specific nouns? List the ones you think are particularly vigorous or specific.

Answers will vary. Sample answers are provided. Students do not need to list as many answers as are given below; we have listed a large number to represent most of the options students may choose.

1. The best vigorous verbs I see: broke, amputated, manage, lost, taught, tie, cutting, sharpened, cut, frighten, climbing, growing

2. The best specific nouns I see: roof, tiles, elbow, thumb, shoelace, knife, fork, pocket, inconvenience, gardener, ledge, wood-carver, mirror-frames, mantelpiece, fireplace, fruit, foliage, branches, oak

Directions: Next, decide which character traits listed on the chart in **5.6 Adjectives Describe Characters** best describe Roald Dahl's father. Do you think Dahl did a good job of showing but not telling?

3. Character traits I see in Roald Dahl's father: able, active, adventurous, ambitious, bold, brave, busy, confident, curious, daring, determined, eager, energetic, fearless, happy, helpful, industrious, intelligent, inventive, lively, positive, strong

9.4 Vocabulary: My Roots Run Deep

Directions: Here are some new words you may encounter while working on this writing assignment. Write their definitions. Then use some of them to have a conversation about your family history with a parent or sibling. These words are all the same part of speech. Can you name it?

Answers will vary, but should be similar to those below.

1. **ancestry:** the people from whom someone is descended

2. **archives:** collections of documents such as photographs, videos, letters, and other keepsakes that relate to history

3. **census:** an official count of a group of people, usually made by a government

4. **deed:** a legal document, usually showing that someone owns land or property

5. **descendant:** someone born into a family, such as a child or great-grandchild

6. **estate:** land or property belonging to a person and often passed on to family when that person dies

7. **heritage:** traditions and accomplishments passed down through a family or culture

8. **heir:** person who inherits something, such as land or property

9. **kindred:** family and relatives

10. **forebear:** someone who comes before in time, an ancestor

11. **genealogy:** family tree or other document that traces ancestors and descendants

12. **legacy:** something handed down from one's ancestors, such as ideas or cultural patterns

13. **lineage:** descent from an ancestor, such as from a king of England

14. **matriarch:** a woman important in a family line, such as a mother or grandmother

15. **namesake:** person or thing having the same name as another, especially one named after the other

16. **patriarch:** a man important in a family line, such as a father or grandfather

Part of Speech: noun

9.9 Now That Is a Good Question!

Directions: Go back and study **9.3 EXPERT MODEL**. What open and closed questions do you think Roald Dahl asked when he was collecting information about his family's history? Write a few of them below.

Answers will vary. Sample answers of closed questions are provided.

How old was my father when he fell off the roof?

What year was it when my father fell off the roof?

Which arm did my father lose after he fell off the roof?

Where did my father and mother travel to collect alpine plants?

What examples of my father's wood carvings do we have in our house?

Answers will vary. Sample answers of open questions are provided.

How did my father cope with life with only one arm?

What did my mother and father like to do together?

What are some of the most impressive things my father was able to do with only one arm?

MODULE 10

10.3 Interview Etiquette

Directions: Circle the practical ideas on this list that will help you be considerate and professional. Cross out the ideas that will not help you.

1. ~~Arrive ten minutes late for your appointment.~~

2. Call or e-mail a request for an interview in advance.

3. Set the appointment at a time that is convenient for the interviewee.

4. ~~Think up the questions you want to ask during the interview.~~

5. Choose an outfit to wear that is clean and suitable as your Sunday best.

6. ~~Ask the interviewee for a pencil and writing paper.~~

7. Bring an organizer, such as a folder or backpack, to keep all your materials in.

8. ~~Leave your cell phone on during the interview.~~

9. Send a thank-you note by e-mail or mail after the interview.

10. ~~Look around the room while the interviewee is talking.~~

11. Take good notes during your interview so you do not forget any important information.

12. ~~Look bored during the interview.~~

13. Explain the assignment you are working on to the interviewee.

14. Ask the interviewee if he or she has any questions for you.

15. Let the interviewee know how many questions you would like to ask.

16. Ask the interviewee how much time he or she has available for an interview.

17. ~~Let the interviewee know when you disagree with something he or she says.~~

10.8 Meet the Mighty Paragraph

Directions: Look back at **9.3 EXPERT MODEL**. Study the two paragraphs. What central idea do you think Roald Dahl is developing in each one?

Answers will vary. Sample answers are provided.

Paragraph 1: In spite of losing his arm, Dahl's resourceful father found ways to do what he wanted to do.

Paragraph 2: Dahl's father was brave, accomplished, and creative, pursuing exciting hobbies despite his limitation.

MODULE 11

11.1 Review Your Progress

Directions: In module 4, you visited the Writer's Workshop for the first time. Before you learn the new information in this module, review what you already know about sentence parts.

1. subject, predicate
2. who, what
3. subject
4. verb
5. compound
6. compound
7. simple

Directions: In module 8, you visited the Writer's Workshop again. Review what you learned in that module.

1. subject and predicate
2. complement
3. predicate
4. conjunction
5. linking
6. action

11.5 Roald Dahl's Adjectives

Directions: Look at some of Roald Dahl's sentences about his father again. All the adjectives are indicated in purple for you in the Student Text and Workbook and in bold in the excerpt below. Circle the noun that is modified by each adjective. Some nouns are described, limited, or clarified by more than one adjective.

YOUR TURN

1. When **my** father was **fourteen**, which is still more than **one hundred** years ago, he was up on the roof of **the family** house replacing **some loose** tiles when he slipped and fell. He broke **his left** arm below the elbow . . . This was in 1877 and **orthopaedic** surgery was not what it is today. So they simply amputated **the** arm at the elbow, and for **the** rest of **his** life **my** father had to manage with **one** arm. Fortunately, it was **the left** arm that he lost and gradually, over **the** years, he taught himself to do more or less anything he wanted with just **the four** fingers and thumb of **his right** hand. He could tie a shoelace as quickly as you or me, and for cutting up **the** food on **his** plate he sharpened **the bottom** edge of a fork so that it served as both knife and fork all in one. He kept **his ingenious** instrument in **a slim leather** case and

Continued on next page »

carried it in **his** pocket wherever he went.

2. He was also **an accomplished** wood-carver, and most of the mirror-frames in **the** house were **his own** work. So indeed was the entire mantelpiece around **the** fireplace in **the** living-room, **a splendid** design of fruit and foliage and intertwining branches carved in oak.

11.6 Where Can You Use Them?

Directions: Study the sentences below. The adjectives are indicated for you in purple in the excerpt in the Student Text and Workbook and in bold in this Answer Key. Circle the noun or pronoun that is modified by each adjective.

1. **The** (barn) was very **large**. (It) was very **old**. It smelled of **the** (perspiration) of **tired** (horses) and **the wonderful sweet** (breath) of **patient** (cows)

   (*Charlotte's Web* by E. B. White, page 13)

2. **Her** (face) was **plain**, **her** (complexion) **ruddy**, and **her** (hair) **light brown** and **stringy**. She was not **a** real **young** (person). . . . She wore **a patchwork** (shirt), **a baggy brown** (sweater) and overalls.

   (*Ida Early Comes Over the Mountain* by Robert Burch, pages 3–4)

3. (He) was **big**, but **skinny**; you could see **his** (ribs) And there were **bald** (patches) all over him, places where he didn't have **any** (fur) at all. Mostly, he looked like **a big** (piece) of **old brown** (carpet) that had been left out in **the** (rain)

   (*Because of Winn-Dixie* by Kate DiCamillo, page 11)

4. I have **a gorilla's shy** (gaze), **a gorilla's sly** (smile). I wear **a snowy** (saddle) of fur, **the** (uniform) of **a** (saddleback). When **the** (sun) warms **my** (back), I cast **a gorilla's majestic** (shadow.)

   (*The One and Only Ivan* by Katherine Applegate, page 4)

11.7 Now You Try

Directions: Fill in the blanks below with adjectives that answer the question below the line.

Answers will vary. Sample answers are provided.

YOUR TURN

1. The _____four_____ squirrels chattered angrily from the
   <small>How many?</small>

   _____oak_____ tree.
   <small>What kind?</small>

2. Betty insisted that _____those_____ shoes were the ones she
   <small>Which?</small>

   wanted to buy.

3. The _____red_____ box and the _____green_____ bag were
   <small>What kind?</small>   <small>What kind?</small>

   filled with _____many_____ gifts for Saul.
   <small>How many?</small>

4. The _____resplendent_____ knights and _____majestic_____ horses
   <small>Your choice</small>   <small>Your choice</small>

   looked _____fearsome_____ as they lined up for battle on the
   <small>Your choice</small>

   _____high_____ ridge.
   <small>Your choice</small>

5. The _____twelve_____ _____dancing_____ princesses wore
   <small>Your choice</small>   <small>Your choice</small>

   _____scarlet_____ gowns and _____satin_____ gloves.
   <small>Your choice</small>   <small>Your choice</small>

11.8 Sensory Words

Directions: Study the chart below. It contains examples of adjectives you can use to describe what your five senses experience. Add three of your own words to each column.

Answers will vary. Sample answers are provided.

Sensory Words				
See	**Hear**	**Smell**	**Taste**	**Touch**
blue	loud	spicy	bitter	rough
bright	husky	musty	delicious	dry
large	low	perfumed	sweet	crusty
square	shrill	spoiled	rotten	sharp
young	high-pitched	sweaty	salty	damp
small	howling	pungent	fresh	oily
speckled	clanging	lemony	sour	jagged
thin	quiet	fragrant	juicy	lumpy

MODULE 12

12.12 Unit Review

Directions: You may write your answers to the questions below in the space provided, or you can talk about these questions with a parent, teacher, or writing coach. You can also look over all the information in the modules you have completed to help you decide upon your answers. Use the unit review to help you master the writing tips and tricks you learned about in these modules.

1. Explain the difference between closed and open questions in an interview. (2 points)

    Closed questions have one specific answer and can be answered with only a brief statement. An open question has many possible answers.

2. List five things you can do to be courteous to someone you are interviewing. (1 point for each thing, maximum of 5 points)

    Answers will vary, but student responses should include some of the following:

    Call or e-mail a request for an interview in advance.

    Set the appointment at a time that is convenient for the interviewee.

    Choose an outfit to wear that is clean and suitable as your Sunday best.

    Bring an organizer, such as a folder or backpack, to keep all your materials in.

    Send a thank-you note by e-mail or mail after the interview.

    Take good notes during your interview so that you do not forget any important information.

    Explain the assignment you are working on to the interviewee.

    Ask the interviewee if he or she has any questions for you.

    Let the interviewee know how many questions you would like to ask.

    Ask the interviewee how much time he or she has available for an interview.

3. What is a paragraph? (4 points)

    A paragraph is a group of sentences that develop a central idea. Typically the central idea is stated at the beginning of the paragraph in a topic sentence.

4. What is a topic sentence? (3 points)

    The topic sentence is the sentence that states the central idea of a paragraph.

5. Every sentence in a paragraph should provide information about the paragraph's central idea. (3 points)

6. List two ways to show that a new paragraph has started. (2 points)

    Indent five spaces or one-half inch; skip a line.

7. Describe what the subject and the predicate do in a sentence. (4 points)

    The subject tells who or what the subject is about.

    The predicate tells something about the subject of the sentence.

8. Adjectives are used to describe which two parts of speech? (2 points)

    Adjectives can be used to describe nouns and pronouns.

9. List three questions you can ask a reader in order to get ideas for improving your writing. (3 points)

    Answers will vary. Sample answers are provided.

    What do you think are the strengths and weaknesses of this piece?

    Did you want to keep reading?

    How can I do a better job of showing but not telling?

10. When you wrote about the dragon, you used sensory words to create a lively picture of the dragon. What were a few of your favorite sensory words from that assignment? (2 points)

    Answers will vary.

Unit 4

MODULE 13

13.10 Vocabulary: A Writer's Life for Me

Directions: Find out what type of writing each career below requires by looking up the word in a dictionary. Write a brief description for each type of writer on the line provided. Circle the three that interest you most.

1. biographer: someone who writes true stories of other people's lives

2. columnist: a person who writes a regular series of articles for a newspaper or magazine

3. critic: a writer who produces reviews of food, music, literature, or other types of art

4. editor: someone who reviews and improves a writer's work, making the final decision about what content to include in a published work

5. ghostwriter: someone who writes material for books produced by others without being named as the author

6. journalist: a writer who works for a newspaper or magazine

7. lyricist: a writer who creates words for composers to put to music

8. playwright: a person who creates plays

9. satirist: a writer who pokes fun at things, especially weakness or foolishness in politics or culture

10. novelist: someone who writes book-length works of fiction

11. speechwriter: a person who writes formal addresses for others, such as the president or another public figure

12. copywriter: someone who writes words for advertisements

MODULE 14

14.3 Is It a Topic or an Opinion?

Directions: Look over the following statements. Decide whether each one states a topic or an opinion and fill in the chart.

Statement	Topic or Opinion
A five-car crash occurred yesterday on the Pennsylvania Turnpike.	● Topic ○ Opinion
I hate ice cream.	○ Topic ● Opinion
Our family took a trip to Disney World last summer.	● Topic ○ Opinion
Roald Dahl is the author of seventeen books for children.	● Topic ○ Opinion
Patricia MacLachlan is my favorite author because her characters remind me of people I know.	○ Topic ● Opinion
The Reading Royals is the worst team in the league.	○ Topic ● Opinion
I think we should go to the mountains for a vacation.	○ Topic ● Opinion

Directions: Look back through the list above and find the statements that only name the topic but do not include an opinion about it. Use the space below to rewrite those statements to include an opinion.

Answers will vary, but student responses should contain an opinion about each of the following topics. Sample answers are provided.

I think the five-car crash on the Pennsylvania Turnpike was caused by ice.

Our family trip to Disney World last summer was our best vacation in five years.

Roald Dahl is one of the most dramatic children's writers I have ever read.

14.8 Info in the Intro

Directions: The writer in the expert model has opened her essay with a surprising fact about her favorite author's life. What is it?

> C. S. Lewis didn't have his own children, even though he wrote some of the most beloved children's books of all time.

MODULE 15

15.1 Review Your Progress

Directions: In module 4, you visited the Writer's Workshop for the first time. Before learning the new information in this module, review what you already know about sentence parts.

1. subject, predicate

2. who, what

3. subject

4. verb

5. compound

6. compound

7. simple

Directions: In module 8, you again visited the Writer's Workshop. Review what you learned in that module.

1. Name the sentence parts used to build all of the sentences below: a. The baby cried. b. Pauline scored. c. Matt laughed. d. Our dog died.

   subject and predicate

2. The sentence part that renames or describes the subject is called a complement.

3. Is the sentence part named in question 2 a part of the subject or the predicate?

   predicate

4. What part of speech is used to connect sentence parts? conjunction

5. Verbs that connect the subject of the sentence with a complement that describes or renames the subject are called linking verbs.

6. Verbs that name the action completed by the subject are called action verbs.

15.3 Modify with Adverbs

Directions: Study the adverbs in the sentences in the preceding examples. What do many of them have in common? Write it down. Words that end this way are usually adverbs.

They end in -ly.

15.5 Work Those Adverbs

Directions: Have some fun creating sentences using a form of each verb below. Modify the verb with the types of adverbs requested in the parentheses.

Answers will vary. Sample answers are provide, and the suggested adverbs are underlined.

1. dance (how) Amber danced energetically to the band's syncopated beat.

2. cry (how) My neighbor cried dramatically when she found out the carousel was closed.

3. swim (where) We swam near the dolphins.

4. spoke (how) We spoke softly as we escaped the dark castle.

5. cook (when) Mom cooked continuously at the family reunion.

6. whisper (to what extent) We whispered constantly during the concert.

7. visit (when) We visited late, but they still let us in to see the elephants.

8. build (when and where) We immediately built a shelter nearby.

9. sing (how and when) The people sang enthusiastically tonight.

10. laugh (when, where, how, or to what extent) We laughed loudly.

15.6 Connect with Adverbs

Directions: In the following sentences, fill in the blanks with adverbs.

Answers will vary. Sample answers are provided.

1. My cat is quite the mouser. <u>Therefore</u>, my neighbor doesn't mind her frequent visits to his barn.

2. On Saturday we plan to visit the science museum. <u>In addition</u>, we may visit the amusement park.

3. I took a bad fall from a stepladder once. <u>Consequently</u>, I no longer volunteer to help with spring clean-up at the church.

4. Maybe I should work on my essay today; <u>otherwise</u>, I might not be able to go to the game tomorrow night.

5. Kevin isn't riding the bus with us tomorrow; <u>instead</u>, he plans to walk.

15.8 More Than One Part of Speech

Directions: Now you try. Identify the part of speech for each word in boldface in the sentences below.

1. **Next**, I will discuss the reasons I think beagles are the best breed. adverb

2. We are leaving the **next** day for Flanders. adjective

3. We are leaving **next** for Flanders. adverb

4. That was a **first**. noun

5. He is our **first** son. adjective

6. We **first** visited Washington, D.C., when I was eight. adverb

7. Over the summer, our **well** went dry. noun

8. I like my steak **well** done. adverb

9. I am **well**, thank you. adjective

10. Tears **welled** up in my eyes when my cat returned home. verb

15.9 Mastery Test

Directions: Study the excerpt from *Charlotte's Web* by E. B. White on the next page. How many nouns, verbs, adjectives, adverbs, and conjunctions can you identify? Fill out the chart with some of the words you find in each category. (The words in gray are parts of speech we have not studied yet.)

Answers will vary. Sample answers are provided.

Proper Nouns	Common Nouns	Verbs	Adjectives	Adverbs	Conjunctions
Fern	school	was	little	now	and
July	barn	lay	grass	quietly	
Mr. Zuckerman	stool	were hitched	big	calmly	
Avery	morning	fell	high	round	
	grass	would be hoisted	cutter	down	

Mark-up is provided to indicate all the parts of speech students might list in their charts. Students were not required to mark up the expert model.

EXPERT MODEL

adv.   n.   v.   adv. n.   v.   adj. n.   adv.
Now that school was over, Fern visited the barn almost

adj. n.   adv.   adj. n. adj.   n.   v.
every day, to sit quietly on her stool. The animals treated

adj. n.   adj. n.   v. adv.   adj. n.
her as an equal. The sheep lay calmly at her feet.

adj. n.   n. adj. adj.   n.   v.
Around the first of July, the work horses were hitched

adj. adj.   n.   conj.   n.   v.
to the mowing machine, and Mr. Zuckerman climbed into

adj. n. conj. v.   adj. n. adj.   n.   v.
the seat and drove into the field. All morning you could

adj.   n. adj.   n.   v.   adv. conj. adv.
hear the rattle of the machine as it went round and round,

while the tall grass fell down behind the cutter bar in long
adj. adj. n. v. adv. adj. adj. n. adj.

green swathes. Next day, if there was no thunder shower,
adj. n. adj. n. v. adj. adj. n.

all hands would help rake and pitch and load, and the hay
adj. n. v. conj. v. conj. v. conj. adj. n.

would be hauled to the barn in the high hay wagon, with
v. adj. n. adj. adj. adj. n.

Fern and Avery riding at the top of the load. Then the hay
n. conj. n. v. adj. n. adj. n. adv. adj. n.

would be hoisted, sweet and warm, into the big loft, until
v. adj. conj. adj. adj. adj. n.

the whole barn seemed like a wonderful bed of timothy and
adj. adj. n. v. adj. adj. n. n. conj.

clover. It was fine to jump in and perfect to hide in. And
n. v. adj. adv. conj. adj. adv. conj.

sometimes Avery would find a little grass snake in the hay,
adv. n. v. adj. adj. adj. n. adj. n.

and would add it to the other things in his pocket.
conj. v. adj. adj. n. adj. n.

(page 42)

MODULE 16

16.7 Organization: Order of Importance

Directions: List some of the words in each paragraph that help you to recognize the author is organizing her examples in order of importance.

Answers will vary, but student answers might include some of the following:

during college, first intellectual defense, that observation convinced me, also, however, influenced me most

16.14 Unit Review

Directions: You may write your answers to the questions below in the space provided, or you can talk about these questions with a parent, teacher, or writing coach. You can also look over all the information in the modules you have completed to help you decide upon your answers. Use the unit review to help you master the writing tips and tricks you learned about in these modules.

1. Writers support their opinions with facts, examples, and details. (3 points)

2. An essay begins with an introductory or opening (either is correct) paragraph, continues with body or supporting (either is correct) paragraphs, and ends with a concluding paragraph. (3 points)

3. What's the difference between a topic statement and an opinion statement? (3 points)

    A topic statement expresses a fact or facts, while an opinion statement expresses a belief or judgment about something.

4. An opinion statement needs to be broad enough to include what? (2 points)

    An opinion statement should be broad enough to include all the individual reasons for your opinion that you will discuss later in the essay.

5. List the three organizational patterns you have learned so far in *Writers in Residence*. (3 points)

    I have learned chronological order, topical order, and order of importance.

6. What do adverbs modify? (3 points)

    Adverbs modify verbs, adjectives, and other adverbs.

7. List two questions an adverb can answer. (4 points)

    Students should list any two of the following questions:

    How was the action done?

    When was the action done?

    Where was the action done?

    How often was the action done?

    How little or how much was the action done?

8. What does it mean to close the circle in your conclusion? (2 points)

    It means to link your concluding points back to your introduction and opinion statement.

9. What two things do transitions do? (4 points)

    Students should list any two of the following answers:

    Transitions signal to readers the type of new idea or new information that is coming up next.

    Transitions show readers how ideas and information are connected to each other.

    Transitions signal to readers the organizational pattern the author has chosen to use.

10. What is your favorite example from your opinion essay? (3 points)

    Answers will vary.

Unit 5

MODULE 17

17.10 Vocabulary: A Sense of Place

Directions: The following words can be used to describe places. Define each one and name a place that might be appropriately described with that adjective.

Answers will vary. Sample answers are provided.

1. **ancient:** (adj.) very old
    Example: Jerusalem is ancient.

2. **bustling:** (adj.) busy
    Example: New York City is bustling.

3. **charming:** (adj.) delightful or pleasant
    Example: My grandmother's garden is charming.

4. **contemporary:** (adj.) modern, happening in the present or recent times
    Example: That office building's design is contemporary.

5. **cosmopolitan:** (adj.) including people from many different countries
    Example: London is a cosmopolitan city.

6. **fascinating:** (adj.) intriguing, compelling, holding the attention
    Example: Yellowstone National Park is a fascinating place.

7. **lively:** (adj.) exciting or active
    Example: The skating rink is always lively.

8. **rural:** (adj.) relating to the countryside
    Example: The edge of my county is rural, full of farms and unpaved roads.

9. **picturesque:** (adj.) charming or quaint, like a picture
    Example: The white country church building is picturesque.

10. **sparse:** (adj.) spare or austere
    Example: A prairie in winter feels sparse and cold.

11. **tranquil:** (adj.) peaceful or free from disturbance
    Example: The woods in my backyard are tranquil.

12. **weathered:** (adj.) worn by weather over time
    Example: The mountaintop is weathered.

MODULE 18

18.3 Paint the Picture

Directions: Now you try. Revise the sentences on the next page as directed to paint a more vivid image in your readers' minds. When you have finished, compare your sentences with the sample sentences below. Then add descriptive details and action words to the rough draft of your autobiography that will paint a more vivid picture in your readers' minds.

Answers will vary. Sample answers are provided.

1. The garden is filled with beautiful flowers. (What kinds of flowers are in the garden? What colors are they?)

   The garden is filled with yellow snapdragons and red coneflowers.

2. The children are playing games outside. (What games are the children playing? Where outside are they playing?)

   The children are playing hopscotch and baseball in the small park by Conewago Creek.

3. The girl danced across the room. (Tell readers what the girl looks like. Make the action more precise and vivid. Describe the type of room.)

   The short girl with dark hair pirouetted across the marble ballroom with the soaring ceilings.

4. The knight rode into the castle courtyard. (How much detail and action can you add to this sentence? Be creative.)

   The knight in bronze armor thundered into the crowded castle courtyard on his black charger.

18.4 Somewhere in Time

Directions: Do the same for the other expert models. How many clues do Sid Fleischman and Mary Pope Osborne include about where and when their stories occurred? Notice that they not only tell readers where they were living when the action occurred, but they also let readers know about historical events that affected their lives.

Answers will vary. Sample answers are provided.

Author	Where did this story occur?	When did this story occur?
Sid Fleischman	• San Diego, California • Vast blue harbor • Precise place: vacant store next door, changed to look like a theater	• The Great Depression is one year old (makes this about 1930). • Autumn
Mary Pope Osborne	• Daytona Beach, Florida • Near the ocean • Pink stucco house • Place with lizards, spiders, and water bugs • Yard with only small, scrubby trees	• One spring night • Eight years after the Korean War

18.6 The Story Arc

Directions: Look up the definition of the word *arc*. Write the one for *arc*, the noun, and the one for *arc*, the verb.

Answers will vary. Sample answers are provided.

1. **arc:** (n.) a line or shape that is curved like part of a circle

2. **arc:** (v.) to follow an arc-shaped course

MODULE 19

19.1 Review Your Progress, Part 1

Directions: In module 4, you visited the Writer's Workshop for the first time. Before learning the new information in this module, review what you already know about sentence parts.

1. subject, predicate
2. who, what
3. subject
4. verb
5. compound
6. compound
7. simple

Directions: In module 8, you again visited the WRITER'S WORKSHOP. Review what you learned in that module.

1. Name the sentence parts used to build all the sentences below: a. The baby cried. c. Matt laughed. b. Pauline scored. d. Our dog died.

   subject and predicate

2. The sentence part that renames or describes the subject is called a complement.

3. Is the sentence part named in question 2 a part of the subject or the predicate?

   predicate

4. What part of speech is used to connect sentence parts? conjunction

5. Verbs that connect the subject of the sentence with a complement that describes or renames the subject are called linking verbs.

6. Verbs that name the action completed by the subject are called action verbs.

19.6 Expert Model

Directions: Underline the prepositional phrases in the following excerpt. Circle the object of the preposition. Remember that the object of a preposition is the noun or pronoun that follows the preposition. The words in gray are not used as prepositions in this excerpt.

YOUR TURN

When it came to getting the two of us in trouble, Soup was a regular genius. He liked to whip apples. But that was nothing new. Every kid did. The apples had to be small and green and hard, about the size of a golf ball. The whip had to be about four to five foot long, with a point on the small end that you'd whittle sharp with your jackknife. You held the apple close to your chest with your left hand and pushed the pointed stick into the apple but not so far as it'd come out the yonder side. No matter how careful you speared the apple, a few drops of juice would squirt on your shirt. They dried to small, tiny brown spots that never even came out in the wash.

(pages 14–15)

19.7 Answer the Questions

Directions: Use prepositional phrases to answer the following questions.
Can you use more than one prepositional phrase to answer the questions?
The first one is done for you.

Answers will vary. Each answer should include more than one prepositional phrase.
Sample answers are provided, and prepositional phrases are underlined as examples.

1. When do dragons usually dine?
    The dragons usually dine <u>by the seaside</u> <u>in the late morning</u> except <u>on Wednesdays</u>. Then they dine <u>at home</u>.

2. Which cave is the best one for napping?
    The cave <u>in the mountains</u> is the best <u>for napping</u> <u>in the winter</u>, but the cave <u>at the beach</u> is cooler <u>in the summer</u>.

3. What time does the dragon dance start?
    The dragon dance starts <u>after dark</u> <u>under the stars</u>.

4. Where does the dragon prefer to buy his shoes?
    The dragon prefers to buy his shoes <u>from the silversmith</u> who lives <u>above the bridge</u>.

5. How long will the dragon usually sleep?
    The dragon will usually sleep <u>until noon</u> <u>on weekdays</u>, and he sleeps <u>until evening</u> <u>on the weekends</u>.

6. Where is the dragon's treasure hidden?
    The dragon's treasure is hidden <u>by the ruined gate</u> <u>beside the silver tree</u> <u>below the cave's roof</u>.

7. Who is coming to slay the dragon?
The knight <u>in shining armor</u> who lives <u>across the wild seas</u> is coming to slay the dragon.

8. Which sword will the dragon slayer use?
The dragon slayer will use the sword <u>of Odin</u> made <u>by Valmir</u> <u>in the forge</u> <u>of Skene</u>.

19.8 Track the Prepositional Phrases

Directions: How many prepositional phrases can you find in Psalm 23? Underline each one. There are sixteen. Can you find at least ten? (The word *for* is used as a conjunction, so it appears in lime green.)

YOUR TURN

Psalm 23

¹ The LORD is my shepherd; I shall not want.

² He makes me lie down <u>in green pastures</u>.

He leads me <u>beside still waters</u>.

³ He restores my soul.

He leads me <u>in paths</u> <u>of righteousness</u>

<u>for his name's sake</u>.

⁴ Even though I walk <u>through the valley</u> <u>of the shadow</u> <u>of death</u>,

I will fear no evil,

for you are <u>with me</u>;

your rod and your staff,

they comfort me.

⁵ You prepare a table <u>before me</u>

Continued on next page »

YOUR TURN

> in the presence of my enemies;
>
> you anoint my head with oil;
>
> my cup overflows.
>
> 6   Surely goodness and mercy shall follow me
>
> all the days of my life,
>
> and I shall dwell in the house of the LORD
>
> forever.

19.10 Revisit

Directions: Go back to the mastery test in **15.9.** How many of the words in gray can you now identify as prepositions?

on, as, at, around, of, to, into, while, behind, in, with, at, like

MODULE 20

20.8 Voice: How I Felt

Directions: What part of speech is used to convey emotion in the examples above?

adverbs

Directions: List the words from the example above that give you the biggest clues about how the writer feels.

Answers will vary, but student answers should include some of the following.

I didn't wait

slipped quickly

speed dialed

"I'm in"

looking up

grabbed

lucky glove

fast-talk

Directions: Look at the expert models in **17.3** one more time. Study each sentence carefully. How does each writer feel about the events described in the excerpts? Underline the words that give you clues about the writer's feelings. Write the emotion implied by the clues in the margins of each paragraph. Explain your decisions to a parent, teacher, or writing coach.

Answers will vary. Sample answers are provided. Parent, teacher, or writing coach: Ask the student to explain his or her answers to you.

This is excerpted from Beverly Cleary's *A Girl from Yamhill: A Memoir*. Her autobiography focuses on growing up in Oregon during the 1920s and 1930s.

EXPERT MODEL

On Sunday, we walked through the misty rain down the muddy road to the white church, where I attended Sunday school in the basement and learned that Jesus loved me, and Pharaoh's daughter rescued a little baby boy she found in a basket in the bullrushes. Then the children joined their parents upstairs for the hard part of church, the endless *boredom* sermon. Hymnbooks had no pictures. Finally, when I thought I could not stand it one more minute, the sermon *relief* ended, and we were released into watery sunshine under a ragged sky. There, once more, was a rainbow that ended not *excitement* far away, at a wild crab apple tree blooming by the side of the road. I ran down the steps, past the buggies and restless horses, past automobiles, and on down the road. *excitement*

"Beverly!" Mother called out. "Where do you think you're going?"

"To get the pot of gold at the end of the rainbow." Silly *amusement* Mamma. Couldn't she see the end of this rainbow was close enough to reach?

"Come back this minute," ordered Mother. Reluctantly *reluctance* I returned to face the affectionate laughter of the dispersing congregation. Mother explained that a pot of gold was something you read about in fairy tales.

In Yamhill we did not have fairy tales, but from bits of overheard adult conversation I was beginning to understand that gold was something like money, and money was needed to buy all we did not grow.

(page 34)

Here is an excerpt from author Sid Fleischman's autobiography, *The Abracadabra Kid*.

EXPERT MODEL

skepticism

I became a writer quite by accident. In school I was being properly formatted to become a productive member of society, but I decided to become a magician instead.

worry

sadness

I was in the fifth grade. The Great Depression was a dismal year old. Even a child could sense that something was wrong, for many of the downtown shops had fallen dark as tombs. Still, San Diego, with its vast blue harbor,

hope

was luckier than most cities. It was the nesting place for the U.S. Navy Eleventh Fleet, and mercifully sailors on shore

relief

liberty had a few bucks to spend. . . .

anticipation

One autumn day the large vacant store next door was hung like a stage set with gaudy canvas signs. A ten-in-one sideshow troop had moved in. The numbers described the procession of bizarre and wonderful features you could

curiosity

witness for a single admission.

excitement

My father gave me a fateful nickel to tour this storefront extravaganza, and my life changed forever. I was allowed past the velvet curtain. There, under the blazing lights, the first performer was about to drive a gleaming six-inch spike

awe

up his nose. I watched without the slightest inclination to go home and do likewise. What I envied about the spike

interest

man were the dove gray spats he wore tightly buckled over his shoes. They struck me as worldly and theatrical.

desire

(pages 2–3)

The final model comes from "All-Ball," an essay by Mary Pope Osborne.

But one spring night when I was eight, **sadness** bad news **sadness** changed everything. . . . I was sitting on the edge of the tub while the water ran, and Dad was standing in the doorway, wearing his summer khaki uniform. "Sis"—he always called me Sis or Little Bits—"in six weeks, Daddy is going to Korea."

I looked at him and **sadness** burst into tears. I knew we wouldn't **sadness** be going with him. Though the Korean War had ended eight years earlier, U.S. soldiers were still sent there for tours of duty—without their families. **shock**

"Don't cry," he said. "I'll only be gone for a year."

shock *Only a year?*

"While I'm gone, you'll live in Florida, in Daytona Beach, near the ocean."

Daytona Beach? Away from an army post?

"You'll have a wonderful time."

"No I won't!" I hated this news. And to prove it, I **anger** pushed him out of the bathroom.

Of course, I was right and he was wrong. A few weeks later, when Dad drove our family to Daytona Beach to get us settled, I didn't find our new life wonderful at all.

Our house was low to the ground, flamingo-pink, and made of stucco. There were no kids in the whole **disgust** neighborhood. There were no real trees in our small yard— just a few scrubby ones. There was no wide open parade field to play on.

I recoiled from this new life—especially when I discovered lizards scampering across our cement driveway, **disgust** a huge water bug scuttling across the floor of the TV room, and a gigantic black spider hovering in the corner of the garage.

(pages 10–11)

20.14 Unit Review

Directions: You may write out your answers to the questions below in the space provided, or you can talk about these questions with a parent, teacher, or writing coach. You can also look over all the information in the modules you have completed to help you decide on your answers. Use the unit review to help you master the writing tips and tricks you learned about in these modules.

1. Writers choose events to write about that are surprising, funny, and dramatic. (3 points)

2. Explain these terms: (3 points)

    a. main character The main character is the most important character in a story, around whom all the action revolves.

    b. major character A major character is a character who has a significant influence on the main character or the plot.

    c. minor character A minor character is a character who appears in a story but does not have as strong an influence on the plot or main character as the major characters do.

3. What is an autobiography? (3 points)
    An autobiography is the true story of a person's life written by that person.

4. What is a story arc? (4 points)
    A story arc is the pattern writers use to hook readers emotionally, create suspense, build to a climax, and resolve the tension with an ending that satisfies readers' curiosity.

5. Name two important jobs of a title. (4 points)
    The title tells readers what they can expect the story to be about.
    The title makes readers curious about the story to follow.

6. Prepositional phrases often answer questions about what two things? (2 points)
    Prepositional phrases often answer questions about time and place.

7. Writers use phrases to add information about the subject, simple predicate, and complements. (4 points)

8. What is voice? (3 points)
    Voice is the combination of characteristics of your writing that distinguish you from every other writer.

9. Name three ways that writers develop their unique voice in their writing. (3 points)
    Writers develop voice by using dialogue, by using internal monologue, and by adding emotion to their writing.

10. Look at some of the prepositional phrases you used in your "History of Me." Write your favorites below. (1 point)
    Answers will vary.

Unit 6

MODULE 23

23.7 Voice Again

Directions: Below are some pieces of dialogue from the expert model. Match each bit of dialogue with the person who says it by drawing a line between the dialogue and the character.

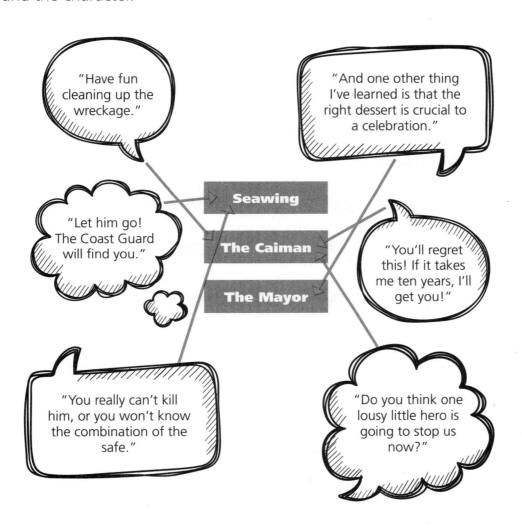

23.9 Interjections

Directions: Add interjections to the beginnings or ends of the following sentences.

Answers will vary. Sample answers are provided. Any interjection added to the beginning or the end of the sentence is a sufficient answer.

1. Yikes! That masked figure is my archenemy.

2. The bridge is about to blow up. Help!

3. Oh no! How will I escape?

4. What? The city is in danger.

5. Watch out! You could get hurt.

6. Seawing is coming. Wow!

7. I finally got my chocolate cake. Yes!

MODULE 24

24.4 Talking Transitions

Directions: Now practice writing some transitions. On the next page is the same part of the story, with blanks left for your own transitions. You can choose any transitions you want. If you get stuck, some of the words in **16.9 COMMON TRANSITIONS** may be helpful, especially the ones related to time. Fill in your own transitions on the blank lines.

Answers will vary. Sample answers are provided.

YOUR TURN

The Caiman was perched on the harbor railing, the mayor flailing in his arms. Seawing rushed toward them, _____

____but the Caiman shouted to her____.

He growled, "You'll never catch me now, Seawing! Have fun cleaning up the wreckage."

____Without another word_____,

the Caiman dove off the edge and vanished. Seawing shot higher into the air, hoping for a glimpse of what had happened.

24.5 Action Transitions

Directions: Several spaces have been left where transitions appear in the original expert model. Fill in the spaces with transitions of your own. They can be in the same structure as the original or a different structure if you prefer.

Answers will vary. Sample answers are provided.

YOUR TURN

Seawing didn't wait long. The menacing ridges of the Caiman's submarine were rising above the water. The hatch was opening. The men in midnight blue came first, then the unhappy mayor with his hands cuffed behind him, then the Caiman himself.

From above, Seawing eyed

the razor-sharp claws on the Caiman's gloves and the crushing strength of his grip. Seawing thought. Rescuing the mayor was going to be tough. What else did she see? As she looked, she spotted something. One of the men in dark blue held a massive gun, shaped differently from the others. That must have been where the fireballs had come from.

Seawing knew she had to act fast.

If they got the mayor inside the fortress, she'd never be able to get him out. At least surprise was on her side. She launched into the air and swooped down, reaching out to grab the mayor.

24.13 Unit Review

Directions: You may write your answers to the questions below and on the next two pages in the space provided, or you can talk about these questions with a parent, teacher, or writing coach. You can also look over all the information in the modules you have completed to help you decide upon your answers. Use the unit review to help you master the writing tips and tricks you learned about in these modules.

Answers will vary. Sample answers are provided.

1. The climax of the story should be the point that is most
    dramatic, intense, uncertain, full of emotion. (3 points)

2. What is one question you can use to build your plot? (3 points)
    Either of the questions below is an acceptable answer.
    How does your superhero try to solve the problem?
    What makes the problem worse or adds a new problem?

3. Should the resolution of the story answer questions or raise them? (3 points)
    The resolution should answer questions.

4. In addition to giving your character skills and traits that can help solve
    the problem, you will also want to give the character other traits. Why?
    (4 points)
    The other character traits may help the reader relate to the character.
    Other character traits will make the character more exciting or
    compelling.

5. Does a story arc need to stay exactly the same as when you first write down
    your ideas? Or are you allowed to change it after fleshing out your characters?
    (3 points) You are allowed to change the story arc you originally wrote
    down, and it's often a good idea to do so.

6. Give one reason why it's important to have a good archenemy in a story. (4 points) A good archenemy will make the problem more challenging to solve, which will in turn make the hero's actions more impressive.

7. Add proper quotation marks and punctuation where needed to the following sentences of dialogue. Also write capital letters above the regular letters to show where things should be capitalized. (4 points)

                 "B   T
   The superhero said, blast! there goes a nice day of swimming.
   I hope I can save the bridge!"

                                                         "G
   The archenemy gave a deep, villainous laugh. He bellowed, good
   luck, Mr. Hero! You'll never get there in time!"

8. You should form a new paragraph every time you switch speakers in dialogue. (2 points)

9. Why should you use transitions in fiction as well as nonfiction? (3 points) Transitions help readers to follow the story when the author switches between dialogue and action. Transitions help readers to understand when the author switches from one action scene to another. Transitions help readers move smoothly from one part to another.

10. What is your favorite line of dialogue that you wrote for your superhero or your archenemy? (1 point)
Answers will vary.

Suggested Daily Schedule

Week	Day 1	Day 2	Day 3	Day 4
1	**Introduction** ☐ Welcome to Writers in Residence! Spotlight on Christian Writers Study infographics.	**Intro to Unit 1** ☐ Discuss "Meet Bill Myers." Read "Intro to Unit 1." Study the rubric.	**Module 1** ☐ Writer's Questions –1.5	**Module 1** ☐ 1.6 – 1.9
2	**Module 1** ☐ 1.10 – 1.13	**Module 1** ☐ 1.14 – Checklist 1	**Module 2** ☐ Writer's Questions –2.3	**Module 2** ☐ 2.4 – 2.7
3	**Module 2** ☐ 2.8	**Module 2** ☐ 2.9 – 2.11	**Module 2** ☐ 2.12 – Checklist 2	**Module 3** ☐ Writer's Questions – 3.6
4	**Module 3** ☐ 3.7 – 3.10	**Module 3** ☐ Do 3.11 over the next week. 3.12 – Checklist 3	**Module 4** ☐ Writer's Questions – 4.5	**Module 4** ☐ 4.6 – 4.8
5	**Module 4** ☐ 4.9 – 4.10	**Module 4** ☐ Finish 3.11. 4.11 – Checklist 4	**Intro to Unit 2** ☐ Discuss "Meet Amy Green." Read "Intro to Unit 2." Study the rubric.	**Module 5** ☐ Writer's Questions – 5.4
6	**Module 5** ☐ 5.5 – 5.7	**Module 5** ☐ 5.8 – 5.10	**Module 5** ☐ 5.11 – 5.12	**Module 5** ☐ 5.13 – Checklist 5
7	**Module 6** ☐ Writer's Questions – 6.4	**Module 6** ☐ 6.5 – 6.7	**Module 6** ☐ 6.8 – 6.11	**Module 6** ☐ 6.12 – Checklist 6

Suggested Daily Schedule

Week	Day 1	Day 2	Day 3	Day 4
8	**Module 7** Writer's Questions – 7.3	**Module 7** 7.4 – 7.5	**Module 7** 7.6 – 7.9 Do 7.8 over the next week.	**Module 7** 7.10 – Checklist 7
9	**Module 8** Writer's Questions – 8.5	**Module 8** 8.6 – 8.9	**Module 8** 8.10 – 8.11	**Module 8** Finish 7.8. 8.12 – Checklist 8
10	Intro to Unit 3 Discuss "Meet Irene Howat." Read "Intro to Unit 3." Study the rubric.	**Module 9** Writer's Questions – 9.3	**Module 9** 9.4 – 9.5 Start 9.6.	**Module 9** 9.6 – 9.9
11	**Module 9** 9.10 – Checklist 9	**Module 10** Writer's Questions – 10.3	**Module 10** 10.4 – 10.5	**Interviews**
12	**Interviews**	**Module 10** 10.6 – 10.9	**Module 10** 10.10 – 10.12	**Module 10** 10.13 – Checklist 10
13	**Module 11** Writer's Questions – 11.5	**Module 11** 11.6 – 11.8	**Module 11** 11.9 – 11.10	**Module 11** 11.11 – Checklist 11
14	**Module 12** Writer's Questions – 12.5	**Module 12** 12.6 – 12.7	**Module 12** 12.8	**Module 12** 12.9 – 12.10
15	**Module 12** Do 12.11 over the next week. 12.12 – Checklist 12	Intro to Unit 4 Discuss "Meet Jason Lethcoe." Read "Intro to Unit 4." Study the rubric.	**Module 13** Writer's Questions – 13.4	**Module 13** 13.5 – 13.8

Suggested Daily Schedule

Week	Day 1	Day 2	Day 3	Day 4
16	**Module 13** 13.9 – 13.10	**Module 13** Finish 12.11. 13.11 – Checklist 13	**Module 14** Writer's Questions – 14.3	**Module 14** 14.4 – 14.5
17	**Module 14** 14.6 – 14.7	**Module 14** 14.8 – 14.9	**Module 14** 14.10 – 14.11	**Module 14** 14.12 – Checklist 14
18	**Module 15** Writer's Questions – 15.1	**Module 15** 15.2 – 15.5	**Module 15** 15.6 – 15.8	**Module 15** 15.9 – Checklist 15
19	**Module 16** Writer's Questions – 16.4	**Module 16** 16.5 – 16.6	**Module 16** 16.7 – 16.9	**Module 16** 16.10 – 16.11
20	**Module 16** 16.12	**Module 16** Do 16.13 over the next week. 16.14 – Checklist 16	**Intro to Unit 5** Discuss "Meet Amy Parker." Read "Intro to Unit 5." Study the rubric.	**Module 17** Writer's Questions – 17.3
21	**Module 17** 17.4 – 17.6	**Module 17** 17.7	**Module 17** 17.8 – 17.9	**Module 17** 17.10 – 17.11
22	**Module 17** Finish 16.13. 17.11 – Checklist 17	**Module 18** Writer's Questions – 18.3	**Module 18** 18.4 – 18.7	**Module 18** 18.8 – 18.10
23	**Module 18** 18.11 – 18.12	**Module 18** 18.12 – Checklist 18	**Module 19** Writer's Questions – 19.3	**Module 19** 19.3 – 19.6
24	**Module 19** 19.7 – 19.10	**Module 19** 19.11 – Checklist 19	**Module 20** Writer's Questions – 20.4	**Module 20** 20.5 – 20.7

Suggested Daily Schedule

Week	Day 1	Day 2	Day 3	Day 4
25	**Module 20** 20.8 – 20.9	**Module 20** 20.10 – 20.11	**Module 20** 20.12	**Module 20** 20.12
26	**Module 20** Do 20.13 over the next week. 20.14 – Checklist 20	Intro to Unit 6 Discuss "Meet Phil Vischer." Read "Intro to Unit 6." Study the rubric.	**Module 21** Writer's Questions – 21.4	**Module 21** 21.5 – 21.7
27	**Module 21** 21.8 – 21.9	**Module 21** Finish 20.13. 21.10 – 21.11	**Module 21** 21.12	**Module 21** 21.13 – Checklist 21
28	**Module 22** Writer's Questions – 22.4	**Module 22** 22.5 – 22.6	**Module 22** 22.7 – 22.9	**Module 22** 22.10 – 22.11
29	**Module 22** 22.11	**Module 22** 22.12 – Checklist 22	**Module 23** Writer's Questions – 23.4	**Module 23** 23.5 – 23.7
30	**Module 23** 23.8 – 23.10	**Module 23** 23.11 – Checklist 23	**Module 24** Writer's Questions – 24.4	**Module 24** 24.5 – 24.7
31	**Module 24** 24.8 – 24.9	**Module 24** 24.10 – 24.11	**Module 24** 24.11	**Module 24** Do 24.12 over the next week. 24.13 – Checklist 24
32	**Final Review**	**Final Review**	**Final Review**	**Final Review**

Unit 1 Student Rubric

Rubric Point System:

5 points – This is the best I've ever done.

4 points – This is a strength in this piece.

3 points – I improved here in this assignment.

2 points – I remembered to pay attention to this.

1 point – I need to improve in this area.

In the appendix of the Student Text and Workbook, you will find REVIEWER'S RUBRIC 3.9, which readers can use to give the student feedback on the assignment.

Rubric for "When I Was Young"	
Traits of Good Writing	**Points Earned**
Ideas • I wrote about just one place.	
• My memories are specific and vivid.	
Organization • My sentences are in chronological or topical order.	
• I like the way the order of my sentences makes pictures in my mind.	
• My readers like the way I have organized my sentences.	
Word Choice • All my nouns are as specific as they can be.	
• I have used vigorous verbs to describe the action.	
Conventions • I have capitalized all the proper nouns and the first word of each sentence.	
• I have remembered to put a period at the end of each sentence.	
• I have checked to make sure all my words are spelled correctly.	
Total	

Unit 1: 50 points possible

Unit 2 Student Rubric

Rubric for "Very Truly Yours"	
Traits of Good Writing	**Points Earned**
Ideas • I think my letter will interest a child of the age and gender I have selected.	
• I have left clues in my letter to keep my readers interested.	
• I included examples and details that show but don't tell my character traits.	
• Readers of my letter can tell what people, places, and things in my life are important to me.	
Organization • I like the way the order of my sentences makes pictures in my mind.	
• My readers like the way I have organized my sentences.	
Word Choice • All my nouns are as specific as they can be.	
• I have used vigorous verbs to describe the action.	
Conventions • I have followed the rules for capitalization carefully.	
• I have punctuated my personal letter correctly.	
• I have checked to make sure all my words are spelled correctly.	
• I have formatted the personal letter properly.	
Total	

Rubric Point System:

5 points – This is the best I've ever done.

4 points – This is a strength in this piece.

3 points – I improved here in this assignment.

2 points – I remembered to pay attention to this.

1 point – I need to improve in this area.

In the appendix of the Student Text and Workbook, you will find REVIEWER'S RUBRIC 7.6, which readers can use to give the student feedback on the assignment.

Unit 2: 60 points possible

Unit 3 Student Rubric

Rubric Point System:

5 points – This is the best I've ever done.

4 points – This is a strength in this piece.

3 points – I improved here in this assignment.

2 points – I remembered to pay attention to this.

1 point – I need to improve in this area.

In the appendix of the Student Text and Workbook, you will find REVIEWER'S RUBRIC 12.9, which readers can use to give the student feedback on the assignment.

Rubric for "My Family Hall of Fame"	
Traits of Good Writing	**Points Earned**
Ideas • I have celebrated one relative in each of my pieces.	
• I have included examples and details that show but don't tell my hall of famer's traits.	
• Readers of my paragraphs can tell what makes the relative I have chosen a family hall of famer.	
Organization • I have organized my research into paragraphs.	
• Each of my paragraphs has a central idea that is fully developed.	
• Each paragraph has a topic sentence.	
Sentence Structure • Each sentence fulfills a clear purpose in the paragraph.	
• Each sentence adds information about the preceding sentence or introduces new information.	
Word Choice • All my nouns are specific.	
• I have used vigorous verbs to describe the action.	
• I have carefully chosen adjectives that add descriptive details.	
• I have used sensory words that appeal to all five senses.	

Rubric for "My Family Hall of Fame"	
Traits of Good Writing	**Points Earned**
Conventions • I have followed the rules for capitalization carefully.	
• I have punctuated the end of each sentence correctly.	
• I have indented to show where a new paragraph begins.	
• I have checked to make sure all my words are spelled correctly.	
Total	

Unit 3: 80 points possible

Unit 4 Student Rubric

Rubric Point System:

5 points – This is the best I've ever done.

4 points – This is a strength in this piece.

3 points – I improved here in this assignment.

2 points – I remembered to pay attention to this.

1 point – I need to improve in this area.

In the appendix of the Student Text and Workbook, you will find REVIEWER'S RUBRIC 16.11, which readers can use to give the student feedback on the assignment.

Rubric for "My Favorite Author"	
Traits of Good Writing	**Points Earned**
Ideas • I have a clear statement of opinion that explains why this author is my favorite.	
• I have included distinguishing facts about this author's life and work.	
• I have three important examples that show why this author is my favorite.	
• I have developed my examples with details from his or her work.	
Organization • I have organized my essay into paragraphs.	
• My introductory paragraph includes my opinion statement and background information about my author.	
• Each of my paragraphs has a central idea that is fully developed.	
• Each paragraph has a topic sentence.	
• My conclusion sums up my opinion and gives my readers a better understanding of why this author's books are important to me.	
Sentence Structure • Each sentence fulfills a clear purpose in the paragraph.	
• Each sentence adds information about the preceding sentence or introduces new information.	
• I have used transitional words and phrases to connect my ideas.	

Rubric for "My Favorite Author"	
Traits of Good Writing	**Points Earned**
Word Choice • All my nouns are specific.	
• I have used vigorous verbs to describe the action.	
• I have carefully chosen adjectives that add descriptive details.	
• I have used adverbs to connect my ideas.	
• I have used adverbs to answer questions about the action.	
Conventions • I have followed the rules for capitalization carefully.	
• I have punctuated the end of each sentence correctly.	
• I have indented to show where a new paragraph begins.	
• I have checked to make sure all my words are spelled correctly.	
Total	

Unit 4: 105 points possible

Unit 5 Student Rubric

Rubric Point System:

5 points – This is the best I've ever done.

4 points – This is a strength in this piece.

3 points – I improved here in this assignment.

2 points – I remembered to pay attention to this.

1 point – I need to improve in this area.

In the appendix of the Student Text and Workbook, you will find REVIEWER'S RUBRIC 20.11, which readers can use to give the student feedback on the assignment.

Rubric for "The History of Me"	
Traits of Good Writing	**Points Earned**
Ideas • I have chosen a title that creates interest.	
• I have a repeated idea or theme in my life history.	
• I have focused on events from my life that are surprising, humorous, or dramatic.	
• I have included clues that give my readers a vivid sense of time and place.	
• I have developed my cast of characters.	
Organization • I have a beginning, middle, and end.	
• My opening hooks my readers.	
• I build suspense and create uncertainty.	
• I develop one event in detail to build to a climax.	
• In the end, I resolve the tension and answer all my readers' questions.	
• I close the circle with my conclusion.	
Sentence Structure • Each sentence fulfills a clear purpose in the paragraph.	
• Each sentence adds information about the preceding sentence or introduces new information.	
• I have used transitions to connect my ideas.	
• I have used prepositional phrases to build better sentences.	

Rubric for "The History of Me"	
Traits of Good Writing	**Points Earned**
Word Choice • All my nouns are specific.	
• I have used vigorous verbs to describe the action.	
• I have carefully chosen adjectives that add descriptive details.	
• I have used adverbs to connect my ideas.	
• I have used adverbs to answer questions about the action.	
Voice • I have added dialogue to important moments in my autobiography.	
• I have included an internal monologue in several places to show my readers what I thought and felt.	
• I have added emotion to my writing.	
Conventions • I have followed the rules for capitalization carefully.	
• I have punctuated the end of each sentence correctly.	
• I have indented to show where a new paragraph begins.	
• I have checked to make sure all my words are spelled correctly.	
Total	

Unit 5: 135 points possible

Unit 6 Student Rubric

Rubric Point System:

5 points – This is the best I've ever done.

4 points – This is a strength in this piece.

3 points – I improved here in this assignment.

2 points – I remembered to pay attention to this.

1 point – I need to improve in this area.

In the appendix of the Student Text and Workbook, you will find REVIEWER'S RUBRIC 24.10, which readers can use to give the student feedback on the assignment.

Rubric for "Zap! Pow! Kazam!"	
Traits of Good Writing	**Points Earned**
Ideas • I have a dramatic central problem for my hero to solve.	
• My hero has skills and traits that will help to solve the central problem.	
• I have a compelling hero with traits that are dramatic or easy to relate to.	
• I have a frightening villain who can make the central problem worse.	
Organization • The story starts at a dramatic moment.	
• I build suspense by making the problem worse or adding new ones for my hero to solve.	
• My story arc builds toward an intense climax.	
• My story has a satisfying resolution that answers readers' questions.	
Sentence Structure • I have used transitional words and phrases to make smooth shifts between scenes, action, dialogue, and thoughts.	
• I have chosen good places to add interjections.	
Word Choice • All my nouns are specific.	
• I have used vigorous verbs to describe the action.	
• I have carefully chosen adjectives that add descriptive details.	
• I have used adverbs to answer questions about the action.	

Rubric for "Zap! Pow! Kazam!"	
Traits of Good Writing	**Points Earned**
Voice • Each character's speaking style is different.	
• When my characters carry on internal monologue, it is consistent with their voices in the dialogue.	
• I have used interjections effectively to add emotion.	
Conventions • I have used quotation marks to show when a character starts or stops speaking.	
• I have used end punctuation correctly within lines of dialogue.	
• I have capitalized correctly in sentences with dialogue.	
• I have started a new paragraph when a new speaker starts to say something.	
Total	

Unit 6: 105 points possible

Checklist for Module 1

Directions: When you have completed a task, make a ✔ in the "Done" column. Ask a parent, teacher, or writing coach to award you points for each task using the checklist point system. Grid in the points you have earned on the APPRENTICE LOG in the appendix.

Checklist Point System:

1–6 points may be awarded by a parent, teacher, or writing coach for each task completed. Here are the recommended guidelines:

6 – exemplary in quality *and* effort

5 – exemplary in either quality *or* effort

4 – acceptable in quality *and* effort

3 – acceptable in either quality *or* effort

2 – needs improvement in quality *and* effort

1 – incomplete

Tasks	Done ✔	Points Earned
1.5 Panning for Gold • Write the name of the special place from your childhood you are most interested in writing about.		
1.6 Gather Your Best Ideas • Use the strategies in 1.5 PANNING FOR GOLD to help you recall specific events and experiences that occurred in your special place.		
• Talk about your memories with others to help you generate lots of details about your special place.		
1.7 Memory Chart • Use the memory chart to collect the memories from your special place.		
• Check to make sure your memories came from one place.		
1.9 Write Your Memory Sentences • Write at least ten memory sentences.		
• Follow Cynthia Rylant's sentence pattern from *When I Was Young in the Mountains*.		
1.10 Vigorous Verbs • List more specific verbs for *run, hit,* and *cut.*		
1.11 Practice • Replace the red verbs with more vigorous verbs.		

Tasks	Done ✔	Points Earned
1.12 Vocabulary: Walk This Way • Practice the different manners of walking on the vocabulary list.		
1.13 The Sandbox • Invent a short story about a fictional version of yourself as an action hero. Create an archenemy too.		
• Use a lot of vigorous verbs to describe the action. Include some from the vocabulary list in 1.12.		
1.14 Revise: Verbs • Underline the verbs you used to describe the action in each of your memory sentences.		
• Replace at least five verbs in your memory sentences with more specific, vigorous verbs.		
1.15 Word Sleuth • Add spelling words and new words to your WORD COLLECTION.		
1.16 Revisit: Writer's Questions • Discuss your answers to the WRITER'S QUESTIONS from the beginning of the module with a parent, teacher, or writing coach.		
Total		

Module 1: 96 points possible

Checklist for Module 2

Directions: When you have completed a task, make a ✔ in the "Done" column. Ask a parent, teacher, or writing coach to award you points for each task using the checklist point system. Grid in the points you have earned on the APPRENTICE LOG in the appendix.

Checklist Point System:

1–6 points may be awarded by a parent, teacher, or writing coach for each task completed. Here are the recommended guidelines:

6 – exemplary in quality *and* effort

5 – exemplary in either quality *or* effort

4 – acceptable in quality *and* effort

3 – acceptable in either quality *or* effort

2 – needs improvement in quality *and* effort

1 – incomplete

Tasks	Done ✔	Points Earned
2.3 Who Is This and What Is That? • Name at least twenty-five things from your memory place that you can see in your mind's eye.		
• Underline and label the nouns in Cynthia Rylant's sentences (PR for person, PL for place, or TH for thing).		
2.5 From Fuzzy to Focused • List more specific nouns that name types of things included in the general category.		
2.6 Here We Go on a Noun Hunt • Make a list of every *person* you name in your memory sentences.		
• Make a list of every *place* you name in your memory sentences.		
• Make a list of every *thing* you name in your memory sentences.		
• Ask a parent, teacher, or writing coach to compare your lists to your memory sentences to find nouns you may have missed.		
2.7 Revise: Nouns • Draw a line through the nouns in your memory sentences in 1.9 that you can replace with more specific nouns, and then write a new noun above each one you crossed out.		
• Write a second draft of your memory sentences.		

Tasks	Done ✔	Points Earned
2.8 The History of Your Name • Write your full name on the line provided.		
• Research the history of your name and write down what you find out about it.		
2.9 Common and Proper Nouns • Write down what writers do to proper nouns to let readers know they are talking about something that is one of a kind.		
2.11 Practice • Draw three lines under the first letter of each word in the paragraph that should be capitalized.		
• Write two sentences that include both common nouns and proper nouns.		
2.12 Inspect • Check to make sure all personal names in your memory sentences are capitalized.		
2.13 Word Sleuth • Add new words and spelling words to your WORD COLLECTION.		
2.14 Revisit: Writer's Questions • Discuss your answers to the WRITER'S QUESTIONS from the beginning of the module with a parent, teacher, or writing coach.		
Total		

Module 2: 102 points possible

Checklist for Module 3

Directions: When you have completed a task, make a ✔ in the "Done" column. Ask a parent, teacher, or writing coach to award you points for each task using the checklist point system. Grid in the points you have earned on the APPRENTICE LOG in the appendix.

Checklist Point System:

1–6 points may be awarded by a parent, teacher, or writing coach for each task completed. Here are the recommended guidelines:

6 – exemplary in quality *and* effort

5 – exemplary in either quality *or* effort

4 – acceptable in quality *and* effort

3 – acceptable in either quality *or* effort

2 – needs improvement in quality *and* effort

1 – incomplete

Tasks	Done ✔	Points Earned
3.4 Time after Time • Put the events of the story in chronological order.		
3.5 Here a Topic, There a Topic • Decide what topics some of your sentences have in common. List some of these topics on the lines provided.		
• If you like, write some additional memory sentences about these topics.		
3.6 Strips of Sentences • Write your memory sentences in the ten boxes provided.		
• Cut out the boxes to create a sentence strip for each sentence.		
3.7 Everybody Do-Si-Do • Arrange your sentences in chronological order. Read this arrangement aloud. Do you like the way this arrangement sounds?		
• Arrange your sentences by the topics they share. Then decide how you want to organize the topics. Read this arrangement aloud. Do you like the way this arrangement sounds?		
3.8 Test Drive • Have at least two people read your arrangements aloud. Ask them to help you decide which arrangement is the best.		

Tasks	Done ✔	Points Earned
3.9 Rubric for "When I Was Young" • Study the rubric carefully before you write your final draft.		
3.10 The Final Draft • Write the final draft of your memory sentences.		
• Share the final version of your memory sentences with as many readers as you can.		
• Place your final draft in your WRITER'S PORTFOLIO.		
3.11 You Be the Judge • Together with a parent, teacher, or writing coach, use RUBRIC 3.9 to evaluate the final version of your memory sentences.		
3.12 Unit Review • Write your answers to the questions or talk about them with a parent, teacher, or writing coach. Record your score in the Points Earned column on the right.		
3.13 Word Sleuth • Add new words and spelling words to your WORD COLLECTION.		
3.14 Revisit: Writer's Questions • Discuss your answers to the WRITER'S QUESTIONS from the beginning of the module with a parent, teacher, or writing coach.		
Total		

Module 3: 90 points possible, plus 30 points for Unit Review

Checklist for Module 4

Directions: When you have completed a task, make a ✔ in the "Done" column. Ask a parent, teacher, or writing coach to award you points for each task using the checklist point system. Grid in the points you have earned on the APPRENTICE LOG in the appendix.

Tasks	Done ✔	Points Earned
4.3 Let's Start at the Very Beginning • Write what all the sentences have in common.		
4.4 Find the Subject • Circle the subject of each sentence.		
4.5 Find the Predicate • Underline the entire predicate of each sentence.		
• Double underline the simple predicate of each sentence.		
4.6 Is the Thought Complete? • Capitalize the first word and put a period at the end of each group of words that forms a complete sentence.		
4.7 Compound Subjects • Complete the sentences using the compound subjects provided.		
• Write two original sentences with compound subjects.		
4.8 Compound Predicates • Complete the sentences using the compound predicates provided.		
• Underline the complete predicate and mark each verb with a "v." above it.		
4.9 Review • Draw a line connecting each grammar term to its example.		
4.10 Mastery Test • Write sentences that fit the patterns requested.		

Tasks	Done ✔	Points Earned
• Make each sentence about you with a superpower or about your archenemy.		
4.11 Word Sleuth • Add new words and spelling words to your WORD COLLECTION.		
4.12 Revisit: Writer's Questions • Discuss your answers to the WRITER'S QUESTIONS from the beginning of the module with a parent, teacher, or writing coach.		
Total		

Module 4: 84 points possible

Checklist for Module 5

Directions: When you have completed a task, make a ✔ in the "Done" column. Ask a parent, teacher, or writing coach to award you points for each task using the checklist point system. Grid in the points you have earned on the APPRENTICE LOG in the appendix.

Checklist Point System:

1–6 points may be awarded by a parent, teacher, or writing coach for each task completed. Here are the recommended guidelines:

6 – exemplary in quality *and* effort

5 – exemplary in either quality *or* effort

4 – acceptable in quality *and* effort

3 – acceptable in either quality *or* effort

2 – needs improvement in quality *and* effort

1 – incomplete

Tasks	Done ✔	Points Earned
5.2 The Power of Questions • Set a timer for sixty seconds and imagine the family you would like to have someday.		
• Write twenty questions you can ask yourself about your future family.		
5.5 Detective Work • List some of the reasons why you stop reading a book.		
• If you wrote "because it is boring," think about what makes a story boring and write that down too.		
• Write or discuss your answers to the questions in this section.		
5.6 Adjectives Describe Characters • Circle some of the traits that best describe you.		
5.7 Vocabulary Work: I Am What I Am • Define each of the vocabulary words.		
• Give an example of a person you know or a character from a book, a movie, or the Bible who shows each character trait.		
5.8 Show but Don't Tell • Write down a character trait for Sarah suggested by each sentence from her letters.		
5.9 Character Traits Chart • Give at least two examples for at least three traits you circled in 5.6.		

Tasks	Done ✔	Points Earned
5.10 Here We Go on a Noun Hunt . . . Again! • Circle the nouns in Sarah's letters.		
• Fill out the chart with some of the people, places, and things mentioned in Sarah's letters.		
• Fill out the chart with some of the people, places, and things in your life.		
5.11 Practice • Fill out a Character Traits chart for you, the superhero, and for the archenemy you created in 1.13.		
5.12 The Sandbox • Write an episode for your superhero story. Use the action to show your readers the character trait you chose for your superhero and your archenemy in 5.11.		
• Ask several readers to name the character traits revealed.		
• Put your draft in your WRITER'S PORTFOLIO.		
5.13 Word Sleuth • Add spelling words and new words to your WORD COLLECTION.		
5.14 Revisit: Writer's Questions • Discuss your answers to the WRITER'S QUESTIONS from the beginning of the module with a parent, teacher, or writing coach.		
Total		

Module 5: 114 points possible

Checklist for Module 6

Directions: When you have completed a task, make a ✔ in the "Done" column. Ask a parent, teacher, or writing coach to award you points for each task using the checklist point system. Grid in the points you have earned on the Apprentice Log in the appendix.

Checklist Point System:

1–6 points may be awarded by a parent, teacher, or writing coach for each task completed. Here are the recommended guidelines:

6 – exemplary in quality *and* effort

5 – exemplary in either quality *or* effort

4 – acceptable in quality *and* effort

3 – acceptable in either quality *or* effort

2 – needs improvement in quality *and* effort

1 – incomplete

Tasks	Done ✔	Points Earned
6.3 Conventions of the English Language • List several reasons why it is important to play by the rules when playing a game with friends.		
6.5 Capitalize Place Names • Circle the capital letters in 6.4.		
• Write three possible rules for capitalization that apply in 6.4.		
6.7 Practice • Draw three lines under the first letter of each word that should be capitalized.		
6.8 Punctuate! • Draw a supersize version of each punctuation mark in the chart.		
• Study the punctuation in 6.4. Read the letter aloud. Think about how punctuation marks help you understand the letter.		
6.9 Using Commas in a Personal Letter • Draw a box around every comma in 6.4.		
6.11 Draft Your Letters • Choose an age, gender, and name for each child you write to.		
• Imagine what you would like to know about a parent's childhood. Add your own ideas in the space provided.		
• Use the information from the charts you completed in 5.9 and 5.10 to help you decide what to include in your letters.		

Tasks	Done ✔	Points Earned
• Draft at least two letters to your future children.		
• Use proper capitalization, punctuation, and formatting in your drafts.		
6.12 Word Sleuth • Add spelling words and new words to your WORD COLLECTION.		
6.13 Revisit: Writer's Questions • Discuss your answers to the WRITER'S QUESTIONS from the beginning of the module with a parent, teacher, or writing coach.		
Total		

Module 6: 84 points possible

Checklist for Module 7

Directions: When you have completed a task, make a ✔ in the "Done" column. Ask a parent, teacher, or writing coach to award you points for each task using the checklist point system. Grid in the points you have earned on the APPRENTICE LOG in the appendix.

Checklist Point System:

1–6 points may be awarded by a parent, teacher, or writing coach for each task completed. Here are the recommended guidelines:

6 – exemplary in quality *and* effort

5 – exemplary in either quality *or* effort

4 – acceptable in quality *and* effort

3 – acceptable in either quality *or* effort

2 – needs improvement in quality *and* effort

1 – incomplete

Tasks	Done ✔	Points Earned
7.3 Readers Needed • Ask two friends or family members to read the first drafts of your two letters.		
• Take notes on their answers to the questions.		
7.4 Revise • Write down several ways you will revise your letters based on their feedback on your drafts.		
7.5 Detective Work • Circle all the nouns in your letters. Make sure you have included all the people, places, and things you care about.		
• Revise to make your nouns more specific and vivid.		
• Include examples that show but don't tell your character traits.		
• Draw three lines under each capital letter. Make sure you have capitalized every proper noun.		
• Make sure you have all the commas you need in the right places.		
• Make sure you have formatted all the parts of your letter correctly.		
• Write a second draft of each letter based upon the information you gathered from your test readers and detective work.		

Tasks	Done ✔	Points Earned
7.6 Rubric for "Very Truly Yours" • Study the rubric carefully before you write your final version of your letters.		
7.7 Spit, Polish, and Shine • Write the final draft of each letter.		
• Make a copy of your final versions and put the copies in your WRITER'S PORTFOLIO.		
7.8 You Be the Judge • Together with a parent, teacher, or writing coach, use RUBRIC 7.6 to evaluate the final version of each letter.		
7.9 Address and Mail • Properly address an envelope for each letter, add stamps, and mail them.		
• Record the date mailed and the date received.		
7.10 Unit Review • Write your answers to the questions or talk about them with a parent, teacher, or writing coach. Record your score in the Points Earned column on the right.		
7.11 Word Sleuth • Add spelling words and new words to your WORD COLLECTION.		
7.12 Revisit: Writer's Questions • Discuss your answers to the WRITER'S QUESTIONS from the beginning of the module with a parent, teacher, or writing coach.		
Total		

Module 7: 108 points possible, plus 30 points for Unit Review

Checklist for Module 8

Directions: When you have completed a task, make a ✔ in the "Done" column. Ask a parent, teacher, or writing coach to award you points for each task using the checklist point system. Grid in the points you have earned on the Apprentice Log in the appendix.

Checklist Point System:

1–6 points may be awarded by a parent, teacher, or writing coach for each task completed. Here are the recommended guidelines:

6 – exemplary in quality *and* effort

5 – exemplary in either quality *or* effort

4 – acceptable in quality *and* effort

3 – acceptable in either quality *or* effort

2 – needs improvement in quality *and* effort

1 – incomplete

Tasks	Done ✔	Points Earned
8.1 Review Your Progress • Fill in the blanks.		
8.5 Answer the Question • Complete each sentence with a word or group of words to answer the question.		
8.6 More Than One Question • Write new sentences that answer the questions.		
8.7 It Has to Be New • Write another sentence about Callie that answers a question with an additional sentence.		
8.9 Link Up • Build four sentences using the subjects, linking verbs, and complements provided.		
8.10 Work Zone • Complete the sentences using the specified building blocks.		
• Capitalize the first word of each sentence and put a period at the end.		
8.11 Mastery Test • Study your written work from 1.13, 5.12, and 7.7.		
• Find the simple sentences in your writing.		
• Find the action verbs.		

Tasks	Done ✔	Points Earned
• Find the compound subjects.		
• Find the compound predicates.		
• Find the complements.		
• Find the compound complements.		
• List questions you answer with other sentence parts in your sentences.		
• Find the linking verbs.		
• Find your three favorite sentences and state what you like best about each.		
8.12 Word Sleuth • Add spelling words and new words to your WORD COLLECTION.		
8.13 Revisit: Writer's Questions • Discuss your answers to the WRITER'S QUESTIONS from the beginning of the module with a parent, teacher, or writing coach.		
Total		

Module 8: 114 points possible

Checklist for Module 9

Directions: When you have completed a task, make a ✔ in the "Done" column. Ask a parent, teacher, or writing coach to award you points for each task using the checklist point system. Grid in the points you have earned on the Apprentice Log in the appendix.

Checklist Point System:

1–6 points may be awarded by a parent, teacher, or writing coach for each task completed. Here are the recommended guidelines:

6 – exemplary in quality *and* effort

5 – exemplary in either quality *or* effort

4 – acceptable in quality *and* effort

3 – acceptable in either quality *or* effort

2 – needs improvement in quality *and* effort

1 – incomplete

Tasks	Done ✔	Points Earned
9.3 Expert Model • List the best vigorous verbs.		
• List the best specific nouns.		
• Write down the character traits you see in Roald Dahl's father.		
9.4 Vocabulary: My Roots Run Deep • Write definitions for each vocabulary word.		
• Have a conversation about your family history with a parent or sibling using the vocabulary words.		
• Name the part of speech each word shares.		
9.5 My Family Tree • Complete your family tree using the graphic organizer provided.		
9.6 Digging Deeper • Gather all the family archives you can find. Decide how to label and store them when you are finished using them.		
9.7 Get Organized • Decide how to organize your family archives.		
• Make a list of categories you will use for organizing information about your family.		
• File your information in chronological order in each category.		

Tasks	Done ✔	Points Earned
9.8 Be Prepared • Make a list of the relatives who can help you collect information about your family.		
• Make a list of the relatives or ancestors you want to learn more about.		
• Begin preparing a list of questions to ask in your interviews.		
9.9 Now That Is a Good Question! • Study 9.3 EXPERT MODEL.		
• Make a list of open and closed questions you think the writer asked.		
9.10 Your Turn • Draft an equal number of open and closed questions for your interviews—at least twenty questions total.		
• Make sure you ask questions about the topics you chose for your categories.		
• Have a parent, teacher, or writing coach look over the questions you created.		
• Write a final draft of your questions for your interviews.		
9.11 Word Sleuth • Add spelling words and new words to your WORD COLLECTION.		
9.12 Revisit: Writer's Questions • Discuss your answers to the WRITER'S QUESTIONS from the beginning of this module with a parent, teacher, or writing coach.		
Total		

Module 9: 132 points possible

Checklist for Module 10

Directions: When you have completed a task, make a ✔ in the "Done" column. Ask a parent, teacher, or writing coach to award you points for each task using the checklist point system. Grid in the points you have earned on the APPRENTICE LOG in the appendix.

Checklist Point System:

1–6 points may be awarded by a parent, teacher, or writing coach for each task completed. Here are the recommended guidelines:

6 – exemplary in quality *and* effort

5 – exemplary in either quality *or* effort

4 – acceptable in quality *and* effort

3 – acceptable in either quality *or* effort

2 – needs improvement in quality *and* effort

1 – incomplete

Tasks	Done ✔	Points Earned
10.3 Interview Etiquette • Circle the practical ideas that will help you be considerate and professional.		
• Cross out those that won't.		
• Add some of your own.		
10.4 Taking Notes • Write down the note-taking method(s) you will try during your interviews.		
10.5 Conducting an Interview • Do a dry run of an interview with a parent, teacher, or writing coach.		
• Talk through your plans for showing consideration and professionalism.		
• Practice establishing rapport.		
• Ask some questions and demonstrate how you will show you are listening.		
• Test any technical equipment you plan to use.		
• Conduct your interview.		
10.6 After an Interview • Review and organize your notes.		
• Add more details you want to remember.		
• Talk through your interview with a parent, teacher, or writing coach.		

Tasks	Done ✔	Points Earned
10.7 Time to Reflect • Complete a FOLLOW-UP REPORT FOR MY INTERVIEW form for each interview. Record your score in the Points Earned column on the right.		
10.8 Meet the Mighty Paragraph • Identify the central idea for each of Roald Dahl's paragraphs about his father in 9.3.		
10.9 Gather Your Building Blocks • List the relatives you will write about for this assignment.		
• Use the PARAGRAPH PLANNING CHART to plan your paragraphs.		
• Divide large categories into smaller ones.		
10.11 First Drafts • Type or handwrite your first drafts of the paragraphs about your family hall of famers.		
• Write at least three paragraphs about each person.		
10.12 Paragraph Building Checklist • Name the central idea of each paragraph. Make sure every sentence is related to it.		
• Make sure each sentence adds more information about the sentence before it or introduces new information about the central idea.		
• Use strategies from 10.10 to help you develop your sentences.		
10.13 Word Sleuth • Add spelling words and new words to your WORD COLLECTION.		
10.14 Revisit: Writer's Questions • Discuss your answers to the WRITER'S QUESTIONS from the beginning of the module with a parent, teacher, or writing coach.		
Total		

Module 10: 144 points possible, plus points from 10.7 Follow-Up Reports

Checklist for Module 11

Directions: When you have completed a task, make a ✔ in the "Done" column. Ask a parent, teacher, or writing coach to award you points for each task using the checklist point system. Grid in the points you have earned on the Apprentice Log in the appendix.

Checklist Point System:

1–6 points may be awarded by a parent, teacher, or writing coach for each task completed. Here are the recommended guidelines:

6 – exemplary in quality *and* effort

5 – exemplary in either quality *or* effort

4 – acceptable in quality *and* effort

3 – acceptable in either quality *or* effort

2 – needs improvement in quality *and* effort

1 – incomplete

Tasks	Done ✔	Points Earned
11.1 Review Your Progress • Fill in the blanks.		
11.5 Roald Dahl's Adjectives • Circle the noun that is modified by each adjective.		
11.6 Where Can You Use Them? • Circle the noun or pronoun that is modified by each adjective.		
11.7 Now You Try • Fill in the blanks with adjectives that answer the questions.		
11.8 Sensory Words • Add your own sensory words to each column.		
11.9 A Dragon We Can See, Hear, Smell, Taste, and Touch! • Use adjectives to answer the questions.		
11.10 Bring Your Hall of Famers to Life • Review your first draft. Add adjectives that tell which one, whose, how many, in which order, and what kind.		
• Use adjectives to give your readers a multisensory experience.		
• Use a caret to show where you want to insert additional words or sentences.		
• Write a final draft of your paragraph.		

Tasks	Done ✔	Points Earned
11.11 Mastery Test • Write a paragraph that describes what you see in the painting.		
• Underline all the adjectives in your paragraph.		
• Describe what you imagine you might hear if you were in the boat.		
• Describe what you imagine you might feel if you were in the boat.		
• Describe what you imagine you might smell if you were in the boat.		
• Write a final draft of your paragraph.		
11.12 Word Sleuth • Add spelling words and new words to your WORD COLLECTION.		
11.13 Revisit: Writer's Questions • Discuss your answers to the WRITER'S QUESTIONS from the beginning of the module with a parent, teacher, or writing coach.		
Total		

Module 11: 108 points possible

Checklist for Module 12

Directions: When you have completed a task, make a ✔ in the "Done" column. Ask a parent, teacher, or writing coach to award you points for each task using the checklist point system. Grid in the points you have earned on the APPRENTICE LOG in the appendix.

Checklist Point System:

1–6 points may be awarded by a parent, teacher, or writing coach for each task completed. Here are the recommended guidelines:

6 – exemplary in quality *and* effort

5 – exemplary in either quality *or* effort

4 – acceptable in quality *and* effort

3 – acceptable in either quality *or* effort

2 – needs improvement in quality *and* effort

1 – incomplete

Tasks	Done ✔	Points Earned
12.5 Inspect and Improve: Paragraphs • Write down the evidence that shows how you honor each relative you've chosen. List what you will add to improve this.		
• Write down what you have included that should please the person this is about. Or list what you will add to improve this.		
• Write down the details that show why each relative is famous in your family history. Or list what you will add to improve this.		
• Write down what your readers will remember about each relative. Or list what you will add to improve this.		
• List the central idea of each paragraph.		
• Highlight the topic sentence of each paragraph. Or use a caret to show where you will insert one.		
12.6 Inspect and Improve: Sentences • Make sure each sentence contributes to the central idea of the paragraph.		
• Identify the strategy you use for each sentence in the paragraph. Put the number of the strategy you used at the end of every sentence in your drafts. Or rewrite the sentence to match one of the strategies listed.		
• Add more sentences to any ideas that you can explain more completely.		
12.7 Inspect and Improve: Words • Make sure you have used many specific nouns.		
• Make sure your nouns tell the reader who, what, when, and where.		
• Add more nouns and replace weak ones.		
• Make sure your verbs are vigorous and your paragraphs are packed with action.		

Tasks	Done ✔	Points Earned
• Make sure your adjectives add details and sensory words.		
• Write a second draft of your paragraphs.		
12.8 Readers Needed • Ask Reader 1 to go through the same process you did to inspect and improve your paragraphs.		
• Ask Reader 2 to go through the same process you did to inspect and improve your paragraphs.		
• Ask Reader 3 to go through the same process you did to inspect and improve your paragraphs.		
12.9 Rubric for "My Family Hall of Fame" • Study the rubric for this assignment before you write the final draft of your paragraphs.		
12.10 Finally, Final Draft • Write or type your final versions of your paragraphs.		
12.11 You Be the Judge • Together with a parent, teacher, or writing coach, use Rubric 12.9 to evaluate the final version of each set of paragraphs you wrote about your family hall of famers.		
12.12 Unit Review • Write your answers to the questions or talk about them with a parent, teacher, or writing coach. Record your score in the Points Earned column on the right.		
12.13 Word Sleuth • Add spelling words and new words to your Word Collection.		
12.14 Revisit: Writer's Questions • Discuss your answers to the Writer's Questions from the beginning of this module with a parent, teacher, or writing coach.		
Total		

Module 12: 138 points possible, plus 30 points for Unit Review

Checklist for Module 13

Directions: When you have completed a task, make a ✔ in the "Done" column. Ask a parent, teacher, or writing coach to award you points for each task using the checklist point system. Grid in the points you have earned on the APPRENTICE LOG in the appendix.

Checklist Point System:

1–6 points may be awarded by a parent, teacher, or writing coach for each task completed. Here are the recommended guidelines:

6 – exemplary in quality *and* effort

5 – exemplary in either quality *or* effort

4 – acceptable in quality *and* effort

3 – acceptable in either quality *or* effort

2 – needs improvement in quality *and* effort

1 – incomplete

Tasks	Done ✔	Points Earned
13.3 Expert Model • Note what is different about each of the paragraphs.		
• Note what is similar about some of the paragraphs.		
• Look up words you do not know and add them to your WORD COLLECTION.		
• Talk about the expert model with a parent, teacher, or writing coach.		
13.6 Choose a Topic: Make a List and Check It Twice • Choose at least two authors to compare.		
• List your sources of facts about each author's life and career.		
• List the possible reasons you will give for choosing each author.		
• List some sources of examples and details that support your reasons.		
13.7 Choose a Topic: Are You Interested? • Name the favorite author you will write about for this assignment.		
13.8 Gather Your Resources • List the resources you will use to help you develop your opinion essay.		
13.9 Think It Through • Take notes while you research and think about your author's life and work.		

CHECKLISTS

Tasks	Done ✔	Points Earned
13.10 Vocabulary: A Writer's Life for Me • Write a brief description of each type of writer.		
• Circle the three that interest you most.		
13.11 The Sandbox • Find two books you really like and write (or type) the opening for each.		
• Cross out and replace all the proper nouns.		
• Cross out and replace some of the common nouns.		
• Cross out and replace the action verbs.		
• Read the opening of your new stories aloud to someone.		
• With a parent, teacher, or writing coach, talk about the differences between the openings you chose.		
13.12 Word Sleuth • Add spelling words and new words to your WORD COLLECTION.		
13.13 Revisit: Writer's Questions • Discuss your answers to the WRITER'S QUESTIONS from the beginning of this module with a parent, teacher, or writing coach.		
Total		

Module 13: 126 points possible

Checklist for Module 14

Directions: When you have completed a task, make a ✔ in the "Done" column. Ask a parent, teacher, or writing coach to award you points for each task using the checklist point system. Grid in the points you have earned on the APPRENTICE LOG in the appendix.

Checklist Point System:

1–6 points may be awarded by a parent, teacher, or writing coach for each task completed. Here are the recommended guidelines:

6 – exemplary in quality *and* effort

5 – exemplary in either quality *or* effort

4 – acceptable in quality *and* effort

3 – acceptable in either quality *or* effort

2 – needs improvement in quality *and* effort

1 – incomplete

Tasks	Done ✔	Points Earned
14.3 Is It a Topic or Opinion? • Decide whether each statement is a topic or an opinion.		
• Rewrite each statement that only names a topic to include an opinion.		
14.5 Think Deeply • List all of your reasons for selecting an author as your favorite.		
• Ask a parent, teacher, or writing coach to help you choose one reason that best sums up many of the reasons why he or she is your favorite.		
• Write the opinion statement you will use as the foundation for your essay.		
14.6 Facts, Examples, and Details • Make a list of facts, a list of examples, and a list of details you can use in your essay.		
14.7 Blueprint for Success • Write a working outline for your opinion essay.		
14.8 Info in the Intro • Write the surprising fact the writer uses to open her essay in 13.3 EXPERT MODEL.		
14.9 Write the Introductory Paragraph • Write or type the first draft of your introductory paragraph.		
• Introduce your favorite author to your readers.		
• Capture your readers' interest with a surprising fact about the author.		

Tasks	Done ✔	Points Earned
• Explain why the author is your favorite in your opinion statement.		
• Include facts and details about the author's life and work that distinguish him or her.		
• Check off each item as you include it in your introductory paragraph.		
14.10 Build Your Body Paragraphs • Write or type the first draft of your body paragraphs.		
• Use one of the examples that supports your opinion statement as the central organizing idea of each body paragraph.		
• Provide specific, vivid details.		
• Highlight the topic sentence and the supporting details of each paragraph.		
14.11 Readers Needed • Ask a parent, teacher, or writing coach for feedback on what you have written so far, using the questions provided.		
• Ask a few others readers some of the same questions.		
• Ask your readers some of your own questions.		
• List the most helpful advice you received from your readers.		
14.12 Word Sleuth • Add spelling words and new words to your WORD COLLECTION.		
14.13 Revisit: Writer's Questions • Discuss your answers to the WRITER'S QUESTIONS from the beginning of this module with a parent, teacher, or writing coach.		
Total		

Module 14: 144 points possible

121

Checklist for Module 15

Directions: When you have completed a task, make a ✔ in the "Done" column. Ask a parent, teacher, or writing coach to award you points for each task using the checklist point system. Grid in the points you have earned on the APPRENTICE LOG in the appendix.

Checklist Point System:

1–6 points may be awarded by a parent, teacher, or writing coach for each task completed. Here are the recommended guidelines:

6 – exemplary in quality *and* effort

5 – exemplary in either quality *or* effort

4 – acceptable in quality *and* effort

3 – acceptable in either quality *or* effort

2 – needs improvement in quality *and* effort

1 – incomplete

Tasks	Done ✔	Points Earned
15.1 Review Your Progress • Answer the questions about module 4.		
• Answer the questions about module 8.		
• Write about a favorite Bible story. Use adjectives to describe what you might hear, smell, taste, touch, and see.		
15.2 Language of the Trade • Review the sentence parts you have learned about so far.		
• Put a check mark beside the sentence parts you have used in the rough draft of your essay.		
15.3 Modify with Adverbs • Write down what many of the adverbs in the example sentences have in common.		
15.5 Work Those Adverbs • Create a sentence using a form of each verb provided.		
• Modify each verb with the type of adverb requested.		
15.6 Connect with Adverbs • Fill in the blanks with adverbs that show a connection between the sentences or sentence parts.		
15.7 What's Your Style? • Look over some of your past writing assignments and see how many adverbs you can find.		

Tasks	Done ✔	Points Earned
• Write down some of your sentences with adverbs.		
• If you cannot find any adverbs, then add some adverbs to a few of your sentences and write them down.		
15.8 More Than One Part of Speech • Identify the part of speech for each word in boldface in the sentences.		
15.9 Mastery Test • List some of the proper nouns you can find in the excerpt from *Charlotte's Web*.		
• List some of the common nouns you can find in the excerpt.		
• List some of the verbs you can find in the excerpt.		
• List some of the adjectives you can find in the excerpt.		
• List some of the adverbs you can find in the excerpt.		
• List some of the conjunctions you can find in the excerpt.		
15.10 Word Sleuth • Add spelling words and new words to your WORD COLLECTION.		
15.11 Revisit: Writer's Questions • Discuss your answers to the WRITER'S QUESTIONS from the beginning of this module with a parent, teacher, or writing coach.		
Total		

Module 15: 126 points possible

Checklist for Module 16

Directions: When you have completed a task, make a ✔ in the "Done" column. Ask a parent, teacher, or writing coach to award you points for each task using the checklist point system. Grid in the points you have earned on the APPRENTICE LOG in the appendix.

Checklist Point System:

1–6 points may be awarded by a parent, teacher, or writing coach for each task completed. Here are the recommended guidelines:

6 – exemplary in quality *and* effort

5 – exemplary in either quality *or* effort

4 – acceptable in quality *and* effort

3 – acceptable in either quality *or* effort

2 – needs improvement in quality *and* effort

1 – incomplete

Tasks	Done ✔	Points Earned
16.3 Why Do I Need a Conclusion? • Write down your answers to the questions about conclusions.		
• Talk with a parent, teacher, or writing coach about the answers to the questions if you need help.		
16.4 What Is Your Goal? • Write down the goal of your opinion essay.		
16.5 Close the Circle • Discuss the questions with a parent, teacher, or writing coach.		
16.6 Write a Conclusion • Write a conclusion for your essay.		
• Link your conclusion to your introduction and opinion statement.		
• Add new information that helps readers understand your point of view.		
• Add some parts that will be memorable for your readers.		
• Revise your introduction as necessary to fit your conclusion.		
16.7 Organization: Order of Importance • List some of the words in each paragraph that help you recognize that the author is organizing her examples in order of importance.		

Tasks	Done ✔	Points Earned
• Explain how you will organize the middle paragraphs of your essay and why.		
16.8 Transitions: Knitting It All Together • Read aloud only the words and phrases in boldface.		
• Notice the transitional words the writer uses to show you the connection to the information that comes before.		
• Notice the transitional words the writer uses to prepare you for the type of information that comes next.		
16.10 Inspect and Improve • Ask other readers to be a part of your revision team.		
• Inspect your paragraphs, sentences, and words.		
• Use the questions to guide yourself and your team of readers.		
• Use feedback from your revision team to write a new draft of your essay.		
• Add transitional words and phrases to your essay to knit your ideas together and to show your readers what is coming next.		
16.11 Rubric for "My Favorite Author" • Study the rubric before you write your final draft for this assignment.		
16.12 Finally, Final Draft • Write or type your final version of your opinion essay.		
16.13 You Be the Judge • Together with a parent, teacher, or writing coach, use Rubric 16.12 to evaluate the final version of your essay.		

Checklist Point System:

1–6 points may be awarded by a parent, teacher, or writing coach for each task completed. Here are the recommended guidelines:

6 – exemplary in quality *and* effort

5 – exemplary in either quality *or* effort

4 – acceptable in quality *and* effort

3 – acceptable in either quality *or* effort

2 – needs improvement in quality *and* effort

1 – incomplete

Tasks	Done ✔	Points Earned
16.14 Unit Review • Write your answers to the questions or talk about them with a parent, teacher, or writing coach. Record your score in the Points Earned column on the right.		
16.15 Word Sleuth • Add spelling words and new words to your WORD COLLECTION.		
16.16 Revisit: Writer's Questions • Discuss your answers to the WRITER'S QUESTIONS from the beginning of the module with a parent, teacher, or writing coach.		
Total		

Module 16: 144 points possible, plus 30 points for Unit Review

Checklist for Module 17

Directions: When you have completed a task, make a ✔ in the "Done" column. Ask a parent, teacher, or writing coach to award you points for each task using the checklist point system. Grid in the points you have earned on the APPRENTICE LOG in the appendix.

Tasks	Done ✔	Points Earned
17.4 Plot Points • List the most exciting events of your life so far. Put a star by the *most* exciting event.		
• List the most difficult challenges of your life so far. Put a star by the *most* challenging experience.		
• Mark the high and low points of your life so far on the graph. Connect the points with a line.		
17.5 The Surprising, the Humorous, and the Dramatic • List the most surprising events of your life so far.		
• List the most humorous events of your life so far.		
• List the most dramatic events of your life so far.		
• List the events of your life that your readers will find most interesting because they are surprising, humorous, or dramatic. Make sure they appear on your graph in 17.4.		
17.6 Cast of Characters • List the most influential people in your life so far. Put a star beside the person who has influenced you the most.		
• Decide who the major characters in your autobiography will be.		

Checklist Point System:

1–6 points may be awarded by a parent, teacher, or writing coach for each task completed. Here are the recommended guidelines:

6 – exemplary in quality *and* effort

5 – exemplary in either quality *or* effort

4 – acceptable in quality *and* effort

3 – acceptable in either quality *or* effort

2 – needs improvement in quality *and* effort

1 – incomplete

Checklist Point System:

1–6 points may be awarded by a parent, teacher, or writing coach for each task completed. Here are the recommended guidelines:

6 – exemplary in quality *and* effort

5 – exemplary in either quality *or* effort

4 – acceptable in quality *and* effort

3 – acceptable in either quality *or* effort

2 – needs improvement in quality *and* effort

1 – incomplete

Tasks	Done ✔	Points Earned
• Decide who the minor characters in your autobiography will be.		
17.7 Make a Story Wheel • Use the story wheel to plan the beginning, middle, and end of your autobiography.		
• Write down information or an event for each of the eight sections.		
• List some characters who will appear in each event or in the information you write about.		
17.8 Title Your Autobiography • Decide which expert model's title you like best and why.		
• Write at least four possible titles for your autobiography.		
• Ask at least five people to tell you which title they like best.		
• Based upon their feedback, put a star by the title you think is best for your autobiography.		
17.9 First Draft • Use the story wheel to guide you through the process of writing the first draft of your autobiography.		
• Double-space so you will have room to make changes and additions when you revise.		
17.10 Vocabulary: A Sense of Place • Write definitions for the adjectives you can use to describe places.		
• Name a place you know that might be appropriately described with each adjective.		
17.11 The Sandbox • Write a descriptive paragraph about one of the pictures.		

Tasks	Done ✔	Points Earned
• Let several people read your paragraph and ask them to guess which picture you are describing.		
17.12 Word Sleuth • Add spelling words and new words to your WORD COLLECTION.		
17.13 Revisit: Writer's Questions • Discuss your answers to the WRITER'S QUESTIONS from the beginning of this module with a parent, teacher, or writing coach.		
Total		

Module 17: 150 points possible

Checklist for Module 18

Directions: When you have completed a task, make a ✔ in the "Done" column. Ask a parent, teacher, or writing coach to award you points for each task using the checklist point system. Grid in the points you have earned on the APPRENTICE LOG in the appendix.

Checklist Point System:

1–6 points may be awarded by a parent, teacher, or writing coach for each task completed. Here are the recommended guidelines:

6 – exemplary in quality *and* effort

5 – exemplary in either quality *or* effort

4 – acceptable in quality *and* effort

3 – acceptable in either quality *or* effort

2 – needs improvement in quality *and* effort

1 – incomplete

Tasks	Done ✔	Points Earned
18.3 Paint the Picture • Revise the sentences as directed to paint a more vivid image in your readers' minds.		
• Add descriptive details and action words to your rough draft that will paint a more vivid picture in your readers' minds.		
18.4 Somewhere in Time • Find the clues Sid Fleischman and Mary Pope Osborne include about where and when in their stories.		
18.5 Add Clues • Add clues to your rough draft that show but don't tell readers where and when each event in your autobiography takes place.		
• Show the changes you made in 18.3 and 18.5 to a parent, teacher, or writing coach. Ask for input about where to add more clues.		
18.6 The Story Arc • Write definitions for the word *arc* used as a noun and as a verb.		
18.7 Hook Your Readers • Write down some facts about your life that readers might find surprising.		
• Decide which opening from 17.3 you like best and why.		
• List four ways you could hook the reader at the beginning of your autobiography.		

Tasks	Done ✔	Points Earned
• With the help of a parent, teacher, or writing coach, decide which opening will work best.		
18.8 Build Suspense • Decide what questions to leave unanswered during your autobiography.		
• Organize your stories in such a way that you create uncertainty. Ask a parent, teacher, or writing coach to help you do this.		
18.12 Checklist for Second Draft • Put your first draft in your WRITER'S PORTFOLIO.		
• Use the checklist to help you carefully write the second draft of your "History of Me."		
18.13 Word Sleuth • Add spelling words and new words to your WORD COLLECTION.		
18.14 Revisit: Writer's Questions • Discuss your answers to the WRITER'S QUESTIONS from the beginning of the module with a parent, teacher, or writing coach.		
Total		

Module 18: 96 points possible

Checklist for Module 19

Directions: When you have completed a task, make a ✔ in the "Done" column. Ask a parent, teacher, or writing coach to award you points for each task using the checklist point system. Grid in the points you have earned on the APPRENTICE LOG in the appendix.

Checklist Point System:

1–6 points may be awarded by a parent, teacher, or writing coach for each task completed. Here are the recommended guidelines:

6 – exemplary in quality *and* effort

5 – exemplary in either quality *or* effort

4 – acceptable in quality *and* effort

3 – acceptable in either quality *or* effort

2 – needs improvement in quality *and* effort

1 – incomplete

Tasks	Done ✔	Points Earned
19.1 Review Your Progress, Part 1 • Review what you have learned by filling in the blanks.		
19.2 Review Your Progress, Part 2 • Write a paragraph about a favorite meal.		
• Use adjectives to describe what you might hear, smell, taste, touch, and see.		
19.3 Review Your Progress, Part 3 • Write a story about a sporting event such as the Olympic Games or the Super Bowl.		
• Use adverbs to answer questions about when, where, how, and to what extent in your story.		
• Underline the adverbs you use.		
19.4 Language of the Trade • Put a check mark beside the sentence parts you have already used in your "History of Me."		
19.5 Prepositional Phrases • Say each of the prepositions aloud, followed with "the [noun of your choice]."		
19.6 Expert Model • Underline the prepositional phrases in the excerpt from *Soup*.		
• Circle the object of the preposition in each phrase.		

Tasks	Done ✔	Points Earned
19.7 Answer the Questions • Use prepositional phrases to answer the questions.		
19.8 Track the Prepositional Phrases • Underline at least ten prepositional phrases in Psalm 23.		
19.9 What's Your Style? • Find the prepositional phrases in your autobiography.		
• Write some of your sentences with prepositional phrases on the lines provided.		
• Add some sentences with prepositional phrases if you cannot find many in your draft.		
19.10 Revisit • Go back to the mastery test in 15.9. Identify as many prepositions as you can.		
19.11 Mastery Test • Rewrite a section of your best writing on the lines provided.		
• Label the parts of speech you recognize in your own writing.		
• Underline the prepositional phrases.		
19.12 Word Sleuth • Add spelling words and new words to your WORD COLLECTION.		
19.13 Revisit: Writer's Questions • Discuss your answers to the WRITER'S QUESTIONS from the beginning of this module with a parent, teacher, or writing coach.		
Total		

Module 19: 126 points possible

Checklist for Module 20

Directions: When you have completed a task, make a ✔ in the "Done" column. Ask a parent, teacher, or writing coach to award you points for each task using the checklist point system. Grid in the points you have earned on the APPRENTICE LOG in the appendix.

Checklist Point System:

1–6 points may be awarded by a parent, teacher, or writing coach for each task completed. Here are the recommended guidelines:

6 – exemplary in quality *and* effort

5 – exemplary in either quality *or* effort

4 – acceptable in quality *and* effort

3 – acceptable in either quality *or* effort

2 – needs improvement in quality *and* effort

1 – incomplete

Tasks	Done ✔	Points Earned
20.3 Voice: A Writer's Fingerprints • List the clues you use to recognize the voices of three members of your family.		
20.4 What's My Personality? • With the help of your family members, fill out the personality chart.		
20.7 What Did We Say? • Identify four places in the current draft of your autobiography where you can add dialogue and/or internal monologue.		
• Try to capture the sound of your voice at the age you were when the events happened.		
• Write these new sections on a separate piece of paper.		
• Use the expert models in 17.3 to help you punctuate your dialogue.		
20.8 Voice: How I Felt • Read the sentences aloud, each time putting a different emotion into your voice.		
• Name the part of speech used to convey emotion in the examples.		
• List the words in the example that give you the biggest clues about how the writer feels.		
• Underline the words in the expert models in 17.3 that give you clues about how the writer is feeling.		

Tasks	Done ✔	Points Earned
• Write the emotion implied by the clues you underline in the margin.		
• Explain your decisions to a parent, teacher, or writing coach.		
20.9 One More Time with Feeling • Read your autobiography aloud to test for emotions.		
• Use some of the strategies in 20.6 to add emotion to your autobiography. Ask a parent, teacher, or writing coach to help you do this.		
• Write or type a third draft of your "History of Me." Be sure to include the dialogue sections and words that add emotion.		
20.10 Inspect and Improve • Use the revision process you learned in unit 3 to inspect and improve your autobiography at the paragraph, sentence, and word levels.		
• Ask other readers, including one adult, to be a part of your revision team.		
• Add transitional words and phrases to help you knit your ideas together and show your readers what type of new information is coming next.		
• Use the questions to guide you and your team of readers through this process.		
20.11 Rubric for "The History of Me" • Before you write the final draft for this assignment, study the rubric.		
• Circle one element under each trait you want to work on the most to improve your final draft.		

Checklist Point System:

1–6 points may be awarded by a parent, teacher, or writing coach for each task completed. Here are the recommended guidelines:

6 – exemplary in quality *and* effort

5 – exemplary in either quality *or* effort

4 – acceptable in quality *and* effort

3 – acceptable in either quality *or* effort

2 – needs improvement in quality *and* effort

1 – incomplete

Tasks	Done ✔	Points Earned
20.12 Finally, Final Draft • Write or type your final version of your autobiography. Place this in your WRITER'S PORTFOLIO.		
20.13 You Be the Judge • With a parent, teacher, or writing coach, use RUBRIC 20.11 to evaluate the strengths and weaknesses of your autobiography.		
20.14 Unit Review • Write your answers to the questions or talk about them with a parent, teacher, or writing coach. Record your score in the Points Earned column on the right.		
20.15 Word Sleuth • Add spelling words and new words to your WORD COLLECTION.		
20.15 Revisit: Writer's Questions • Discuss your answers to the WRITER'S QUESTIONS from the beginning of this module with a parent, teacher, or writing coach.		
Total		

Module 20: 150 points possible, plus 30 points for Unit Review

Checklist for Module 21

Directions: When you have completed a task, make a ✔ in the "Done" column. Ask a parent, teacher, or writing coach to award you points for each task using the checklist point system. Grid in the points you have earned on the APPRENTICE LOG in the appendix.

Tasks	Done ✔	Points Earned
21.3 Expert Model • Read the beginning and identify the main problem the superhero needs to solve.		
21.4 Pick Your Problems • Jot down at least one problem your hero could face under each heading in the chart.		
21.5 Pick Just One Problem • Circle the problems on your chart that best answer the questions.		
• Write the problem that best answers all three questions on the lines provided.		
21.7 Hook the Reader • Write the central problem on your STORY ARC CHART: BEGINNING.		
• Choose a hook for the beginning of the story and write it on your STORY ARC CHART: BEGINNING.		
21.9 Expert Model • Read the story and look for how the superhero tries to solve the problem, how the problem gets worse, and how she tries to solve the continuing problems.		
21.10 Building Your Plot • On the STORY ARC CHART: MIDDLE, write down what your hero does to try to solve the problem, and then what makes the problem worse.		

Checklist Point System:

1–6 points may be awarded by a parent, teacher, or writing coach for each task completed. Here are the recommended guidelines:

6 – exemplary in quality *and* effort

5 – exemplary in either quality *or* effort

4 – acceptable in quality *and* effort

3 – acceptable in either quality *or* effort

2 – needs improvement in quality *and* effort

1 – incomplete

Checklist Point System:

1–6 points may be awarded by a parent, teacher, or writing coach for each task completed. Here are the recommended guidelines:

6 – exemplary in quality *and* effort

5 – exemplary in either quality *or* effort

4 – acceptable in quality *and* effort

3 – acceptable in either quality *or* effort

2 – needs improvement in quality *and* effort

1 – incomplete

Tasks	Done ✔	Points Earned
21.11 Can You Repeat the Question? • Keep answering the questions as long as you want by writing plot events on your STORY ARC CHART: MIDDLE.		
21.12 Create a Climax • Answer the questions given to create your climax.		
• Write your idea for the climax in your STORY ARC CHART: CLIMAX AND RESOLUTION.		
21.13 Resolve the Tension • Use the questions given to decide what will happen in your resolution.		
• Write your idea for the resolution in your STORY ARC CHART: CLIMAX AND RESOLUTION.		
21.14 Vocabulary: Knockout Verbs • Study the vigorous verbs given.		
• Practice using them in a conversation about superheroes.		
21.15 Word Sleuth • Add spelling words and new words to your WORD COLLECTION.		
21.16 Revisit: Writer's Questions • Discuss your answers to the WRITER'S QUESTIONS from the beginning of the module with a parent, teacher, or writing coach.		
Total		

Module 21: 102 points possible

Checklist for Module 22

Directions: When you have completed a task, make a ✔ in the "Done" column. Ask a parent, teacher, or writing coach to award you points for each task using the checklist point system. Grid in the points you have earned on the APPRENTICE LOG in the appendix.

Tasks	Done ✔	Points Earned
22.3 What Kind of Hero? • List some skills or traits needed for your hero to solve your story's central problem.		
22.4 Superhero Identity • Choose a name for your superhero.		
22.5 Superhero Suit • Fill in the chart to design your superhero's suit.		
22.6 An Alter Ego • Fill in the superhero's alter ego chart.		
22.7 Your Superhero's Archenemy • Write down some skills and traits your archenemy could have that would make your superhero's problem worse.		
• Write down some skills and traits your archenemy could have that would counteract the skills and traits of your superhero and make the story more exciting.		
22.8 Archenemy Identity • Fill in the chart to design your archenemy's identity.		
22.9 Archenemy Appearance • Fill in the chart to describe your archenemy's appearance.		
22.10 Inspect and Improve: Your Plot • Decide whether you want to change your plot now that you know more about your characters.		

Checklist Point System:

1–6 points may be awarded by a parent, teacher, or writing coach for each task completed. Here are the recommended guidelines:

6 – exemplary in quality *and* effort

5 – exemplary in either quality *or* effort

4 – acceptable in quality *and* effort

3 – acceptable in either quality *or* effort

2 – needs improvement in quality *and* effort

1 – incomplete

Checklist Point System:

1–6 points may be awarded by a parent, teacher, or writing coach for each task completed. Here are the recommended guidelines:

6 – exemplary in quality *and* effort

5 – exemplary in either quality *or* effort

4 – acceptable in quality *and* effort

3 – acceptable in either quality *or* effort

2 – needs improvement in quality *and* effort

1 – incomplete

Tasks	Done ✔	Points Earned
• If you want, cross out things you want to change in the plot and write in different plot points.		
• Be sure that they all still work together in a sensible sequence of events.		
22.11 Write Your Rough Draft • Write your rough draft.		
• Start with an exciting and dramatic event that introduces the central problem.		
• Make the problem worse or introduce a new one. Show how your superhero tries to solve each new problem.		
• Build to a climax and spend extra time developing it.		
• Write a resolution that answers all the questions raised by the story and satisfies your readers.		
22.12 Word Sleuth • Add spelling words and new words to your WORD COLLECTION.		
22.13 Revisit: Writer's Questions • Discuss your answers to the WRITER'S QUESTIONS from the beginning of the module with a parent, teacher, or writing coach.		
Total		

Module 22: 108 points possible

Checklist for Module 23

Directions: When you have completed a task, make a ✔ in the "Done" column. Ask a parent, teacher, or writing coach to award you points for each task using the checklist point system. Grid in the points you have earned on the APPRENTICE LOG in the appendix.

Tasks	Done ✔	Points Earned
23.1 Review Your Progress • Explain the job of each sentence part to a parent, teacher, or writing coach.		
23.2 Language of the Trade • Review the grammar terms you have learned about so far in the Writer's Workshop.		
• Look over the current draft of your superhero story. Put a check mark beside the sentence parts you have already used.		
23.4 Punctuate Dialogue • Write dialogue on the blanks provided. Follow the instructions given.		
23.5 To Question or Exclaim • Write a sentence of dialogue for your superhero or your archenemy, ending with a question mark or exclamation point.		
23.6 Paragraphing Dialogue • Write several lines of dialogue in correct paragraph form.		
23.7 Voice Again • Match the dialogue with the character who says it.		
• Write two lines of dialogue for your hero and two lines of dialogue for your archenemy, making sure they sound different.		
• Ask a parent, teacher, or writing coach to identify the characteristics that make each character's voice distinctive.		

Checklist Point System:

1–6 points may be awarded by a parent, teacher, or writing coach for each task completed. Here are the recommended guidelines:

6 – exemplary in quality *and* effort

5 – exemplary in either quality *or* effort

4 – acceptable in quality *and* effort

3 – acceptable in either quality *or* effort

2 – needs improvement in quality *and* effort

1 – incomplete

Checklist Point System:

1–6 points may be awarded by a parent, teacher, or writing coach for each task completed. Here are the recommended guidelines:

6 – exemplary in quality *and* effort

5 – exemplary in either quality *or* effort

4 – acceptable in quality *and* effort

3 – acceptable in either quality *or* effort

2 – needs improvement in quality *and* effort

1 – incomplete

Tasks	Done ✔	Points Earned
23.8 That Voice in My Head • Write a few lines of internal monologue for your superhero. Match it in content and style to your superhero's dialogue so that your character's voice is consistent.		
23.9 Interjections • Add interjections to the beginnings or ends of the sentences.		
23.10 Voice Warm-Up • Use the chart to describe your superhero's voice.		
23.11 Mastery Test • Write a short conversation between your superhero and your archenemy. Be sure to switch speakers at least three times.		
• Use the correct conventions of capitalization and punctuation.		
• Remember to start a new paragraph each time you switch speakers.		
• Include several interjections.		
23.12 Word Sleuth • Add spelling words and new words to your WORD COLLECTION.		
23.13 Revisit: Writer's Questions • Discuss your answers to the WRITER'S QUESTIONS from the beginning of the module with a parent, teacher, or writing coach.		
Total		

Module 23: 108 points possible

Checklist for Module 24

Directions: When you have completed a task, make a ✔ in the "Done" column. Ask a parent, teacher, or writing coach to award you points for each task using the checklist point system. Grid in the points you have earned on the APPRENTICE LOG in the appendix.

Tasks	Done ✔	Points Earned
24.4 Talking Transitions • Read the expert model excerpt aloud, leaving out the transitions.		
• Fill in the blanks with your own transitions.		
24.5 Action Transitions • Study the transitions in the expert model.		
• Fill in the blanks with your own transitions.		
24.6 Add Your Own: Dialogue and Transitions • On your current draft of your superhero story, mark places to add dialogue with a "D."		
• On your story draft, mark places to add transitions with a "T."		
24.7 Filling It In • Find the places where you wrote a "D" or a "T" on your story draft, and add dialogue and transitions.		
• Make sure your superhero and archenemy sound like themselves.		
• Make sure your dialogue uses quotation marks and proper punctuation and capitalization.		
• Make sure your transitions are clear.		
24.8 Add Your Own: Interjections • Write an "I" anywhere you want to add an interjection. (Choose at least three places.)		
• Add your interjections.		
• Write or type a new draft of your story.		

Checklist Point System:

1–6 points may be awarded by a parent, teacher, or writing coach for each task completed. Here are the recommended guidelines:

6 – exemplary in quality *and* effort

5 – exemplary in either quality *or* effort

4 – acceptable in quality *and* effort

3 – acceptable in either quality *or* effort

2 – needs improvement in quality *and* effort

1 – incomplete

Checklist Point System:

1–6 points may be awarded by a parent, teacher, or writing coach for each task completed. Here are the recommended guidelines:

6 – exemplary in quality *and* effort

5 – exemplary in either quality *or* effort

4 – acceptable in quality *and* effort

3 – acceptable in either quality *or* effort

2 – needs improvement in quality *and* effort

1 – incomplete

Tasks	Done ✔	Points Earned
24.9 Inspect and Improve • Use the revision process you learned in unit 3 to inspect and improve your story at the paragraph, sentence, and word levels.		
• Ask other readers, including one adult, to be a part of your revision team.		
• Add transitional words and phrases to knit your ideas together and show your readers what type of new information is coming next.		
• Use the questions to guide you and your team of readers through this process.		
24.10 Rubric for "Zap! Pow! Kazam!" • Before you write the final draft for this assignment, study the rubric.		
• Under each trait, circle one element you want to work on the most to improve in your final draft.		
24.11 Finally, Final Draft • Write or type your final version of your superhero story. Place this in your WRITER'S PORTFOLIO.		
24.12 You Be the Judge • With a parent, teacher, or writing coach, use RUBRIC 24.10 to evaluate the strengths and weaknesses of your story.		
24.13 Unit Review • Write your answers to the questions or talk about them with a parent, teacher, or writing coach. Record your score in the Points Earned column on the right.		
24.14 Word Sleuth • Add spelling words and new words to your WORD COLLECTION.		
24.15 Revisit: Writer's Questions • Discuss your answers to the WRITER'S QUESTIONS from the beginning of the module with a parent, teacher, or writing coach.		
Total		

Module 24: 138 points possible, plus 30 points for Unit Review

feng shui
in a weekend™

SIMON BROWN

feng shui
in a weekend™

transform your life and
home in a weekend or less

hamlyn

contents

1
using feng shui

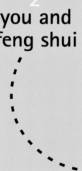

2
you and feng shui

First published in Great Britain in 2002
by Hamlyn, a division of
Octopus Publishing Group Ltd
2–4 Heron Quays, London E14 4JP

Book design and illustrations © Octopus
Publishing Group Ltd 2002
Text © Simon Brown 2002

Distributed in the United States and
Canada by Sterling Publishing Co., Inc.
387 Park Avenue South, New York,
NY 10016

"In a Weekend" is the trademark
property of Sterling Publishing Co., and
is used by permission.

The moral right of Simon Brown to
be identified as the author of this work
has been asserted in accordance with
the Copyright, Design and Patents Act
of 1988.

ISBN 0 600 60378 4

A CIP catalogue record for this book is available from the British Library
Printed and bound in China
10 9 8 7 6 5 4 3 2 1

using feng shui

introduction

Feng shui is part of an ancient philosophy and can be applied
to a wide range of practices including tai chi, the I ching, acupuncture, shiatsu,
macrobiotics and astrology. Chi energy, yin and yang, the five elements and the eight
trigrams are common to all these philosophies and practices making them
a binding force that together offer a complete approach to life.

Feng shui is only one part of the jigsaw puzzle of life. Personally I use
many different things to help overcome challenges. Apart from eastern practices
I have also found western influences such as NLP, modern therapy
and scientific research helpful in understanding the world.

The place you live in has a significant influence on your life. I remember
as a child moving from London to a large house in the country where there
was a special feeling of empowerment and optimism and as a family we
all succeeded in different ways during our time there.

Since then I have lived in four different homes in London and each has added its own
dimension to my life. Moving into our current home coincided with me beginning to work
for myself which has exceeded my expectations bringing success through publishing,
exciting feng shui consultancies and invitations to give many talks and lectures.

Our home is very bright, sunny and fresh. The rooms are a mixture
of shapes and, being at the top of the building gives a sense of space.
It mixes modern and antique styles offering balance to our home.

Interestingly my mother's cottage has turned out to have the
ideal family atmosphere and we spend most weekends there. It is the children's
utopia! I do not think you can have everything in one place.

Feng shui has given me a much greater feeling of control over my environment
along with a better understanding of why various patterns of events happen in life.
Although our home would not stand out as being unusual or different a lot of
thought has gone into everything that is in it. As a result it is a special place that is
tuned to provide the best possible environment for both myself and my family.

Simon Brown

Feng shui is based on the idea that we are connected to everything in the universe and that we are all part of a huge web.

Consequently, events in one place will eventually effect everyone in the web. Some things will have a greater influence and be more noticeable than others. The different phases of the moon, the sun and the seasons, along with the local weather, have a more obvious effect on us. Our behaviour, moods and thinking can all be altered according to the changes in these aspects of our natural environment. To understand how this works it is useful to understand the basic principles.

Chi in the body

Everyone has an energy field moving through and around his or her body. In China this is called chi, which is a subtle flow of electromagnetic energy that carries your emotions, thoughts and beliefs. So if you are feeling excited you will send an excited chi energy through your body.

The chi energy around you

The chi energy field extends beyond the skin by about 10cm–1m (4–40in), depending on the current state of both your physical and emotional being. Someone in a rage will find their chi energy field extends further than when they are feeling depressed. This external energy field is called your aura and can be photographed by a process known as Kirilian Photography. It is this part of your chi energy that is most easily influenced by the atmosphere around you.

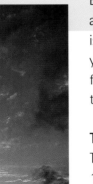

What is feng shui?
Feng shui translates into English as wind and water. It uses the forces of nature – ebb and flow of tides and wind currents – so they work for you.

orientate your home

To help you **orientate** your home, observe the movement of the sun throughout the day, making notes of where it comes into your home and at what time. You will need to work on a normal summertime schedule.

At **sunrise**, make a note of the time where the sun enters your home. This will be east. Next **calculate** the time halfway between sunrise and midday. For example, if sunrise is at 6.00 a.m., then halfway will be at 9.00 a.m. At this time the sun will be in the south-east. Observe how the south-eastern sun comes into your home and make notes. At **midday** the sun will be at its highest point in the sky and to the south. In the winter it will be easier to see this. Calculate **halfway** between midday and sunset, which will be when the sun is in the south-west. Watch the sun as it descends through the sky until sunset. Again, make a note of the time and where the sun comes into your home. This will be **west**.

The **remaining directions**, where you will not see the sun, are opposite to the directions you have observed. So north-west will be opposite south-east, north opposite south and north-east opposite south-west.

A feel for success
Each room will have a unique atmosphere of its own. The idea is to create an atmosphere that you can suceed in.

On a cold wet day the atmosphere becomes more yin (see pages 132–5), and if this yin chi energy pervades your own chi energy field you will become more yin. Eventually this could lead you to feeling more withdrawn. To balance this you would need to make yourself more yang by being active.

Similarly, each building has an atmosphere or energy of its own and this will influence your external chi energy. As a result, spending time in certain buildings will effect the way you feel. Feng shui is the study of how to create an atmosphere inside your home that will allow you to succeed in life.

Various outside factors will influence the chi energy inside a home. For example, if one home is situated high up on the side of a mountain and another identical home is situated low in the valley next to a river, the two houses will have very different atmospheres inside.

The design and interior design of a building will further define the chi energy or atmosphere within. For instance, a large cathedral feels very different from a small cottage, just as a sparsely decorated home with hard surfaces will encourage different emotions compared with an over-furnished home with lots of soft fabrics.

Chi energy around the home
One of the prime influences on a home is the sun. Its solar radiation sends powerful chi energy into a room. As the sun moves through the sky it energizes different parts of your home. Once the sun has moved on, the chi energy in that room will slowly diminish until it is recharged the next day.

The movement of the sun through the sky will create different kinds of chi energy. The rising sun in the east will send more upward energy, associated with the beginning of the day, into the east part of the home. The setting western sun will send more descending energy, associated with the end of the day and completing things, to the west part of the home.

Using this principle the home can be divided into eight different areas. The cardinal compass points – east, south, west and north and those in between – south-east, south-west, north-west and north-east. Each of these directions carries its own type of energy. Spending time in the eastern part of a building will enable you to absorb more eastern chi energy. But, as well as your location, the direction you face will determine which type of energy you absorb more of.

At the top of your head your hair grows in a spiral pattern. This is known as the crown chakra and is where you can most easily take in chi energy. Therefore, if the top of your head points east while you sleep more eastern chi energy will fill your chi energy field, so when you awake you will have more of this kind of energy in your system. Over time, someone who sleeps with their head pointing east will build up eastern energy and the characteristics associated with it inside them. (See page 146 for more details on the eight directions.)

how to **use** feng shui

Ask yourself what you want? Do you want to **improve your life** or do you want to **improve your home?**

Work on yourself

Work on your home

Clear your mind

Go out and return to your home with a clear mind

Think about what you want from life

Walk into and around your home looking for ways to improve it

Decide what you could change about yourself to be more successful

Look up projects for your home to help you make those changes

Make notes and look for projects listed under the appropriate room

how to use this book

There are two aspects to feng shui. One is remedial and problem-solving while the other is preventative. Although the application of these two aspects is quite different, this book is designed to accommodate both.

Remedial feng shui

If you have identified a problem in your life, remedial feng shui can be used to help you solve it. In this scenario, most people **do not want their home disrupted or to spend a great deal on the remedies.** So, if you can find a solution to your problem by simply changing the position of your bed, this is ideal. The art of this style of feng shui is to be as accurate, precise and specific as possible. Less is more.

The second chapter, *You and Feng Shui,* is based on this remedial style of feng shui and contains projects for any part of your home. The projects are relatively simple and designed to help you improve various aspects of your life quickly and easily.

Preventative feng shui

If you have identified a problem in your home, preventative feng shui is applied when you want to **renovate or redecorate your home.** The idea behind this type of feng shui is that if you are going to make a significant change to your home it can also be a great opportunity to improve the atmosphere. Many of the feng shui considerations will not add any cost to the project and should help you make more informed choices on the colours, materials and shapes that you use. In addition, it will provide valuable information on how to arrange your furniture.

The third chapter, *The Feng Shui Home,* deals with one room at a time and includes projects for specific

icons help you find the projects most useful to you

individually devised projects will help you achieve your goal within the time indicated by these symbols

pictures and extended captions develop the theme of the text

half-day

one-day

two-days

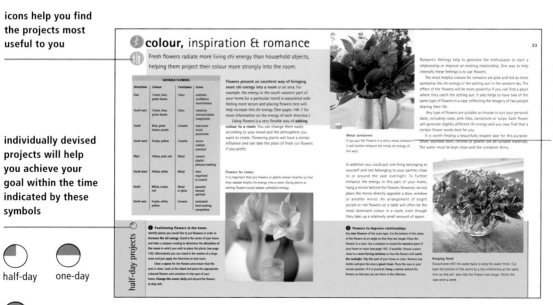

THE ICONS
Icons have been placed throughout the book so that you can flick through the pages and home in on projects that will be most useful to you. These icons are listed below.

 stronger family relationships

 wise, organized and in control – north-west

 health

 balance – yin/yang

 ambition, confidence and assertiveness – east

 peaceful, sensual and spiritual – north

 relaxation

 more settled

 creativity, communication and imagination – south-east

 motivated, hard-working and competitive – north-east

 vitality

 cleaning the atmosphere

 expressive, social and passionate – south-west

 sex

 fresh start

 finances

 secure, realistic and practical – south

 selling your home

 clear head

 improving relationships

 content, playful and pleasure-seeking – west

 feeling good about your home

parts of the home, as well as suggestions for more profound changes.

All of the projects in the book have been given time-bands – an indication of the length of time they could take. Obviously this is only a rough guide, as much will depend on the size of your home and how easy they are for you to implement. However, it is advisable to take your time in order to complete each one successfully. Leave some time between projects, so that you can see how you feel with the change before embarking on the next one.

It is always helpful to be in a good frame of mind. If you feel stressed or negative, leave it for another day. Your commitment and the quality of chi energy you put into the project will also have an effect.

ROOM PLANS
Chapter three, *The Feng Shui Home* contains room plan illustrations as a before and after setting of rooms so that you can visualize how small changes can make all the difference to the chi energy in your home. See below for the meaning of the energy lines used in these illustrations:

fast-flowing energy

energy flowing harmoniously

slow-moving energy, potentially stagnant

potentially harmful energy

what do you **want** from life?

Regular meditation on what you want from life will help you to focus your energy and will make it easier for you to realize your dreams. Think about your long-term and most ambitious goals first and then work backwards to short-term and less ambitious objectives.

To prepare, begin with some gentle stretching exercises. Co-ordinate this with long deep breaths. Lie on your back or sit in an upright posture. Relax and try to empty your mind by concentrating on your breathing. Feel each breath enter and leave your body. Once you feel calm you can begin your meditation.

Imagine you are at the end of your life, feeling content and satisfied as you prepare to move on from this material world. You have completed everything you have ever wanted to do. Try to visualize, feel and hear what it would be like having reached this state. Now think about what you would need to do between now and then to be able to be in that position.

Initially think about broad, big ideas. Once you have these fixed in your mind, begin to work on the practicalities and fill in the details. You may need to keep refining the details until you are satisfied that they are realistic. This can then become the main force that drives you forwards.

You may need to practise this technique several times to get the best results. At the beginning do not worry about what the results are, instead try to develop the ability to focus your mind.

Some people will find that they have one dream that becomes a consistent force in their life, while others may have several. It is also acceptable to change your dreams as your life progresses.

When you have a dream keep it in your mind so that whenever you have a decision to make you can check to see whether it will help you realize your life's ambition.

From time to time review your progress. It is important not to feel disappointed if you go through phases in which you do not make progress. Try to look at new ways to move forward.

Meditation

To meditate sit in a comfortable position so that your spine is straight and you will not be distracted by aches and pains.

questionnaire

Answer the following questions and make a note of what feelings, emotions and states of being you wish to achieve:

- What do you want from life?
- How do you think you will feel once you have achieved it?
- What would this achievement look like?
- What would people say about you and what would you say about yourself?
- What can you change about yourself to help you achieve your goals?

Circle the words below that apply to you, turn to the appropriate pages and see which projects are most practical for you. Remember to focus on the characteristics that will help you attain your dream in life, not those that appeal to you most. You should only consider yourself or young children and let others do their own exercise.

TO BE MORE	SEE PAGES	TO BE MORE	SEE PAGES
assertive enthusiastic confident forceful positive	29, 38–41, 42, 46–7, 56–7, 90–1, 107–11.	romantic playful content youthful	31–3, 38–41, 50, 64–5, 67, 90–1, 125–6.
optimistic communicative creative imaginative	25, 38–41, 46–51, 54–7, 60, 67, 80–3, 86, 90–1, 110–11, 119–20, 126–7.	organized intuitive responsible structured dignified	24, 31, 35, 38–42, 82–3, 90–1, 98, 104, 108–11.
expressive outgoing social emotional spontaneous	36–41, 46–7, 76, 78, 85–7, 90–1, 96.	sexual peaceful spiritual flexible objective	24, 25, 34, 38–41, 44–5, 90–4, 113–17, 122–7.
intimate realistic practical stable	30, 36–41, 43, 53, 54, 74–75, 84, 86, 90–94.	motivated competitive clear-minded decisive sharp	24–2, 30, 38–43, 90–1, 108–11, 121, 124–5.

life & relationships

Feng shui is like any tool for improving your life and relationships. First you need to relax and think carefully about what it is you want, and then work out how you can use the tool to make an improvement.

In feng shui consultations people are not always very clear on what exactly they want or how they could use feng shui to achieve their goals. Sometimes you think you know what you want but then later you realize you wanted something different. Before making any decisions on what you want from life, try talking it over with a valued friend, going for a walk, doing some exercise, deep breathing or meditation (see pages 14–5). It can help to take a blank piece of paper and write down your objectives, visualize the difference they would make to your life and try to imagine how you would feel. Work on these until you are happy with them.

Feng shui is not a magic pill and it will not make you wealthy, get you the perfect relationship or improve your health by itself. You will also need to work at it and try to create the circumstances for it to happen.

The examples on this page and the next show how you could apply this process to different problems.

Relationships

First consider what kind of relationship you would like. Should it be a long-term relationship, more casual or a quick fling? Do you want to live together, get married or have children? Think about the kind of person that might be best suited to that kind of relationship.

Next, work out what you could change about yourself to make it happen. This requires an honest appraisal of how you could have made past relationships more successful. For example, were you too dominating, uncommitted or serious?

Remember you cannot change another person, only yourself, so to blame the other person will not help you improve your ability to enjoy happy relationships.

If you have not been in a relationship, you will need to work out why. Do you go out enough? Do you meet new people and, if so, are they the kind of people you could have a relationship with? Do you get into potentially romantic situations?

Once you have decided which aspects of your character you want to work on, you can use feng shui to help bring about a change. For example, if you want to be more romantic you will need to try the projects associated with romance.

CHARACTERISTIC
See projects on pages

Be more outgoing, expressive and sociable
36–41, 46–7, 76, 79, 85–7, 90–1, 96.

Feel more romantic
31–3, 38–41, 50, 64–5, 67, 90–91, 128–9.

Work towards a long-term relationship
30, 37–41, 43, 53, 55, 74–5, 84, 86, 90–4.

Be more relaxed
24, 25, 34, 38–41, 44–5, 90–4, 113–17, 122–7.

Have more fun
31–3, 38–41, 50, 64–5, 67, 90–1, 126–7.

To help make a commitment
24, 31, 35, 38–42, 82–3, 90–1, 99, 105, 108–11.

Feel more secure and intimate
30, 37–41, 43, 53, 55, 74–5, 84, 86, 90–4.

health & wealth

Health

Good health is made up of many factors including diet, lifestyle, attitude to life and exercise. In addition, your home will have a direct effect, for instance, it is more difficult to remain healthy in a home that is dark, damp or dusty. Generally, a bright, sunny home with plenty of plants and natural materials will be one in which it is easier to maintain good health.

There are other factors in your home that could adversely affect your health. Mildew, electromagnetic fields (EMF), synthetic materials that release toxic fumes, and materials that carry a charge of static electricity can all compromise your health, according to feng shui theory.

Indirectly, an uplifting atmosphere in your home will encourage you to eat well, remain positive in the face of adversity and be motivated to exercise. A home with a depressing energy will make this harder to achieve.

Make a list of how you feel at home. For example, do you sleep well, feel relaxed and feel generally happy at home? Try to identify aspects of your home that could be contributing to poor health and then look through the projects to see which ones could help.

Wealth

Think through ways in which you can increase your income. It is unlikely that feng shui will make money come from nowhere. Do you need to earn more, save more or spend less? If you need to earn more you will need to consider ways of making this happen. For instance, could you get a promotion, ask for an increase in salary or do you need to change your job?

How do you see yourself increasing your long-term wealth? Are you working on something that could bring in a large one-off payment?

When you have a clear idea of how you can become wealthier, build up your self-motivation in order to take advantage of any opportunities that arise with regard to making money. If you have tried before and failed, you will have more experience to draw on next time.

Make a list of characteristics that you could change so as to make it easier to be wealthy. For example, do you need to be more assertive, work harder, have a more ruthless streak, concentrate on profits more, be better at completing projects, save more money or value yourself more.

CHARACTERISTIC
See projects on pages:

Depression
29, 38–1, 42, 46–7, 56–7, 90–1, 107–11.

Insomnia
24, 25, 34, 38–1, 44–5, 90–4, 113–17, 124–9.

Headaches
24–7, 76, 94–5.

Stress
24–5, 28–30, 38–1, 46–7, 90–4, 119–20, 124–9

Lethargy
25, 38 –41, 46–51, 54–7, 61, 67, 81–3, 87, 90–91, 110–11, 119–20, 126–7.

CHARACTERISTIC
See projects on pages:

To complete projects and focus on profits
31–3, 38–41, 50, 64–5, 67, 90–1, 126–7.

To value yourself and be more assertive
29, 38–41, 42, 46–7, 56–7, 90–1, 107–11.

To be more careful with money
30, 37–41, 43, 53, 55, 74–5, 84, 86, 90–4.

To work harder, be more motivated and more opportunistic
24–5, 30, 38–43, 90–1, 108–11, 121, 126–7.

your **home**

When you have lived in a home for a while it is easy to loose your objectivity. The interior style gradually forms piece-by-piece over time and, as the years go by, you can often over-furnish and clutter your home. In addition, when people move into a home they are often inspired to put a lot of energy into ambitious projects. Inevitably this enthusiasm wanes and projects remain unfinished.

We are usually good at casting a critical eye over someone else's home on our first visit and, occasionally, it can be helpful to do this in your own home. Take a fresh look on a sunny day in spring, as this is a helpful time to start new projects on your home.

To begin this exercise, take yourself for a long walk or to a café so that you can think about what you want your home to do for you. For example, should it be more relaxing, do you want to feel more inspired or be more organized?

When you return to your home pretend you are viewing it for the first time. If you travel by car, park in the road. Walk towards your home and carefully look at the front garden, exterior and front door. These make an important first impression and continue to make an unconscious impression each time you come home.

Walk around your home taking in the overall feeling. At this point you do not need to focus on details. Make a mental note of any rooms that do not feel right. Once you have completed this journey repeat the process looking at specifics. You may find it easier to look at one aspect of your home each time you walk around. For example, try looking only at clutter, then observe the colours in each room, next consider any pictures, paintings or photographs you may have, and each time you go around make notes of anything that you could improve upon. This is a very helpful exercise when you are selling or renting a home.

Checklist when observing your home:

Once you have a list of things that you would like to improve in your home look through this book for helpful ideas. You may find that repeating this process, say, once a year helps keep your home fresh and allows it to grow with you. Photocopy this checklist so that you can make notes beside each category.

Clutter	**Plants**	**Materials**
Colours	**Furnishing**	**Lighting**
Artwork	**Arrangement of furniture**	**Cleanliness**

With practice you can feel chi energy between your hands. Once you have achieved this you can go on to feel the chi energy in your home.

Stand up and rub your hands together vigorously until they feel warm all over. Breathe in, take one step forwards and stretch your arms above your head. Bring your arms down and, with your other foot, step forwards and repeat the stretches at least three times.

Vigorously shake your hands keeping your wrists and fingers relaxed and loose. Try to imagine you are shaking the blood right down to the tips of your fingers.

Hold the base of your thumb firmly with your other thumb and index finger and massage all the way up to your thumbnail. Squeeze your thumb at each side of the base of the nail and breath in. Pull gently as you breathe out and quickly pull your thumb and index finger away from your thumb. As you do this imagine you have a multi-coloured flame of energy around your thumb and that you are extending it. Repeat with each finger.

Put the palms of your hands together in front of your chest or neck. Each time you breathe in imagine you are breathing a powerful colour, feeling or sound

Breathing
Long deep breaths into your abdomen will help move your chi energy into your hands.

into your body. For example, a strong red colour, a warm feeling or the roar of a lion. Breathe deeply so that your lower abdomen expands as you breath in and imagine the powerful colour, feeling or sound filling your lower abdomen. As you breathe out imagine the powerful colour, feeling or sound moving up into your hands. Repeat this approximately 12 times.

If your hands feel damp, dry them on a cotton cloth. Give the palms a vigorous rub together for at least ten seconds. Now hold your hands about 2cm (¾in) apart and start to move them closer and further apart. Be very sensitive to any feeling in the palms of your hands. Do the same with your hands further apart. Experiment and play by gently moving your hands together and apart. Try doing it very slowly, slightly quicker, with very small distances apart and with larger movements.

See if you can detect any of the following:
• A feeling of warmth between your hands as you bring them closer together. You may be able to almost pull this field of warmth apart as you slowly move your hands in opposite directions.
• A tingling sensation in your hands and fingers.
• Feeling that your hands are being pulled and pushed together almost as though you have little magnets in the palms of your hands.

Once you have mastered this, try using your hands to feel the chi energy present around your home. Experiment by moving your hands up and down near a doorway, across a corner or near a window.

tools of the trade

Convex mirrors

These round, fish eye, mirrors help disperse chi energy. Use this type of mirror when your staircase leads straight down to your front door or in a long corridor.

Water features

These are used to bring more vitality into your home and are best placed in the eastern or south-eastern part of your home or room. You can choose from small indoor waterfalls, fountains, aquariums, or a simple bowl of fresh water refilled daily. Moving water will add more yang, vibrant energy whereas still water will add more yin, calming energy. The water must be clean, and fresh, and changed frequently.

Candles

Although softer than electric lighting, candles add more fiery energy to a space, helping to make a passionate, intimate atmosphere. They are best in the south, south-west or north-east. Position in pairs if you want to improve or start a relationship.

Sea salt

This is helpful for cleansing and stabilizing the flow of energy through your home. Put two tablespoons of sea salt in a small ramekin dish and place in the north-eastern and south-western parts of your home. Alternatively sprinkle on the floor before you go to bed and vacuum up the next day.

Mirrors

To help redirect and keep energy moving, use mirrors around your home. They are ideal in rooms that are dark, small or narrow. Avoid positioning mirrors so that they are directly opposite a door, window or another mirror. Keep mirrors in your bedroom to a minimum and avoid having a mirror facing your bed.

Crystals

These will reflect natural light into the colours of the rainbow and spread these colours around the room. Crystals are excellent for dark rooms where you want to bring in more natural chi energy. Ideally, place them in the western, north-western, northern, eastern and south-eastern parts of your home.

Fresh flowers

For more living energy and colour, use flowers to brighten up a room. Brighter colours will create a more lively atmosphere and pale shades a more relaxed feel. Discard them as soon as they begin to wilt.

Plants

A variety of plants brings more natural energy into your home. They are suitable for all rooms as long as they can remain healthy. Plants also help to reduce air pollution and noise.

Wind chimes

The sound of wind chimes sends out ripples of energy, which helps to move and disperse energy. Ideally, hang them above a door so that the door knocks the bottom of the chimes each time it is opened. Metal wind chimes are best situated in the south-west, north-east, centre, west, north-west and north. Use wooden wind chimes in the eastern, south-eastern and southern parts of your home.

Clocks

Apart from telling the time, clocks are good for adding rhythm to a space, which, in turn, can make it easier to be more organized and add structure to your life. Ideally, choose a clock with a pendulum and as many metal parts as possible. Place in the western, north-western or northern part of your home.

Lighting

Electric lighting, although not as natural as daylight or candles, adds energy to a room. For example, uplights help make ceilings feel higher, indirect lighting is soft, direct spot or halogen lights create a bright, exciting atmosphere, and table lights with shades encourage a cosy, intimate feel.

Coins on a red cloth

A collection of shiny coins on a red cloth can help you put more energy into improving your finances. Place in the western part of your home.

Charcoal

If you have a fireplace, cooker or boiler in the western or north-western part of your home, put some artists charcoal in a clay pot and place nearby in order to help harmonize the energy.

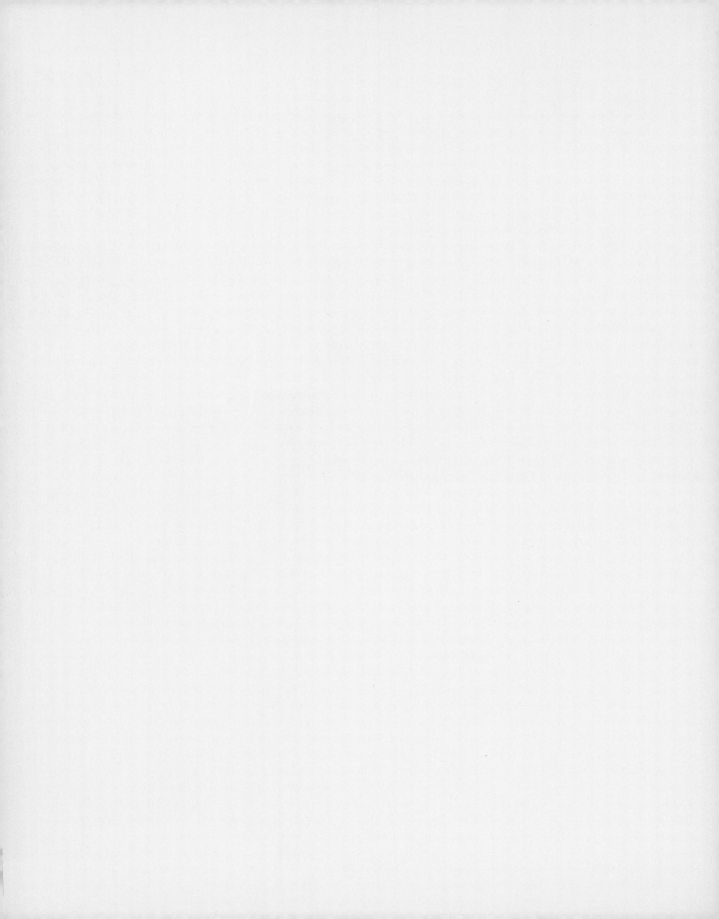

you and feng shui

renewing the atmosphere

One way of changing the atmosphere of a room is to use your own chi. If you walk into a room feeling happy or excited, some of that inner energy will radiate into the room. This can help to disperse any bad atmosphere that is still present after, say, someone has expressed strong emotions or following a violent argument.

Some of that disruptive energy will remain in the room and it needs to be cleared so that everyone can move on.

You can do this consciously by meditating and focusing your mind on positive thoughts. To help spread your energy through the room you can use sound waves. Like ripples spreading across a pond, sound will help spread your positive energy. Hand bells, gongs, clapping, chanting, or your favourite piece of uplifting music are common ways to spread harmonious energy.

Happy children playing games or a contented pet will also radiate their own chi energy, altering the atmosphere of the room. The sound of genuine laughter will quickly pick up the energy.

Using candles

A candle can help disperse chi energy. As you meditate you can imagine sending your thoughts into the flame so that they disperse throughout the room.

half-day projects

❶ Change the energy

Choose a room in which you want to change the energy. Wait until you feel generally **happy, strong** and **focused**. A walk in the fresh air, stretching or exercise may help.

Sit comfortably in the room and focus on want you want from life or from the room. It may help to **light a candle** and place it in front of you so that you can stare into the flame. Do this for as long as it feels right. The time is not important.

Everytime you have a good thought take a deep breath and imagine exhaling those thoughts into the room.

❷ Sounds to clear bad energy

Empty your mind and feel the room. Sense if any areas are **fresh** or **stale. Clap your hands** several times in stagnant areas. Use a **hand bell** to disperse the energy in areas that feel too chaotic. The sound of a large **gong** will move the energy around the room. Once the reverberations have faded the room should feel revitalized.

Use your **voice** to spread your own chi energy throughout the room and cleanse and refresh your own chi. Breathe deeply several times and then let out a long 'aah, oo, mmm' sequence of sounds. Relax, leave the room and return later to see if you can feel the change in atmosphere (see also page 30).

creating harmony

Wind chimes spread and disperse chi and can be helpful where energy is compressed. Much of a home's chi flows in through the doors. Chi can become constrained in these small gaps where there is often fast-flowing energy. If these spaces are especially small or cluttered it will be easier for the energy to get congested.

Metal chimes
These are the most common type of wind chime. These make a deep powerful sound. They are best used in the south-western, western, north-western, northern and north-eastern parts of your home.

Wind chimes also add a natural sound to a quiet room. The sound should have a crisp tone that refreshes the energy of the room as well as the energy of the people in the room, and it is important to hang them so that they chime frequently. Hang them near a door so that the top of the door strikes the tag hanging below the chimes each time you open the door. Alternatively hang them where they will be activated by wind or a draft, for instance, next to a window or in your garden.

Wind chimes are either made of metal, wood, china or glass. It is important to listen carefully and choose ones that have a sound you like. Metal wind chimes are the most common. Wooden wind chimes produce a lighter sound and are most effective in the northern, eastern, south-eastern and southern parts of your home. China wind chimes create a higher pitch of sound and are best used in the southern, south-western, north-eastern, western and north-western parts of your home. Glass wind chimes radiate a tinkling sound which is helpful in the north, east and south-east.

half-day projects

❶ Wind chimes by windows

Walk around your home and see if any room feels **low in energy** or is uncomfortable to be in. Use a **compass** to find which direction the window faces, see page 144, or use the method explained on page 9.

Attach a hook at the top of the window frame or into the recess or wall above the window. Measure from the hook downwards and note how long the **wind chimes** should be. They should not touch the window when they are hanging. Buy the appropriate size and type of wind chime, referring to the information above in order to get the most harmonious material for the direction your window faces.

❷ Wind chimes in doors and gardens

You can also hang wind chimes near any door that **opens to the outside** of your home.

If you enjoy the sound of wind chimes, hang some outdoors so that they **chime in the wind**. Experiment until you find a place where the chime catches the wind easily.

Make sure you can take the wind chimes down easily in case they disturb neighbours or may be damaged in stormy weather.

better health

Everything that uses or transports mains electricity, from a radio to a washing machine, will produce electromagnetic fields or EMF.

Some research has suggested that EMF could be detrimental to your health. The risks range from headaches to cancer. The EMF will certainly distort the earth's local natural magnetic field and they are, therefore, not desirable in feng shui. The best way to reduce your exposure to EMF is to keep as far away from the source as possible. The general rule is that the closer something is and the more electricity it uses the greater your exposure to EMF. For example, an electric hairdryer or electric blanket, if switched on, will subject someone to a relatively strong EMF. In addition, the longer you are exposed to it the greater the risk of health problems.

Minimizing EMF
When arranging a room avoid placing electrical equipment close to places where people will sit.

Potentially harmful
Here the television has been kept well away from the seating area to avoid the potentially harmful flow of electromagnetic energy.

half-day projects

1 Reducing EMF in the home

Walk around your home and make a note of all the **objects** you have that are **powered by electricity**. Think about how close you are to them when they are in operation and for how long.

Next look at the list and see where you can **substitute** a **non-electrical device** for something electrical. For example, replacing an electric blanket with a hot water bottle, an electric cooker with a gas cooker or a hair dryer with fresh air. Whenever you have an opportunity to **unplug a device**, do so, as this will disconnect the transformer and it will no longer create an EMF.

2 Reducing your exposure to EMF

Move any electrical objects that can be placed away from where people will sit. See if you can arrange the room so that you are at least 3m (3¼yd) **away** from the television. Move your computer screen further back from where you sit. The central processing unit **(CPU)** also emits EMF, so distance yourself from this too. If you have a **laptop** keep the **remote transformer** as far from your body as possible. The same applies to a **fax machine** and photocopier.

Where possible grow a peace lily, spider plant or South-American cactus next to electrical objects.

One way to detect disturbances in the earth's magnetic field is with a compass. As the compass passes over a disturbance the needle will turn to realign with the new magnetic field swinging erratically as you move over it. Some items in your home are simply magnetic by nature and anything with iron in it will have a similar effect as electrical items on a compass. Radiators, metal furniture and white goods, along with electrical items will all distort a magnetic field.

TV in the bedroom
Apart from EMF, a television adds more vibrant, yang energy to a room, which can make it less relaxing for sleep.

Your bedroom can be effected by disturbances in the earth's magnetic field and this is of concern because it is where you spend a great deal of time. If you are constantly subjected to these distortions, they will have an accumulative effect. This could increase the risk of nightmares or insomnia.

AVOIDING EMF
Move any electrical or magnetic items further away from your bed. Sometimes even a small increase in distance will make a significant difference. Moving a television from the foot of your bed to the far side of the room will significantly reduce your exposure to EMF. Place an electric alarm clock and a bedside light as far away from the bed as possible. You could replace these items with a mechanical or battery-operated alarm clock and candles. Always take care when using candles and follow common-sense safety procedures.

❸ Finding EMF in the bedroom
Note The following project will not work if you have a metal-framed bed, wire-sprung base or metal-sprung mattress. You can experiment with a compass, but the compass will not remain steady and be true to the earth's magnetic field.

Switch on all electrical items in your bedroom. This could include lights, alarm clock, television and music centre. Take a **compass** and move it slowly over your bed. Be sure to keep the body of the compass aligned with the bed so that you can see any movements of the needle. Note the areas where the needle moves.

❹ Reducing EMF by your bed
Next look for any **cables** that run under your bed or **close to your head**. You may find that the wall socket is next to your headboard. The cables could run under a carpet so you will need to **trace** them from electrical equipment **to the wall sockets**. Where possible resite the cables, keeping them as far from your bed as possible.

Recheck your bedroom with the compass and see if the needle is steadier. You may need to consider moving the bed to another part of the room if the compass still moves erratically as this could be due to cables in the wall or under the floor. Check the alternative spaces with a compass until you find a suitable area with a consistent reading.

relaxation

As chi energy passes a protruding corner, that is, a corner or edge which faces into a room (see glossary, page 155), it will tend to speed up, swirl and change direction.

This fast-flowing energy will predominantly move directly away from the corner. Anyone sitting or sleeping in the path of this energy will feel unsettled and restless. Over a long period of time it could even make it difficult to maintain good health.

If the fast-flowing chi from a protruding corner is directed towards a door or window, the chi energy that naturally flows into your home or room at these points can become erratic and unstable.

The objective is to soften the edge of the offending corner by, say, the introduction of a plant or with the use of fabric or moulding. In addition, you can rearrange your furniture so that you are not sitting or sleeping facing the corner. Corners that point towards where you spend time sleeping or sitting, and towards doors and windows will be of greater importance.

Corners
A tall corner, like the one in this room, will have a much greater influence than the corner of a table.

half-day projects

1 Hiding corners with plants
Note any **protruding corners**, such as those found in an **L-shaped room** or corners on furniture such as wardrobe edges.

Wherever practical **place a plant** in front of the offending corner. The plant will generate its own **living chi** energy, which will help to harmonize the fast-flowing energy from the corner. Ideally, the plant should be as tall as the people living in the home. Where space is limited, use hanging plants so that they drape over and soften the corner's edge.

If you have the skills, you could replaster the corner incorporating a rounded edge. The radius should be about 3cm (1¼in), similar to the rim of a teacup.

2 Hiding corners with fabric
A more simple option is to drape some fabric over a corner. Use a natural cloth, such as pure cotton because synthetic materials will build up a static charge of electricity. Choose colours and patterns that will **enhance your mood** when you are in that part of your home. (See pages 38–41.)

Finally experiment with moving the furniture around so that you are not facing a **protruding** corner. There are many other things to consider with regard to where you sit. (See pages 83, 108–9 for more information.)

feeling **secure**

In feng shui there are four ways that energy surrounds our bodies – in front of us, behind us, to our left and to our right.

the energy around you

- in front
  phoenix
- left **dragon**
- **POSITION**
- right **tiger**
- behind **tortoise**

These positions are symbolized by four animals – the pheonix, the tortoise, the dragon and the tiger (see pages 136–7).

The phoenix rises in front of you while the tortoise protects your back; the dragon and tiger guard your sides. Generally, it is better to sit with your back to a wall so that it is protected by the energy of the tortoise and your front is open to the rising energy of the phoenix. Unfortunately, this is not always possible as you may need to sit with your back to a room, a door or a large window.

The risk of leaving your back exposed is that you will feel less settled and find it harder to relax as chi energy rushes past you. If there is a feature that funnels or directs fast-flowing energy towards you, such as a long corridor or protruding corner, the effect will be worse. One of the remedies for this is to use a screen to protect your back.

Screens may also be used to enclose helpful energy within a specific area or smaller space. For example, you might want to meditate, give someone a massage or rest in a large room. All of these will be easier to do if the energy around you is calm and still.

Screens
The screen protects the person in the arm chair from any fast-flowing energy from the window.

half-day projects

❶ Positioning screens behind chairs

Before you do either of these projects, see pages 82–3, 108–9, which refer to furniture layout. The position of your chairs will effect the outcome of these projects.

Look at the places you or your family sit. See if any seats are **unprotected** at the back by a wall, and if it is possible to protect them with a screen.

There are numerous types of screen – a Japanese-style paper screen (useful if you want to let some light through), a wooden lattice screen, a solid wooden screen or a metal-framed screen with cotton fabric. You can also use tall plants to make a natural screen. Place the screen of your choice behind the chair(s).

❷ Positioning screens in a room

If you are finding it difficult to relax and find **solitude** in a particular room, consider the possibility of using a **screen** or plants to **enclose** part of the room. Once you have set up the screen try to relax there and assess the results.

removing **unpleasant energy**

Sea salt is used in feng shui to absorb old chi energy. Salt is considered to be very yang (see pages 132–3) and has the ability to pull energy into it. Hence it is useful in any situation where you want to get rid of stale chi energy.

It can also be used if you move into a new home and want to remove the energy left by the previous occupants, have had a difficult separation and want to clear the atmosphere when your partner has left or if you feel that your home is possessed by ghosts, as the salt will help absorb some of the old chi energy that keeps a ghost in your home.

Sea salt will also absorb the energy that is left over from a negative experience or feeling. For example, having an argument, feeling very depressed or losing your temper can temporarily change the energy of a room and the salt will help to restore the atmosphere. This can be combined with the projects on page 24.

Sea salt also has the ability to make the chi energy flowing through a home more stable. This is useful in places where energy will naturally wash back and forth more forcefully.

Salt
Always use pure sea salt around the home, which is available from health food stores.

half-day projects

1 Using salt within the home
Before going to bed take a **bowlful of sea salt** to the room in which you wish to change the energy. **Sprinkle the salt** on the floor and leave it over night. The next day vacuum or sweep the sea salt up and **discard it outside** your home. If you wish to combine this with the projects on page 24 you should do those projects before and after sprinkling the salt.

2 Stabilizing the energy in your home
Take a **compass** and stand in the centre of your home. Using the compass, work out which parts of your home are to the north-east and south-west. See page 143 for more advice on using a compass. Fill a **ramekin** or similar dish with approximately two tablespoons of **sea salt** and place in the north-eastern and south-western parts of your home. Replace with fresh salt approximately every **two months**.

love, wealth & wisdom

The western and north-western parts of your home are associated with metal chi energy. According to the theory of the five elements, also explained on pages 138–9, this metal chi energy can be destroyed by fire chi energy when there is a deficiency of soil chi energy.

Using charcoal
This will add more energy associated with being practical and feeling settled.

The western part of your home is also associated with the desire to be wealthy, feeling romantic and being content, while the north-western side relates to feeling in control, being organized and acting with wisdom. These aspects of your life could be disrupted if you have anything that generates fire chi energy, such as a fireplace, boiler or cooker (gas or electric).

The solution to this is to add more soil chi energy to help harmonize the fire and metal chi energies. A convenient and simple option is to use charcoal in a clay pot, which will generate strong soil chi energy. The energy can be further enhanced by placing the pot on a yellow cloth.

Other items made of clay will help, as will yellow objects with low flat shapes. The earth used to pot houseplants carries even more soil energy. A yellow flowering plant in a clay container will harness all these attributes.

Colour and materials
Yellow flowers and clay containers combine the colour and material of soil chi energy which can make a relationship more stable.

(see page 145)

half-day projects

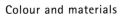

❶ Using charcoal in the home
Break a stick of **artist's charcoal** into chunks and put them in a **clay pot**. Stand in the centre of your home and use a compass to find the western and north-western segments of your home (see page 145). Look in those areas to see if you have any of the items that generate **fire chi** energy, such as a **fireplace**, **boiler** or **cooker**. Place the clay pot containing the charcoal on a **yellow cloth** as close as possible to the item.

❷ Using charcoal near heat
In the case of a **cooker** or **fireplace**, place a pot of charcoal on **either side**. Place the charcoal on a **shelf** or on the floor **below** the boiler and place it in a **cupboard** as near to the oven as possible.

Change the charcoal approximately **every two months** and keep the area around the charcoal clean and uncluttered.

colour, inspiration & romance

Fresh flowers radiate more living chi energy than household objects, helping them project their colour more strongly into the room.

SUITABLE FLOWERS			
Direction	**Colour**	**Container**	**Icons**
East	Cream, blue, green leaves	Glass	ambition confidence assertiveness
South-east	Cream, blue, green leaves	Glass	creativity communication imagination
South	Blue, green leaves, purple	Ceramic	expressive social passionate
South-west	Purple, yellow	Ceramic	secure realistic practical
West	Yellow, pink, red	Metal	content playful pleasure-seeking
North-west	Yellow, white	Metal	wise organized in control
North	White, cream, red	Metal or glass	peaceful sensual spiritual
North-east	Purple, white, yellow	Ceramic	motivated hard working competitive

Flowers present an excellent way of bringing more chi energy into a room or an area. For example, the energy in the south-western part of your home (or a particular room) is associated with feeling more secure and placing flowers here will help increase this chi energy. (See pages 146-7 for more information on the energy of each direction.)

Using flowers is a very flexible way of adding colour to a room. You can change them easily according to your mood and the atmosphere you want to create. Flowering plants will have a similar influence and can take the place of fresh cut flowers if you prefer.

Flowers for colour

It is important that any flowers or plants remain healthy so that they radiate helpful chi energy into a room. Dying plants or wilting flowers could radiate unhelpful energy.

❶ Positioning flowers in the home

Identify places you would like to put **flowers** in order to **increase the chi energy**. Stand in the centre of your home and take a compass reading to determine the **direction of the room** in which you wish to place the plants (see page 145). Alternatively you can stand in the **centre** of a large room and just apply the directions to that room.

Clear a **space** for the flowers and ensure that the area is clean. Look at the **chart** and place the appropriate coloured flowers and container in that part of your home. **Change the water daily** and discard the flowers as they wilt.

Metal containers
If you put the flowers in a shiny metal container, it will further enhance the metal chi energy of the west.

Romantic feelings help to generate the enthusiasm to start a relationship or improve an existing relationship. One way to help intensify these feelings is to use flowers.

The most helpful colours for romance are pink and red as these symbolize the chi energy of the setting sun in the western sky. The effect of the flowers will be more powerful if you can find a place where they catch the setting sun. It also helps to have two of the same type of flowers in a vase, reflecting the imagery of two people sharing their life.

Any type of flowers are suitable so choose to suit your personal taste, including roses, pink lilies, carnations or tulips. Each flower will generate slightly different chi energy and you may find that a certain flower works best for you.

It is worth finding a beautifully shaped vase for this purpose. Silver, stainless steel, chrome or pewter are all suitable materials. The water must be kept clean and the container shiny.

In addition you could put one thing belonging to yourself and one belonging to your partner close to or around the vase overnight. To further enhance the energy in this part of your home, hang a mirror behind the flowers. However, do not place the mirror directly opposite a door, window or another mirror. An arrangement of bright purple or red flowers on a table will often be the most dominant colour in a room, even though they take up a relatively small amount of space.

❷ Flowers to improve relationships
Buy **two flowers** of the same type. Cut the bottom of the stems of the flowers at an angle so that they last longer. Place the flowers in a vase. Use a compass to locate the **western part** of your home or room (see page 145). If possible, choose a place close to a **west-facing window** so that the flowers will **catch the sunlight**. Tidy this part of your home or room. Remove any clutter and give the area a **good clean**. Place the vase in your chosen position. If it is practical, **hang a mirror** behind the flowers so that you can see them in the reflection.

Keeping fresh
Discard and refill the water daily to keep the water fresh. Cut back the bottom of the stems by a few millimetres at the same time as this will also help the flowers last longer. Polish the vase once a week.

sex

Sexual vitality is primarily associated with energy found in the northern part of your home. Northern chi energy is represented by water, the night and winter. Bringing more northern energy into your own chi energy field can help increase your desire for sex. This chi energy also helps you to feel relaxed, intimate and affectionate.

Crystals
Hanging a crystal is an easy way to bring more chi energy into a room and increase intimacy between yourself and your partner.

You can also consider using the chi energy of the south to feel more passionate and of the west to feel more romantic, if these are missing from your life. Other common-sense steps, such as working on your relationship, eating the appropriate diet and resolving any issues you might have about sex by seeking professional advice, can be important factors.

Crystals have the effect of refracting light as it passes through them. A crystal hung in the sunlight will refract light, spreading it throughout the room and helping to bring in more energy. Spherical, multi-faceted crystals are available with a cord already attached.

You can also use rock crystals which are taken from deep within mountains where they have absorbed the earth's chi energy. These crystals emit this chi energy, increasing the energy of a room. Different crystals emit different types of chi energy and you will need to try to find a crystal that best suits your own needs.

Placing either kind of crystal in the northern part of your home or your bedroom will increase sexual energy. You could also add sexually stimulating imagery to this part of the room.

half-day projects

① Using a rock crystal in the home
Use your notes about the **position of the sun** or a compass to determine where the northern part of your home or bedroom is (see pages 9 or 145). **Clear a space** so that the crystal has room to **radiate its chi energy**. If you wish to use a rock crystal place it in a clean, uncluttered area that is facing north.

② Hanging a crystal
If you wish to hang a **spherical crystal,** look in the northern part of your home or room and, ideally, find a window that catches some sunlight from the **east or west**. If you have a choice, the west would be better for **helping a relationship**. Experiment and hang the crystal so that at some time in the day, the sunlight is refracted into the northern part of your home or bedroom. You may need to **adjust the position** of the crystal at different times of the year as the sun changes its position in the sky.

To be well organized we need a certain structure and rhythm to our lives. This can enable us to achieve more with less effort. Rather like dancing where the rhythm of the music can keep us active for long periods of time without tiring, having a rhythm to your life can help you achieve your goals.

Grandfather clocks
Add some healing and calming rhthym to your home with the gentle ticking of a grandfather clock.

Our bodies are based on rhythmic motion. Examples of this are the human heartbeat, breathing and menstruation. We are also easily influenced by other cycles such as the phases of the moon, day and night and the seasons. Women living together will often find their menstrual cycles harmonize.

There are many ways to add rhythm to your life. For example, going to bed and waking at the same time, eating your meals at regular times or exercising at the same time each day. In addition to this it is possible to add rhythm to your home.

Pendulum clocks create rhythm. Fill a room up with pendulum clocks and after a while their pendulums will harmonize and swing together. In a subtle way we can also tune into the rhythm of a clock. The movement of the pendulum, ticking sounds and chimes all make it easier to be more structured and feel organized.

To create this rythmic effect you will need to use a mechanical rather than an electric clock with as many metal parts as possible and a pendulum. It will be most effective in the north-western part of your home or room. If this is not possible, the west or north would be the next best options.

half-day projects

① Positioning clocks
Use the sunlight or a compass (see pages 9 or 145), to determine the **north-western** part of your home or room. Find a suitable site for your clock – either hung on the wall, placed on a shelf or, in the case of a grandfather clock, on the floor. Make sure that the clock is **easily visible** from within the room.

② Maintaining the benefits
To be effective the clock should be **continually working** and you may need to make **periodic adjustments** so that it keeps accurate time. Try to keep any metal parts **polished** and clean where appropriate.

Use several clocks within your home or even in a room, if you feel the need to **strengthen this rythmic influence** which, in turn, can help you develop a more structured life.

adding **excitement**

Lights bring more energy into a space and, therefore, generate a livelier, yang atmosphere (see page 132). Lights also add one of the components of the sun's energy and so are associated with fire chi energy.

Representing the summer and midday energy, fire chi energy is used to help you become noticed, to stand out and shine. It is, therefore, useful if you want greater recognition from a partner or work colleague, to improve your social life or to make new friends. As you absorb more fire chi energy you should find it easier to express yourself and let your feelings shine through.

Direct light

Spotlights help to create a more yang environment. They can be useful if you want to activate the chi energy in a particular room, such as a kitchen or a in a specific part of a room, such as a worktop. They can also be used to illuminate a particular area for work, while allowing the rest of the room to remain in natural light. Similarly, low-voltage halogen lighting produces a bright, high-intensity light that is ideal for increasing the flow of yang chi energy through stagnant places. These can be very flexible and used for up- or down-lighting.

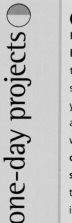

one-day projects

❶ Spotlights

Identify an area you wish to make **more yang using focused lighting**. This will apply primarily to **work areas** and surfaces in the kitchen or study, and to recesses such as **cupboards** or spaces that are not likely to be reached by any natural daylight. If you have the skill, attach a **spotlight** to the ceiling or wall, or ask a qualified electrician to install the light. If you are lighting a work surface, be sure to position the light so that you **do not cast a shadow** over the surface itself. Alternatively, use a **free-standing halogen light** to create the same effect, making sure that the **light source is not blocked** when the work area is in use.

❷ Placing candles

Use a compass or **observe the movement of the sun** to locate the **southern** part of your home (see pages 9 and 145). Place one or more candle in a convenient place in this area of your home depending on your needs: if you want to focus on **yourself** use one candle; if you would like to be in a relationship or improve an **existing relationship** use two candles; if you want to embrace your **whole family** use a candle for each member. This can also apply to loved ones who have passed on. Light these candles each day. Sit facing the candles, so you also face south, and meditate on ways that you can **bring your feelings to the surface**.

Uplighting

Uplighting encourages an upward flow of chi energy which is particularly helpful if you have low or sloping ceilings. Directing the light onto the ceiling helps make the ceiling appear higher.

Light bulbs

Incandescent bulbs are useful for general lighting. They increase the chi energy over a wide area in a relatively even manner. The colour of this light is slightly orange, helping to create a warmer atmosphere. In general, lampshades made from fabric or paper will soften the light and create a more yin atmosphere, while metal or reflective lampshades will create a harder more yang atmosphere.

Candles

Candles are the most yin source (see page 132) of light, radiating a soft orange glow, and having the advantage of not generating any electromagnetic fields (EMF). This type of light is ideal when you want to create a softer, more romantic atmosphere.

Lamplight

Table lamps or floor lamps will make the room feel cosier and more intimate. This is ideal when you want to feel close to someone, have a romantic evening or take your mind off things and relax.

❸ Low or sloping ceilings

Walk around your home and locate any rooms or areas where you have **low or sloping ceilings**. Use a free-standing or fixed halogen light to **direct the light source** onto the appropriate ceiling. When planning this, however, make sure that the light will not shine into your eyes if it is mounted lower than head height. A bright light can be hidden behind a plant or paper screen to **reduce glare**. This also **softens the light** and helps to create a more relaxing **yin** atmosphere appropriate for a bedroom or living room.

❹ Creating different moods

At night turn on the lights and **walk around your home**. Think carefully about where you would like to relax, be more romantic or more intimate – all more yin – and where you wish to be more energetic, lively and alert – all more yang. Fit **fabric** or **paper** lampshades to lights in the areas you wish to make more yin. The thicker the fabric and the larger the shade the more yin it becomes. If you wish to make this area **cosier** keep the light source as close to the floor as possible. Use a **reflective metal shade** in areas you want to make more yang – the more open the shade the **more yang** the space will become.

colours

The colours in a room influence the light frequencies present in it. These light frequencies pass through your outer chi energy field and, as they do this, can change your mood. You can, therefore, choose colours to help you feel the way you want.

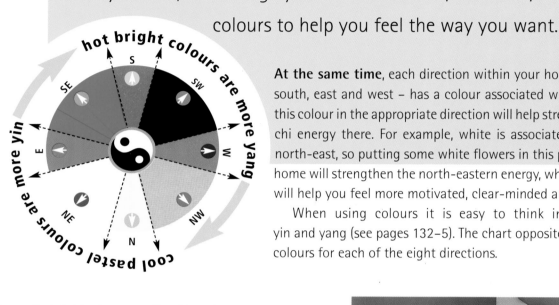

At the same time, each direction within your home – north, south, east and west – has a colour associated with it. Using this colour in the appropriate direction will help strengthen the chi energy there. For example, white is associated with the north-east, so putting some white flowers in this part of your home will strengthen the north-eastern energy, which, in turn, will help you feel more motivated, clear-minded and decisive.

When using colours it is easy to think in terms of yin and yang (see pages 132–5). The chart opposite shows the colours for each of the eight directions.

Generally bright, strong, noticeable colours are more yang and pale, subtle, pastel colours more yin. A room with lots of yang colours will have a more exciting, dramatic and vibrant atmosphere. Yin colours help create a peaceful, relaxing and gentle atmosphere.

Blue
The blue used here is calm and relaxing but equally helpful for feeling inspired and creative.

half-day projects

1 Colour schemes
When redecorating, use the chart above to help you choose colours that will be in **harmony** with the energy of that part of your home. To do this you will first need to work out in which **direction** the room or area is facing (see pages 9 and 145). Next look at the chart to find the colour to match that direction. This would normally be your **first choice**, however, you can **also** use the chart of harmonious colours to provide you with **more choice**. If your room falls into **several directions** choose the colours appropriate for the largest area or a **mixture of all directions**.

2 Think carefully
Consider the **strength of the colour** and make sure that it **balances** with the area that it will cover. A small area of a bright colour, such as **red**, will be more noticeable than a large area of, say, pale blue. So it follows that a bright red window frame in a room with pale colours will be a **dominant feature**.

COLOURS FOR EVERY ROOM

Use the chart below to see the range of colours that are suitable for each of the eight directions. You can then apply this information to the room you wish to decorate.

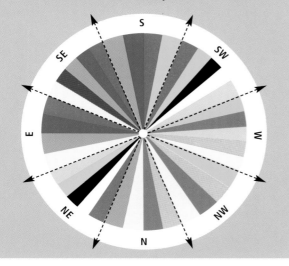

Using the principles of the five elements (see pages 138–9), you can substitute one colour with another colour of the same element. For example, matt-black in the south-west can be substituted with the other soil chi energy colours which are yellow and white. This is helpful if you do not feel comfortable with the colour associated with a particular direction. North and south do not have alternative colours as their element only applies to one direction.

In addition, it is possible to use a colour from the preceding, supporting element or the following, calming element in the five element circle. This brings a greater range of colours to your palette. Use the supporting colours to make it more vibrant and the calming colours to make it more restful.

SUITABLE COLOURS		
Colour	**Direction**	**Influence**
Bright green	EAST	Ambition, confidence, self esteem, energy, enthusiasm
Dark green or blue	SOUTH-EAST	Creativity, imagination, persistence, sensitivity, new ideas
Purple	SOUTH	Being expressive, passion, being social, greater emotion, quick thinking
Matt-black	SOUTH-WEST	Settling down, add quality, being practical, realistic, intimate
Rusty red or pink	WEST	Romance, focused on the end result, financially aware, playful, content
Silver, grey	NORTH-WEST	Self control, dignity, responsibility, feeling in control, being organized
Cream and translucent or glossy finishes	NORTH	Independence, objectivity, feeling sexual, going with the flow, being spiritual
Brilliant white	NORTH-EAST	Motivation, being competitive, quick witted, sharp minded, knowledgeable
Yellow	CENTRE	Feeling powerful, centre of attention, attracting opportunities, making changes

Calming

The blue units in this kitchen act as a calming element against the touches of red.

Apart from decorating, coloured objects can be used to enhance certain aspects of your character or life. All you need to do is place any household object with a strong colour in the appropriate part of your home or room. Typical items that can bring strong colour into a room include cushions, curtains, flowers, flowering plants, paintings, bedspreads, towels, rugs, vases, lampshades or pieces of furniture.

MATERIALS

It is essential that the fabric used for clothing, bedding or seating is natural. Synthetic fabrics can lead to tiredness and loss of concentration, and will eventually compromise your health. Cotton, linen and silk, are more appropriate close to your skin, whereas wool and leather are better away from your skin.

The clothes that you wear can have an even more direct influence, as they are actually within your chi energy field. The same applies to your bedding and the chairs you sit on – the material, colour and, to a lesser extent, the style will all help you feel differently. It is usual to notice a discernible change in the way you feel when changing out of formal work clothes into something more yin and relaxing, just as a change into something formal will make you feel more yang and alert.

HARMONIOUS COLOUR			
Direction	**Supporting element**	**Same element**	**Calming element**
EAST and SOUTH-EAST	Cream, varnish or lacquered surfaces	Any green or sky-blue	Pale purple
SOUTH	Bright green and sky-blue	Bright red or purple	Pale yellow beige brown matt-black
SOUTH-WEST, CENTRE, and NORTH-EAST	Fiery purple	Yellow, matt-black, white, brown or beige	Pink grey off-white
WEST and NORTH-WEST	Bright yellow or brilliant white	Red, pink, grey, silver or off-white	Cream varnish lacquered surface
NORTH	Red, pink, off-white, silver and grey	Cream, translucent or glossy finishes	Pale green blue

half-day projects

USING COLOURS IN CLOTHING

❶ to feel better

Look through the chart on page 39 to find a characteristic that would help you in life. Try incorporating the suggested colours into your daily clothing and see how you feel. You should be aware that people might begin to treat you differently too.

❷ to be more assertive

This can best be achieved by using the more aggressive, confident chi energy of the east. Bright greens, vertical lines and a fitted cut would all make you appear taller and increase the energy associated with being taken more seriously.

❸ to delegate more

Use the organizational and leadership qualities of the north-west to help. Grey colours, round shapes and a prominent metal watch will help to increase these powers.

❹ greater recognition

The chi energy of the south will help you be noticed more and receive greater recognition. Use a bright fiery purple, star shapes and silk.

❺ to be more creative

Greater ability to create and communicate can be achieved by boosting the chi energy of the south-east. Vertical lines, greens

USING COLOURED OBJECTS

① Choosing colours

When choosing the colour of a new household object, first identify where you intend to put it. Use a compass to determine the direction of the room (see page 9 or page 145). Next look at the chart on page 38 to see which colour is best for that part of your home. If you are happy with that colour choose an object of the same colour.

If you do not like the colour look at the harmonious colour chart on page 40 which includes the additional five elements, supporting and calming colours. For example, if you do not want to use green in the east you can try cream, blue or pale purple. The brighter the colour the more yang and energetic it will be, the paler the colour the more yin and relaxing the influence.

② New clothing, bedspread or chair

Look up your nine ki colour on page 149. Choose an item of clothing, a bedspread or chair which has this colour in it. A strong shade will make you feel active and more yang, whereas a pastel shade will help you feel relaxed and more yin.

③ Changing your energy.

Referring to the chart on page 39, look for an aspect of your character that you would like to develop and find the colour associated with it. For example, if you want to be more imaginative and creative choose blue or dark green. Tie a ribbon of this colour in the appropriate part of your home or room. In this case you would need to tie a blue or dark green ribbon in the south-eastern part of your home.

You can also use clothing to adjust your own chi energy and project a particular impression to others. The same principles apply – using more yang bright colours will help you appear alert, dramatic and expressive, whereas more yin pastel colours will contribute to a calmer, softer and more gentle appearance.

When choosing clothing, use the colour chart to decide which aspect of your character you would like to strengthen and then wear clothes of that colour. For example, if you want to feel more expressive, social and passionate wear clothes containing some bright purple. Should you want to appear more reliable try grey, white or black.

Using furniture

By adding a bright chair to the bedroom the atmosphere has completely changed, lifting the cold blue to give a bright, sunny feeling.

and blues along with comfortable harmonious styles will aid the creative process.

⑥ to be more competitive

North-eastern chi energy increases this energy. Crisp white clothing with sharp creases will add more north-eastern chi energy.

⑦ to have greater charisma

This can be achieved with more western chi energy. Use reds, shiny metal jewellery and round shapes to help increase this energy.

⑧ to be able to relax more

More chi energy associated with the north will help you find an inner peace and greater tranquillity. Cream is the ideal colour along with flowing loose clothing.

⑨ to be more caring and considerate

To help bring out these qualities add more south-western chi energy. Yellows, browns and black should increase this energy along with strong horizontal lines.

In addition, you can choose colours according to your nine ki number. By looking for the year you were born on the chart on page 149 you will find a colour that is associated with it. This colour will help revitalize your deepest energy. Apply this colour to clothing or bedding.

letting go

A room or home that contains clutter will be at greater risk of energy stagnating. The clutter will slow down the flow of chi energy making it more difficult to refresh and renew the atmosphere in a room.

Clever cutter
It is much easier to stop clutter accumulating if you have easy to use storage units.

Clutter can cling on to chi energy, keeping it in one place for long periods of time. This can lead to a stuffy feeling which may make you feel less active and unable to do more in life. In extreme cases, the person living in a very cluttered home can feel that their life is stagnating.

During your life you may encounter difficult times that you will have to make a big effort to overcome. It will hinder your progress if you have kept items from this, or other difficult times, as they will act as reminders and will hold you back. For example, if a relationship ended and you were finding it difficult to move on and start a new one it would not help to see reminders of the previous relationship in your home.

During times when you want to move forwards in life and let go of the past it helps to get rid of clutter and open up your home so that it is easier for the chi energy to flow.

It is also good to keep items that remind you of the good times and things that will help your children or grandchildren appreciate their ancestry.

half-day project

① Cleaning the atmosphere

Get a number of large **cardboard boxes** and **label** each one with today's date. Take one box, label it 'long term' and put all the things in it that you think you will not need for some time. Do this in **each room** and include things like old make-up containers you no longer use, unused equipment, books, magazines and non-essential **paperwork**.

Next take a box and mark it 'finished' and put inside all the items that remind you of a part of your history that you wish to leave behind. This could include photographs, non-essential documents, letters and artwork.

Now take another box and mark it '**undecided**' and put into it all the things that clutter your home but you are not sure if you will miss.

After a month throw out, or give to charity, the box marked 'finished' if you have not missed anything. Keep the other two boxes and after a month look through them to see if you can transfer anything from '**undecided**' to '**long term**' or if you need to transfer any of the long-term items to 'undecided'. After three months see if you feel comfortable parting with the contents of the 'long term' box. Repeat this exercise every year to stop new clutter building up.

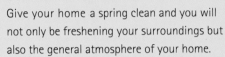

refreshing yourself

Cleaning is a quick and immediate way to change the atmosphere in your home. After a thorough 'spring clean' your home will feel fresher.

Out with the old...
Give your home a spring clean and you will not only be freshening your surroundings but also the general atmosphere of your home.

A clean atmosphere will provide you with more vitality and energy. It is also easier to relax in a clean and tidy environment, particularly if you are the kind of person who feels irritated when things are out of place.

A clean home is also one that can help you to maintain good health. It is important to reduce the risk of mildew or dampness building up, as these will create unhealthy chi energy. The biggest priorities are the kitchen and bathroom.

The best time to give your home a major clean is on a dry, sunny day so that you can open the windows and doors and let fresh, dry air flow through your home. Traditionally cleaning is done in the spring to clear out all the old energy from the autumn and winter.

Fabrics often retain dust and this contributes to a stagnant atmosphere. Each grain of dust retains stale chi energy stored in your home. Cleaning curtains, soft furnishings and carpets will get rid of this old energy allowing fresh new chi energy to enter your home. Cleaning the windows will allow light to shine into your home bringing in even more sunny chi energy.

two-day project

❶ Spring cleaning

Choose a **dry, sunny day** and begin by opening all the windows and, if appropriate, the doors. It may help to play your **favourite music**. Start in the kitchen and then move on to the bathroom, bedrooms, living room and garage as these are the areas where you can make the biggest difference.

Empty all the cupboards, shelves and drawers in each room. Put into practice the clearing clutter exercise on page 42. **Clean** all of the places you cannot usually get access to. For example, **behind the cooker**, refrigerator and washing machine.

Pay **particular attention** to cupboards under sinks or household equipment that uses water, such as washing machines and dishwashers. If there are any signs of a leak you will need to get it rectified. If there is any **dampness** you should dry the area thoroughly before replacing items. Check shower curtains for mildew and wash them carefully.

Wash and **clean any fabrics** you can, including curtains, rugs and chair covers. If possible **shampoo** your carpets. Take fabrics outside and **get rid of as much dust** as possible.

adding sparkle to your life

Mirrors or other reflective surfaces will change the direction of chi energy in the same way that they reflect light in new directions. This is helpful where you want to reflect more chi energy into a stagnant area. Mirrors will speed up the flow of chi energy, creating a dynamic, stimulating and more yang atmosphere.

Mirror

A mirror over a fireplace will reflect more fire energy into the room.

Whenever you use mirrors it is important to avoid hanging them directly opposite a door, window or each other. Mirrors facing a door or window will reflect chi energy entering your home back out again, while two mirrors facing each other will bounce chi energy back and forth, making the environment tense which is not very good for relaxation.

Always try to use one large mirror, rather than several mirrors next to each other or mirror tiles as these can make the image in the reflection seem disjointed and the atmosphere less harmonious.

Mirrors are particularly useful in dark spaces where you want to reflect as much of the available light back into the room as possible. This applies to basement apartments or a room that only receives northern light.

Large mirrors will make a room feel much larger. Ideally, they should be from floor to ceiling. Place large mirrors along one of the long sides to make the room appear twice as wide. The same can be achieved in a corridor or hall by staggering mirrors on each side.

half-day projects

1 Positioning mirrors

Fit a mirror in a **narrow room** or in a corridor. Measure the longest wall or the **corridor** wall in order to determine the size of the mirror you can fit. Remember **not** to hang a mirror directly **opposite a door**. Hang the mirror on the wall and make sure you keep it clean.

Similarly, in any **L-shaped room**, hang a mirror in the narrowest part of the room so that the **proportions** appear more even.

2 Where to put a mirror

If you have any basement rooms or **north-facing rooms** look to see where you can hang mirrors. If possible, position the mirror where it will reflect some of the **daylight** into the rest of the room. In this situation you may need to use several mirrors. However, avoid hanging them directly opposite one another.

Look in your **bedroom** to see if you can remove any mirrors. If there are any remaining mirrors facing your bed try to find a new location for them within the room. You can always **cover** the mirrors with a **cloth** while you sleep.

You may be able to strategically place a mirror so that natural light from a window is reflected back into a dark area of the room or a stagnant corner.

Fast-flowing energy is most likely to occur when the stairs lead down to the front door in a long straight hall, or if the front door is directly in line with the back door. In these situations, the fast-flowing chi energy can make you feel unsettled, tense and irritable. These feelings are intensified if the fast-flowing energy is directed towards your bed or where you sit for long periods of time.

Mirrors in bedrooms

In general, avoid having mirrors in your bedroom as they create a faster, yang environment, which is not ideal for good sleep. If you have a mirror in your bedroom it should not face your bed. During the night you will, ideally, release emotions and chi energy from the previous day, so you that when you awake you will feel refreshed. Reflecting this chi energy back at you will disrupt the process.

Convex mirrors

A convex mirror or any other convex reflective surface will disperse fast-flowing chi energy by reflecting it back in a wide arc. As the convex shape spreads out and disperses the energy, it weakens the force of this unhelpful chi energy.

❸ Mirrors in specific rooms

If you have a hall, take a look at the relationship between the **stairs** and **front door**. If the stairs lead directly down to the front door, hang a small **convex** mirror so that it faces you as you descend the stairs. You will often find that there is a **wall** or **wooden panel** facing you as you start to walk down from the top of the stairs. This is an **ideal** place for a convex mirror. If this is not possible, try hanging the mirror to the side of the front door.

If you have a long hall or corridor running through your home look at each end to determine the best place to put a convex mirror. If one end of the hallway leads onto a bedroom, or somewhere you sit for

long periods of time, the situation is potentially more serious and the mirror must be hung at this end of the corridor. **Hang the mirror** above the door at this end of the hall so that it faces back into the corridor.

Enter your home through your front door and check to see if you can see your back door. If there is a **door in between** open it for this exercise. A situation where all the doors are in a line encourages energy to flow too fast and can be remedied with a convex mirror. Walk from your front door towards the back door looking for a good place to hang a small convex mirror so that it faces you. For example, you could hang it above your back door.

health & happiness

Plants are unique in that they bring natural living chi energy into your home which could otherwise be a dead space.

Healthy, growing plants have been found to be the most effective way of cleaning the air in a room. This has become more important today as rooms are increasingly filled with toxic fumes from materials such as MDF (medium-density fibreboard), plastics and paints. Bushy or leafy plants have also been found to be particularly helpful in reducing noise levels. The leaves absorb the sound waves from the air making a room quieter and more relaxing. Plants with more rigid, stronger and pointed leaves, such as yuccas, will radiate more dynamic yang chi energy. Plants with softer, floppy and rounded leaves, such as some types of ivy generate more relaxing yin chi energy.

A stagnant or lifeless atmosphere can make people feel tired, drained or depressed. Usually you feel this way if your home is deficient in fresh, moving chi energy.

The most effective way to refresh the chi energy in your home is to add plants. They will bring in more vitality to a space. It helps to put plants in all the rooms that benefit from natural light. The rooms you spend more time in, such as your bedroom, will be more important.

PLANTS & EMF
A Swiss institute carried out a two-year research programme to examine the effects of keeping plants next to computers. The most effective was a *Cereus peruvianuf* (cactus) that reduced the incidence of headaches and tiredness. Other researchers have claimed that the peace lily and spider plant have similar properties.

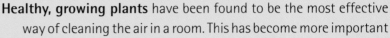

Plants for serenity
A series of bushy plants can make an effective screen for reducing noise and creating a more secluded or quiet area.

① Plants in the home
Walk around your home making notes of where you could have **more plants**. Ideally, each room should have **at least two plants**. Plants are very helpful in bathrooms and kitchens as they **absorb dampness** from the air. Refer to books on houseplants or seek advice if you need help in finding out which plants will grow best in a **certain location**. If you have problems looking after plants, find out what your options are available to help you. For instance, there are products available that automatically water plants. Avoid positioning a plant with **pointed leaves** close to your bed or where you sit for long periods of time.

② Reduce feelings of depression
If you suffer from depression or lethargy, fill your home with healthy plants to increase the energy.

As the atmosphere in your home begins to feel livelier try doing some exercise as this will greatly help reduce feelings of depression. Start off with gentle stretching and short walks, working towards aerobic exercise. You may find it helpful to play some music with a strong beat.

The containers you use can also be matched with the energy in each part of your home:

Earthenware	*South, south-west, west, north-west, north-east*
Cast iron	*South-west, west, north-west, north-east, north*
Wood	*North, east, south-east, south*

Plants have a variety of benefits. They can create harmony by calming the energy in a stressful environment or picking up the energy where it is dull.

It is good practice to use a variety of plants. However, if you use them for a specific task such as to cure depression, which is a more yin condition (see pages 132–5), it would, therefore, help to balance this with a more yang environment created by plants with pointed leaves.

A yin environment at home can contribute to depression. This might be due to damp conditions, coldness or a more yin style of decoration. Plants can be very effective at absorbing dampness from the air, helping to make the environment more yang. The colour of the plants will brighten up a drab interior, especially if some of the plants are in flower.

Plants and containers

Choose natural containers. See the box above if you want to choose a material that is in harmony with the energy of that part of your home. This can also be an opportunity to add colour if you want bright containers.

NASA scientists recently published the results of a two-year study into the ability of plants to absorb environmental pollution from the air in indoor environments. Their effectiveness was so good that they are to be used to clean the air in artificial space environments. The top ten most effective plants are:

Aglaonema modestum
Chamaedorea seifrizii Reed palm
Chrysanthemum morifolium Pot mum
Dracaena 'Janet Craig'
Dracaena Deremensis Group 'Massangeana'
Dracaena Deremensis Group 'Warneckei'

Dracaena marginata
Gerbera jamesonii Barberton daisy
Hedera helix English ivy
Sansevieria trifasciata 'Laurentii' Mother-in-law's tongue
Spathiphyllum 'Mauna Loa' Peace lily

changing your **mood**

Any sound waves vibrating through the air will also pass through and influence your own chi energy field and will help to change your mood.

Telephones
Think about changing your home telephone or, if you can, turn the sound off and attach a metal bell to your telephone that will provide a traditional ringing sound. You would then make a clear distinction between work and home phones.

A soft, gentle, more yin sound will soothe and calm the chi energy around you, making it easier to relax. Whereas, a vibrant, rhythmic, more yang sound will stimulate your chi energy field, making you feel more active. In addition, certain sounds will have a cleansing effect on the atmosphere of a room as well as on the people in it. Certain bells, gongs and special metal bowls are used in monasteries and other spiritual places for this reason (see pages 24–5).

One of the most common sounds at home is music. You probably find that music can quickly alter your mood. A serene piece of a classical music is helpful when you feel tense, while a rhythmic piece of modern dance music will make you feel livelier, if you are feeling low. Think carefully when you play music, as this is an opportunity to help you manage your emotions.

Before you introduce anything that makes a sound into your home make sure it has a tone you like. For example, the electronic sound from modern telephones can be irritating. At the same time, if your telephone at home and work has the same sound, when you are at home you may constantly be reminded of work, which may not be the ideal scenario.

half-day projects

❶ Positive sounds in the home
Listen to the sound of your **telephone ringing** and consider how you feel about it. If it produces feelings of **stress** because it reminds you of work consider changing it. Try the sound of a **natural metal bell**. Change the sound of the ringing tone or buy an old telephone with a natural bell.

Ring your **doorbell** and ask yourself if you are happy with the sound. If not listen to other possible doorbell sounds. When you find a better sounding doorbell, install it in your home.

❷ Moving energy with sounds
To increase energy in a stagnant or dark area, such as a corner under a low or sloping ceiling or in a basement, place something that will generate sound. This could be a telephone, a music centre, an audible clock or a television.

A common cause of stress, particularly when living in a town or city, is noise. When the sounds of traffic, aeroplanes, trains, people in the street or neighbours invade your home, it can make it difficult to relax.

One way to mask irritating sounds is to create white noise. White noise is a sound that contains a wide range of sound frequencies. Some of these sound waves will be opposite to other audible sounds. The result is that the two sound waves cancel each other out removing that particular frequency from the range.

An attractive form of white noise is the sound of running water, which can be introduced inside a room with a small indoor waterfall. However, be aware that it will mask other sounds and may force you to talk a little louder, so it is helpful if the waterfall is easy to turn on and off.

In addition, it helps to have features in your home that absorb sounds. Soft surfaces will do this, while hard surfaces tend to reflect sounds back into the room, adding to the potential for stress. Leafy plants are an excellent way of absorbing sound wave vibrations. To reduce noise add tapestries, thick rugs and full length curtains. Large cushions close to windows will help further.

Reducing noise

Wall hangings, heavy blinds, carpets and other soft furnishings will help eliminate any disturbing noise from outside the home.

❸ Peaceful sounds

Find a **water feature** that produces the sound of falling water and ideally, one which allows you to **adjust** the flow of water and, therefore, the sound. Place the water feature in the **eastern** or **south-eastern** part of the house or room where you want to **reduce** the noise level. Make sure the sound of the water is **not masked** or **stifled** by nearby soft items, such as a sofa or plant. Run the water feature and test the results. You should change at least some of the water every week so that it remains fresh.

❹ Irritating noise

Try to locate the **source of a noise** that irritates you, for example, the sound of traffic coming through the windows. Buy a **bushy plant** and place it close to the windows. In general, the more plants you have in the room the easier it will be to absorb sounds. In addition, add more **soft furnishings** to the room. Cushions, tablecloths, tapestries and rugs will all absorb noise.

stimulating your imagination

Your thoughts can change your chi energy and, therefore, the way you feel. The way to alter your mood is by looking at an image that triggers different thoughts in your mind.

Using images
This relaxed stone statue will remind you to take it easy and enjoy life.

Hanging a romantic picture of a couple in an embrace could make you think about being intimate with someone with the result that you actually feel more loving and affectionate.

Using imagery in this way can be a powerful force in helping you to focus on what you want to achieve in life. Firstly, it is important to know what you want to achieve (see page 14) and, secondly, you need to think about the kind of imagery that would be helpful.

If you are already in a relationship, it is helpful to have pictures in your home that remind you of the best times you have had together. Everyone goes through happy and difficult times in relationships and having reminders of the good times can support both of you when you are going through a challenging period.

Similarly, a single person can think about starting a new relationship when there is positive imagery around to help him or her feel good about meeting someone new. Sometimes the opposite feelings are generated. When a single person who is desperate to start a relationship is surrounded by images of solitary figures, it reinforces his or her lonely situation.

In terms of the energies in your home, it is most effective to put romantic pictures in the south-western, western or south-eastern parts of your home, as these areas relate to long-term relationships, feelings of romance and starting a relationship respectively.

half-day project

❶ Using images in the home

Look through your **photograph albums** for pictures that remind you of your happiest times together. Find an attractive frame to mount them in and, if necessary, get the photographs reprinted and enlarged to the appropriate size. Hang them in the south-western, western or south-eastern parts of your home or room, ideally in a position where you can see them clearly. Make sure this area is kept alive by **updating** the photographs **regularly. Carry a camera** with you and remember to take new photographs of you both having fun together.

If you want to begin a **relationship** look for images that symbolize romance. You may find it is more effective to use paintings or sculptures that are better at **conveying an impression** rather than a photograph of real people. Place the images in the **western** part of your home or room. In general, keep things in **pairs** in your home. For example, **two flowers** sharing a vase or two candles branching out from one stand.

improving **family life**

You can use the principle of changing your mood through imagery to help your whole family. This can be especially empowering for children. Keeping a record of their most successful moments in life will serve to remind them that they can overcome difficulties and challenges through their own efforts.

Message boards
Make sure the boards are easy for your children to reach and use and are placed in a prominent position within the room.

It is important to cultivate an environment where they can feel proud of themselves and do things to a high standard because they care, rather than to please their parents. Once this becomes part of their character it will be easier for them to be self-motivated in later years.

To encourage this, allow your children to have their own space to display photographs, artwork, awards, good reports and other similar material. The space should be clean, tidy and in a prominent position within the house. Try not to interfere even if you would prefer them to choose different items to display. If you have your own well-organized area for positive imagery, they can follow your example.

Another way to improve your children's self-esteem and encourage closer relationships within the family is to have a message board where you can leave spontaneous messages. For instance, 'I love you', 'you should be proud of your latest homework' or 'what a beautiful painting', will help make them feel that little bit more special. They should also be encouraged them to leave messages when they feel like it.

half-day project

1 Pin board
Choose a pin board that will fit into the **space** you have available. Fix it in place and explain to your **children** how to use it. Encourage them to put a **variety** of images there and to renew them from time to time. Add your own family pictures and keep changing them to keep the board fresh and alive.

Find and put up a **noticeboard** that you can write on. Write **spontaneous** messages on the board when the mood takes you. Encourage the rest of the family to feel free to do the same.

FAMILY DISPLAYS
If it is possible, put the family imagery in the south-western part of your home or room as this is where the energy associated with family life is found. Alternatively, the eastern areas relate to new beginnings and working towards the future, so these areas would be equally helpful.

relating to the **outside world**

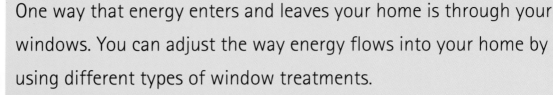

One way that energy enters and leaves your home is through your windows. You can adjust the way energy flows into your home by using different types of window treatments.

Wooden blinds and shutters
Large openings should be flexible so you can close them when you want to restrict the flow of energy.

This will affect the way you relate to the outside world. If you want to feel more secluded you will need a heavier window treatment – to be more outgoing use a lighter window dressing. It is good practice to keep the windows clean and uncluttered so that chi energy can move freely. Ideally, you need to be able to reduce the flow of energy through the windows when you want to settle down and relax and, at the same time, be able to fully open up the windows to allow in as much light as possible when you want the room to feel more active.

In general, it is better to use curtains in situations where you want to calm the flow of energy and create a cosy, comfortable atmosphere. Wooden blinds will make it easier for energy to flow, creating a more dynamic and stimulating atmosphere. These blinds can also be angled to let in light without having to suffer the glare of direct sunlight. The advantage of fabric roller blinds is that they leave the window unobstructed and provide a soft surface when they are pulled down. Other fabric blinds, such as Roman blinds, have the same effect.

Metal blinds are too hard for most residential situations. Only consider using them in a north-eastern, south-western, western or north-western bathroom as here they will encourage a more harmonious flow of energy.

one-day project

① Change of window treatment
Choose a room which would benefit from a **change** of window treatment. Clean the windows and remove any **clutter** from the window-sill. Focus on the **atmosphere** in that room over a few days. Pay particular attention to the way **light** enters the room. Think about what you do in that room and whether the atmosphere is helpful.

First consider whether it would help to make the room more yang and **active**, or more yin and **calm**. To make it more active, fit wooden blinds. To make it more comfortable, add curtains. To create a balance, use fabric roller blinds.

MATERIALS
You can match the material of your window treatment with the different chi energies present in each part of your home.

Wooden blinds	*North, east, south-east and south.*
Fabric roller blinds, Roman blinds or curtains	*South, north-east, south-west, west and north-west.*

Sharp edges or corners from another building can direct fast-flowing chi energy towards your home. The effect of this is that you could feel less settled at home, find it harder to relax and become more easily stressed. Over a long period of time it might even be harder to maintain good health.

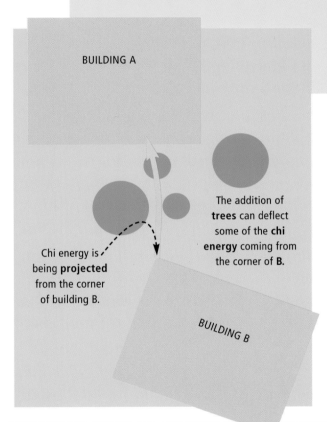

BUILDING A

Chi energy is being **projected** from the corner of building B.

The addition of **trees** can deflect some of the **chi energy** coming from the corner of **B.**

BUILDING B

The closer the corner of another building is to your home and the larger it is, the greater the influence. In addition, a building with hard, flat, shiny surfaces, such as glass, will speed up and direct the chi energy at your home more forcefully than one that is made up of textured, softer materials such as wood or bricks.

To solve this potential problem you need to slow down the chi energy as it approaches your home and deflect some of it away. Chi energy can easily be slowed down by vegetation, including hedges, bushes or trees, and deflected away from your home by using a reflective surface, such as a convex mirror or a brass plaque. An additional option would be to use wind chimes to generate sound waves to help disperse the fast-flowing energy. The ideal solution is to use a variety of remedies. A tree will soften higher sharp energy, bushes lower sharp energy and reflective surfaces will take care of any energy that gets through to your home.

two-day project

1 Sharp energy

Walk around the **outside** of your home looking carefully at nearby buildings. Also walk around the **top floor** of your home, as you will get a better view of the surroundings. If you see the corner of a building **pointing towards you**, make an assessment of the potential harm. If it is another home with one or two floors and further than 100m (109yd) away it will not pose a threat. A large, commercial building with glass outer surfaces and a similar distance away could be a problem.

To reduce the energy from the corner plant a **hedge**, some **bushes** or a **tree** in-between the corner and your

home. Evergreens will provide cover during the winter.

If possible, hang a **convex mirror** or shiny metal convex plaque on the outside of your home so that it **faces** the corner. Position this so that it is **easy to clean or polish** or keep shiny. Alternatively, you can hang a ba gua mirror so that it faces the corner. This is an eight-sided mirror with the trigrams etched into the glass.

Hang some wind chimes between your home and the corner. Find a location where the chime will catch the wind and ring frequently.

personalizing your home

Furniture can influence the chi energy in your home, depending on the material it is made from, its shape and colour. A home filled with modern high-tech furniture made from a hard material, such as metal, will feel very different from a home filled with antiques made from a softer material, such as wood.

In addition, modern furniture will create a different feel to antique items. Modern objects can bring in a fresh new feeling, while antiques have a more solid, established feeling.

When choosing furniture or setting up a new home it is important to think about what you want from life and what you want from your home (see pages 14–18), so that each item helps to create the right atmosphere to make it easier for you to achieve your goals.

The more furniture you have the slower energy will move around the room, and the easier it is to feel settled and comfortable. In a room that has less furniture and big open spaces, energy will move more quickly and, therefore, create a dynamic, active atmosphere.

When choosing chairs, tables or beds, think about when you will use them and what you hope to achieve in the room where

Cushions
Big soft cushions create a more cosy, yin atmosphere and will help you to relax.

one-day project

❶ Using furniture

Write a list of tasks you do in your home that require you to sit on a chair. Use the list in the box to **choose which type of chair** would best suit each task. For example, if you are working on your accounts a stool would help, and if you want to be romantic with someone it might be easier on a low sofa, bean bag or large cushion.

Take a look at the chairs that you use in your home and consider whether an **alternative type of seat** would be helpful and more effective.

Think about how many people sit around your dining room table and if it is more than six consider changing to a round or

oval table, if you do not already have one.

If you have **trouble sleeping**, look at the distance between your bed and the ceiling. If you have a low or sloping ceiling and a high bed, consider changing to a lower bed.

Furniture needs to fit in with the **proportions** of your room, so if you have a high ceiling use taller items and smaller, lower items where the ceilings are low.

It helps to buy furniture with **rounded edges**. Even a small radius can make a big difference. The harder the material the more important it is to have rounded corners.

CHECK LIST
Refer to the following list when you buy new furniture.

MATERIALS
To create a more relaxing atmosphere, use soft, more yin materials. Drape linen or cotton cloths over furniture to make it softer. Hard, more yang, materials will speed up the flow of energy creating a dynamic atmosphere.

COLOURS
Bright, yang colours will make your room feel exciting and inspiring, while pale, yin colours will create a more relaxing and calm atmosphere (see also pages 38–41).

SHAPES
Tall, upright furniture will encourage chi energy to move vertically, which can create an inspiring, more imaginative atmosphere. Whereas low, wide furniture encourages chi energy to move horizontally, which can generate a social and more intimate atmosphere.

POSTURE
The taller the chair, or higher the bed, the more yang and alert it helps you to feel, while a low, soft chair will encourage you to feel more yin and relaxed.

AGE
Consider whether a new or old piece of furniture will be most appropriate in a particular room. Use modern furniture to help with new projects, get out of a rut, or to be more adventurous. Antiques can help you feel more secure, stable and established.

MATERIALS

YIN soft
fabric
softwood
hardwood
stone
metal
glass
YANG hard

COLOURS

YIN relaxing
pale blue
pale green
pink
pale yellow
bright blue
bright green
bright yellow
bright red
YANG exciting

POSTURE

YIN relaxed
large soft cushion
beanbag
sofa
low upholstered chair
office-style chair
standard chair
high upright chair
YANG alert

they will be placed. A chair could be for relaxing, working or eating. Each chair needs to be different to help with each task.

Similarly a bed that is high off the ground can feel dramatic and more yang, while a futon on the floor can help you feel settled and more yin. However, when choosing a bed it is important to consider the amount of space between you and the ceiling. A high bed in a room with a low ceiling is not favourable as it can compress your chi energy field, making it harder to sleep deeply. It is helpful to leave a larger space between you and the ceiling.

When choosing a dining table it is important to consider how many people it will need to seat, as this will help you decide on the shape of the table. If you intend to have more than two people along each side, or more than six people, choose a round or oval table so that everyone can see and communicate with each other easily.

What you sit on
The furniture you sit on will influence your personal chi energy directly, as it defines your posture and your position within the room. For example, it feels very different to sit on a high stool as opposed to a cushion on the floor.

vitality

In oriental medicine the water inside our body, along with the chi energy that flows with it, has a special influence on our health. We are 70 per cent water ourselves and it is believed that the chi energy of the water inside our bodies is virtually the same as the chi energy of the water around us.

Still water
Calm water features are more yin and serene and will help to attain a tranquil atmosphere.

Consequently, any water close to us has the ability to influence the chi energy of the water inside our bodies. It is probably no accident that people throughout history have sought out water to help them heal themselves, convalesce or recuperate. Spa towns with natural springs and seaside towns have been popular locations for some time.

It follows that as water has such an influence on people, having a water feature inside your home or garden will have a similar helpful effect. However, it is essential that the chi energy of any water close to us is healthy, fresh, clean and unpolluted.

When considering the use of a water feature you should first decide on what you want it to achieve. If your aim in life is to be more active you will need a more active yang, water feature with moving water. For example, a fountain, powerful waterfall or an aquarium stocked with quick, active fish. Conversely, to feel calmer you will need a water feature that is slow moving, such as water trickling across a stone or slow-moving fish in an aquarium. Another alternative would be to keep a bowl of fresh water in an appropriate place, although it is important to remember to change the water at the beginning of each day.

one-day project

❶ Water features in the home

Use a **compass** or **watch the sun** (see pages 9 and 145) to locate the eastern or south-eastern part of your home. If possible, find a spot where the morning sun enters the room. You will need to get up at **sunrise** to be able to find the best place. Remember the **position** of the sun in the sky will be different depending on the time of year. Move any clutter away from the area. Place a **clear glass bowl**, filled with water in this spot and put some fresh flowers next to it. Replace the water each morning, **ideally before sunrise**.

Decide on whether you want to create an **active** or **calm** atmosphere and buy an appropriate small indoor water feature.

Locate the east or south-east part of your home or room (see pages 9 and 145), and **install** the water feature. Refresh the water regularly by taking some water out and refilling.

If you are feeling **adventurous** you can make your own indoor water feature. Buy a large glass, metal or ceramic container, a water pump and decorative items such as large stones. The pump will need an electrical socket so choose a location with easy access to **elelctricity**. It will circulate the water within the feature so there is no need for a water supply. Place the pump in the container so that the **output pipe** is above

In fact, whatever water feature you choose you will need to be able to refresh the water regularly. Change some of the water at least once a week simply by taking a few cups out and refilling it.

Moving water has two practical advantages: first, as the water falls it collects dust and sometimes other toxins out of the air, and secondly it generates a multi-frequency sound known as white noise, which can mask other sounds (see pages 48–9).

Placing a water feature to the east or south-east of your home or room is important as it will nourish the tree chi energy of these directions (see pages 138–42). As the chi energy of the east is associated with ambition, confidence and activity a water feature here would make it easier to adopt these characteristics. Alternatively, placing a water feature in the south-east of your home or room will nourish the chi energy associated with communication, creativity and generating new ideas.

The influence of a water feature becomes more yang if the water is exposed to sunlight. If you position it so that it catches the eastern sun as it rises through the sky the water will be further energized.

The sun continues to rise to the south-east and this will also energize the water, although more gently. Both will increase the chi energy associated with vitality.

Fast-flowing water
A waterfall will create a soothing sound and yet stir up the energy around it making the area refreshing to spend time in.

the proposed water level and arrange the stones so they hide the pump and provide an **attractive form** for the water to run across. Fill with water. You can add appropriate plants to your water feature.

Another option is to have an aquarium. You will need expert advice to make sure that it is properly set up so that the fish are healthy. An aquarium with unhealthy fish can be detrimental to the energy of your home. If you have **fast-moving** fish it will help create a dynamic, more yang atmosphere, whereas, an aquarium with **slow-moving fish** will be relaxing and more yin.

The same principles apply to outdoor as indoor water features. First you will need to find an appropriate location to the east or south-east of your **garden** or **outdoor space**. Next decide on the kind of water feature that would be appropriate for your needs. Options include a fountain, waterfall or pond. The greater the movement of water, the more yang the influence of the feature. It is important that the water does not become stagnant, so where there is little movement, such as in a pond, you will need to stock it with **wildlife** to keep the water fresh.

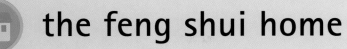 the feng shui home

exteriors

It is good practice in feng shui to feel good about your home, take pride in its appearance and enjoy coming home. Your home is a reflection of yourself and, therefore, it helps to make the exterior of your home something you can be proud of.

After you have lived in a home for a while it is easy to get used to its appearance, even though there may be aspects of it that have deteriorated or that you initially meant to rectify but never got round to doing.

Try to maintain the outside of your home so that it makes a good impression whenever you or anyone else enters. This will also make a difference if you want to sell your home as it will add value.

It is important to fix any dampness due to poor guttering, deteriorating exterior surfaces or blocked drainage as this will cause rot and dampness inside your home, harming the atmosphere.

The path to your door
A wide clear path brings more energy to your home. This could make it easier to feel stimulated at home but hard to relax.

one-day project

❶ Improvements to the exterior

Spend some time away from your home and try to empty your mind so that when you return it is as though you are **seeing it for the first time**. Look at your home with a critical eye and make notes about things you could improve. First look at your home from a distance, pay attention to its colour and the condition of the paintwork. Next observe your gate, make a note of its material, general condition and colour. Walk through the gate and look at the path to your front door. Check the material of the path and **the line it takes**. If you have plants, look at their condition and see if they enhance the outward appearance of your home. Inspect your front door, noting its colour, the type of fittings and its general condition.

Once you have made your initial survey make a list of things you would like to improve. Include projects you cannot do immediately but keep this list so that you can slowly work through it when you have the time and **finances**.

This first project should be to tidy up the outside of your home. Make sure the garden looks well kept. **Prune** back any **plants** that look overgrown. Renew any peeling or **damaged paintwork** and wash walls where appropriate.

Water

A bridge into your home will separate it slightly from the ambient energy, making it easier to lead an independent life.

Coloured front doors

A red front door makes the energy slightly more yang as it enters – making your home more vibrant. The pink flowers close to the door increase the energy associated with romance.

Your front door

A large front door allows energy to flow freely into your home. This only works well if the entrance hall is large, so that it can accomodate this fast-flowing energy. Arches encourage energy associated with spirituality to enter your home.

creating an entrance

The gate to your home marks the beginning of your property. It is where people enter and it can be an important part of everyone's first impression of where you live.

Gates vary from being very grand to being simple and friendly. You need to consider what kind of first impression you wish to make before renewing your gate. It is favourable if the gate is in a similar style to your home. For example, a large ornate metal gate looks best in front of a large house and a small wooden gate in front of a cottage.

The wider the gate the easier it is for chi energy to enter your property and home. This can be helpful if you want a fast-moving, active atmosphere indoors, which is fine for, say, a home with large, relatively empty rooms where the chi energy can move around easily. However, fast-flowing chi energy could make a smaller home feel too hectic, making it more difficult to relax and feel settled.

A small gate with the opening restricted by plants will provide a more secretive, secluded entrance. Here the chi energy will move slowly into your home, making it an ideal place for hideaways, retirement homes or holiday sanctuaries. However, if you are working from home there is a risk that you could feel isolated and out of touch with the world around you. Most people will opt for something in between. You can make subtle changes to the size of your gate depending on how you want to adjust your lifestyle. An opening without a gate will allow energy to move freely and create a very open feel to your property.

Gates

A wooden gate is soft and more yin, giving a friendly appearance, while a metal gate looks more formal.

one-day project

1 Style of gate

Think about whether your life would be improved with a greater flow of chi energy into your property through a large gate or a reduced flow of energy with a smaller gate.

Consider what style of gate would best reflect your personality and home. Look at a large **number of gates** to get ideas. Purchase the **appropriate gate** and have it fitted or have one specially made so that you can influence the design.

GATEWAYS

SMALL GATE: Secluded, private, relaxing, calm, remote, isolated and yin.

LARGE GATE: Active, dynamic, open, social, outgoing, interactive and yang.

SHAPED GATE: A tall gate with spikes can appear intimidating. This could help deter burglars but, at the same time, make it more difficult to create a social and welcoming atmosphere.

coming home

The path to your front door influences the way chi energy moves from the entrance of your property to the entrance of your home.

Pathways
A straight path made of stones will speed up the flow of energy, which is helpful if you want your home to have a more active atmosphere.

The shape of the path, the material and the borders will all make a difference to the flow of energy, and a subtle influence on the atmosphere inside your home. You will also absorb some of the chi energy as you walk along the path. This can have an effect on the way you feel when you leave or return home.

A wide, straight path made of hard, flat stone will allow energy to move quickly and will help to create a dynamic atmosphere. This is appropriate if you have a large home and a long path or drive. An open path with grass each side will allow freer flowing energy and a path bordered with bushes and trees will channel and confine the flow of chi energy.

The first creates a more active atmosphere whereas the latter creates a more intriguing and mentally stimulating approach.

In most situations something in between is ideal. If you feel that your life is too hectic and stressful it may help to slow down the energy along your path by making it more curvacious, adding bushes at the side and using a rougher surface. However, if you want to spice up your life and be more dynamic, it would help to open up your path and use a flat stone surface. Placing lights along the path will attract more attention to you and your home.

 two-day project

① Types of path

Think about how you want to improve your life (see page 14). It may help to draw on the principles of **yin and yang** (see page 132–3). Try to work out if it would help you to be more yang – active, dynamic and alert, or more yin – calm, relaxed and creative.

Take a look at your path, walk along it and concentrate on how you feel. If you want to make the experience more yang

look at ways of achieving this by, say, cutting back or even **moving certain plants**. You could also consider laying a stone path.

If you want to feel more yin, explore ways of softening the edges of the path by making it more curvy. Plant bushes and shrubs with **rounded and soft leaves** close to the path or use a **rough surface**, such as gravel.

plants

The plants in your front garden help to create atmosphere. In general, a well-stocked front garden with a variety of plants will carry a healthy balance of chi energy. You can adjust this to suit your particular needs.

Colour in your garden
Pastel pinks and blues will make your garden tranquil and calm. Use borders and beds to create the right atmosphere for creativity and imagination.

The main consideration is whether you want an open-plan garden where chi energy can move freely, encouraging you to feel dynamic and active, or a more imaginative layout where a labyrinth of different plants forces the chi energy to move in a more convoluted fashion.

An open-plan garden, with a few carefully selected plants and a large lawn allows chi energy to move easily around your garden and into your home. This is preferable if you want to be more outgoing, social and active. It could also help you to be more ambitious, open-minded and broaden your vision.

A garden with many plants, flower beds, bushes, trees and curved paths will create an imaginative atmosphere that could make you feel more creative, artistic and thoughtful. This would be an ideal place for generating original ideas, feeling more inspired and retreating into your own world.

The plants you choose will influence the way you feel in your garden. Plants with spiky, pointed leaves, such as yuccas and palms, will create an exciting atmosphere in your garden, whereas plants with large floppy leaves, such as hostas and ferns generate a calmer feeling.

If you want greater privacy or live near a busy road it will help to grow a hedge at the front of your garden. The higher the hedge the more isolated and private you will be.

half-day project

❶ Siting plants in the garden

Think about any changes you might want to make to your life and, using the above information, how changes to your garden could help you to achieve this. Note the existing balance of plants to open areas and the different kinds of plants in the garden.

If you want an **open-plan garden**, draw up plans to remove some of the existing plants, if necessary, and create a **larger lawn**. Explore the possibility of using more plants with **pointed leaves**. If you have a hedge consider lowering it and also **pruning larger bushes** or trees to allow energy to move more easily.

If your aim is to create a closed and intriguing space, consider the options for introducing a taller hedge and a greater variety of plants. Add plants, shrubs or bushes to places where they will break up any straight lines and enclose open spaces.

paintwork

Some outer surfaces on your home, such as rendering, can be painted. This gives you the opportunity to express yourself and influence the chi energy around the house.

Most chi energy enters and leaves your home through the doors and windows; however, a small amount of chi energy can seep in and out through the walls.

The colour of the outside of your home will influence other people's perception of you and can make you feel a little different each time you see your home. A village or town where the houses are painted in bright colours has an uplifting effect and tends to attract attention and visitors.

It is best to choose a colour according to which direction your home faces (see pages 38–41), or a colour that will improve the way you feel, or nine ki astrology (see pages 148–9). You may find that one particular colour keeps coming up in the exercises below. If this happens, it would be worthwhile trying that colour first. If several different colours come up, you can try painting a small patch of each colour on the wall of your home and see which appeals to you most.

Remember, the brighter the shade the more yang and dynamic the atmosphere around it, and the paler the colour the more peaceful you will feel.

Colouring your walls

The use of punchy cornflower blue on the exterior of a house will give visitors the impression that it is a bright and airy home full of creativity and imagination.

half-day project

① First impressions count

Stand outside with your back to the front of your home and, using a **compass**, make a note of the direction it faces (see page 145). Alternatively, use the method described on page 9. Turn to pages 38–41 to find out which colours **complement** the direction your home faces.

Use the chart on page 148 to discover which colour is harmonious with the chi energy present when you were born, and make a note of it. Identify what you want from life, it may help to work through the **questionnaire** on page 15. Think about how you can change in order to achieve your goals. Turn to the charts on pages 38–41 and see if any of the characteristics associated with various colours would help you. If one set of **characteristics** stands out as being useful, make a note of the respective, complementary colour.

Walk around the area surrounding your home, making a note of the colour of other houses and the general colours that are **predominant**. Look at your home from a distance and think about the different colours in your mind.

window boxes

Window boxes full of plants or flowers are an excellent way of adding colour and living energy to the outside of your building. This is particularly useful as they enhance the chi energy entering your home through the windows.

Window boxes
Window boxes bring natural living chi energy close to your home helping you to achieve greater harmony.

Choose the colours of the flowers according to the kind of chi energy you want to increase and the direction the front of your home faces. See pages 9 and 145 to check the direction and pages 38–41 for advice on colours.

If possible, plant a variety of plants so they will flower throughout the year. You could consider growing herbs in your window boxes as they will emit fragrances and be a healthy source of nutrients in your cooking.

The material your window box is made from can enhance the chi energy around your home. Avoid using plastic window boxes as they can disrupt the flow of energy.

metal window box	*south-west, north-east, west, north-west or north*
wooden window box	*south-west, west, north-west, north-east, north*
earthenware window box	*north, east, south-east, south*

two-day project

① Materials for window boxes

Stand outside with your back to the front of your home and, using a **compass**, make a note of the direction it faces (see page 145). Alternatively, use the method described on page 9.

Use this information and the box above to help you decide on the material for your **window box**. For example, if your home faces north a **wooden** or **earthenware** window box would be ideal. Also use the information on pages 38–41 as a guide to the **colours** of flowers to plant.

Put up the window boxes with specialist advice taking all **safety precautions**. Fill the boxes with the appropriate soil (preferably organic) and plant your flowers at the appropriate time of year. Make sure you keep the window boxes in good order for the best benefits.

front doors

Front and main doors create entrances for chi energy. When someone enters your home they create a current of chi energy and, once inside, their chi displaces some of the energy already in your home.

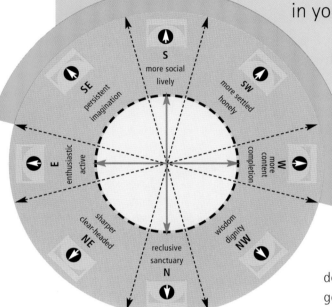

Doors have a very important role in feng shui, as they influence the chi energy entering and leaving a building. The direction your door faces defines the kind of chi energy that enters your home. So, a door that faces the west will bring in more western chi energy, making it easier to complete projects, feel romantic and be playful.

If your main or front door faces a direction that is helpful to you, then a large door is preferable, as it will encourage more of this influential chi energy to enter your home. A smaller door is recommended when it faces a direction which generates unhelpful chi energy.

⬆ FACING SOUTH

A highly active location in which it would be easy to be noticed. Can lead to feeling over emotional and stressed. Purple, bare wood, green and blue with wooden door fittings would be harmonious, however, black or yellow would help calm your emotions. A flat clay pot filled with charcoal would further subdue the chi energy of the south.

⬈ FACING SOUTH-WEST

Exposes the home to chi energy that is slow to settle which can be helpful for long-term relationships and add quality to your life. Ideal colours are black, yellow, beige, rustic red or grey with shiny metal door fittings. A small bowl of sea salt will help stabilize the movement of chi energy.

➡ FACING WEST

Brings in the chi energy associated with pleasure, romance and financial income. Good for completing projects. Harmonious colours are red, black, yellow, and grey with shiny metal fittings.

⬋ FACING NORTH-WEST

Favourable for leadership, organization and feeling in control of your life. Helpful for planning ahead and acting with wisdom. Harmonious colours are grey, black, yellow and red with shiny metal fittings.

⬇ FACING NORTH

Generally quiet and good as a sanctuary if you want to hide away. Can be isolating. A red door with shiny metal fittings will stimulate the flow of chi energy.

⬉ FACING NORTH-EAST

Exposes the home to sharp, quick, piercing chi energy. Good for motivation and clear thinking. A high gloss white door and shiny metal fitting will reflect chi energy. Also consider yellow, black or purple. A small bowl of sea salt inside the door will help subdue the movement of chi energy.

⬅ FACING EAST

Good for young people who wish to build up their careers. Helps confidence and self esteem. A bright green, bare wood, or cream door with wooden door fittings will be harmonious.

⬊ FACING SOUTH-EAST

Helpful for communication and harmonious progress. Good for any creative activities. A dark green, bare wood, blue or cream door with wooden door fittings will be harmonious.

hallway & stairs

The hall is the first place to receive incoming chi energy from your front door. It leads to the other rooms and in feng shui its function is to take in chi and distribute it throughout your home.

BEFORE

Two doors almost **in line** will encourage energy to **flow in and out** of the hall and home rather than **circulate** around your home.

Clutter near the front door will risk **stagnation** and greater **congestion.**

Stairs leading down toward your front door increase the risk of energy flowing between the floors and flowing **straight out** of your home.

Clutter in a corridor can **restrict** the flow of **energy** from the hall into your home.

SUITABLE FLOORS
Stone and polished hardwood stairs encourage energy to move quickly across the surface of the stairs; bare wooden stairs have a more neutral influence; carpets, sea grass and rush matting will slow down the flow of energy.

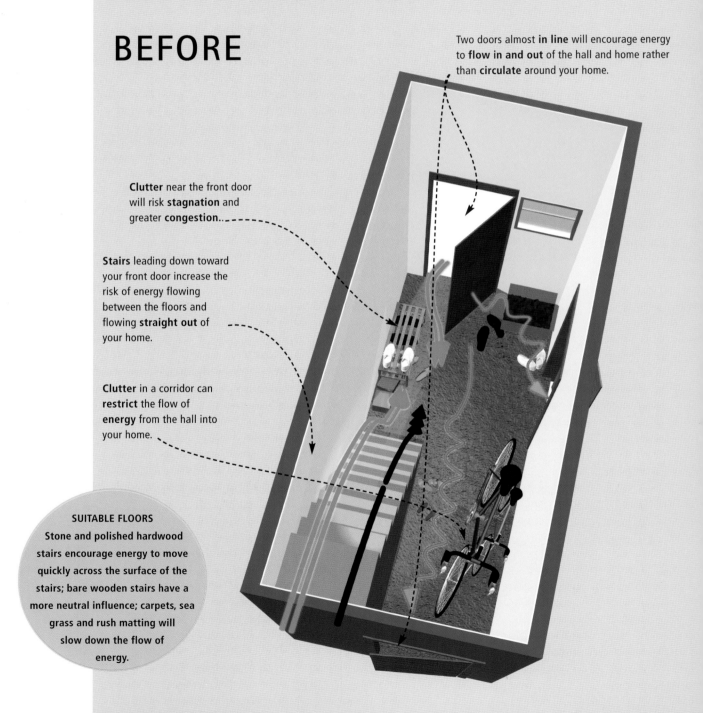

AFTER

Position a wind chime on the inside of your front door so that when opened it will activate it's chime. This will **disperse energy** flowing through the door helping to spread it into the rest of your home.

A plant between the stairs and door will **slow the flow** of energy between the two.

A mirror positioned so you can see **round the door** to make you feel more **secure** on entering or leaving your home.

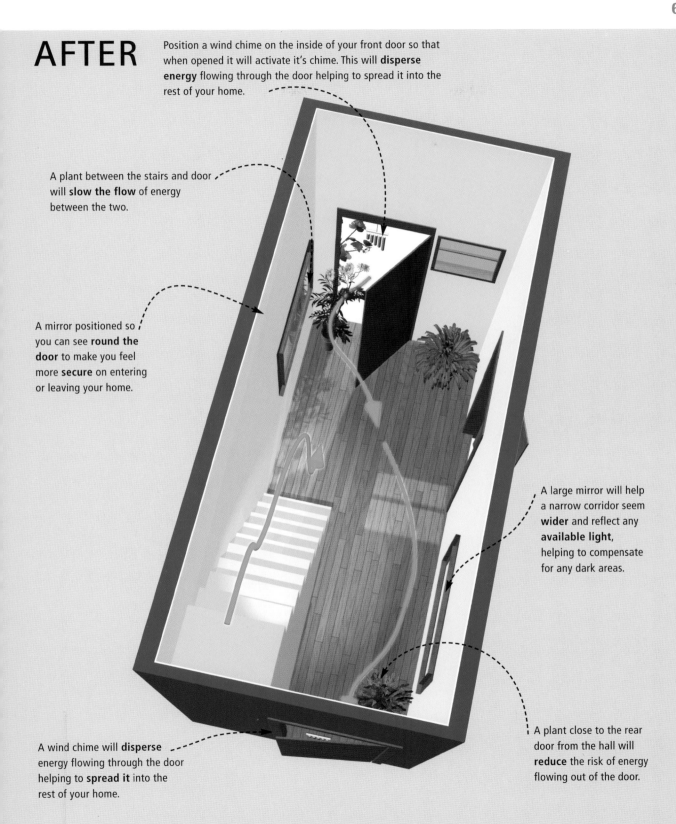

A large mirror will help a narrow corridor seem **wider** and reflect any **available light**, helping to compensate for any dark areas.

A wind chime will **disperse** energy flowing through the door helping to **spread it** into the rest of your home.

A plant close to the rear door from the hall will **reduce** the risk of energy flowing out of the door.

mirrors, plants & wind chimes

If your hall is dark and the energy feels stagnant or flat you can speed up the flow of energy by using mirrors. Large mirrors are also useful if your hall is small or cramped as they can make it feel twice its size.

The ideal place for mirrors is to the left or right as you enter your hall. You should not position a mirror so that it faces your front door, as it will reflect the energy entering your home back out again.

It is often helpful to hang a mirror on the wall that you first see as you begin to open the front door. The advantage of this is that it allows you to see into the hall before you enter, which will be reassuring each time you come home. In addition, when you open the door to a visitor you will be able to see the person before you open the door fully, taking away any anxiety there may be over who is calling.

If your stairs lead straight down to your front door you can use a convex mirror to help disperse the energy back into your home reducing the tendency for this energy to leave your home too easily.

Plants

If your hall feels as though the chi energy is moving too quickly you will need to find ways to slow it down. The energy is most likely to move quickly if the hall leads into a corridor, has a stone floor or the stairs lead down towards the front door.

Bushy plants are one of the most effective ways to slow down the movement, because they generate a chi energy field of their own which any other chi energy will have to flow through. This is rather like water flowing through a sponge.

Using mirrors

The mirror should be as large as possible so that it reflects the whole person – even the tallest visitor to your home. In many cases the hall forms a corridor running through the home and mirrors can be used to make it feel wider. For more on using mirrors, see pages 44–5.

half-day projects

1 Using mirrors to quicken energy

Stand outside your home and open the front door slowly and mark the ideal place to hang a mirror so that it will reflect the hall before you open the door fully.

Step into your hall and if you feel you need to speed up the chi energy there look for suitable **locations** for mirrors. Once you have identified the best locations, **measure the wall** in order to estimate the size of mirror(s) you will need. Always use a single piece of mirror glass and not several pieces joined together. Purchase the **appropriate** mirror(s) and hang them in your hall.

2 Siting plants in the hall

Stand in your hall and look for places where you can grow plants. You will need to take account of the natural light conditions so that you can use the correct plants. Decide whether you want to use **hanging plants** or plants in **containers** on the floor.

If your stairs **descend** towards your front door look for a spot between the foot of the stairs and your front door where you can locate a **plant**. Again you may need to use a hanging plant if space is limited.

In a large hall you will be able to use big plants in containers, however, if you live in a home with a narrow hall you may need to use hanging plants as these do not require any floor space. In some cases there will not be enough natural light for plants. However, in this type of hall the emphasis is usually on speeding up the flow of energy so mirrors are a more helpful feature. For more advice on using plants, see pages 46-7.

Wind chimes

In a small, cluttered or narrow hall it is possible for the chi energy entering your home to get stifled so that it cannot circulate into your home properly. Wind chimes will help to disperse the energy as the sound waves carry the chi energy beyond the hall and into the rest of your home. To be effective wind chimes, should ring each time you open the front door. You can use them on any other door in your home where you feel that energy is congested.

HANGING WIND CHIMES
Measure the distance between the ceiling and the top of the door and buy wind chimes that will fit this space. If necessary, add a longer or shorter cord to the wind chimes. Hang them from the ceiling or buy a bracket and hang them on the back of the door.

Indoor containers

When you use containers try to use ones made of natural materials, such as terracotta, as these will add to the harmonious atmosphere in your home. In a hall where the stairs lead down to your front door, place a bushy plant between the stairs and your front door to slow the flow of chi energy and reduce the risk of it being directed out of the front door.

S
165–195°
Wood or ceramic

SE
105–165°
Wood or glass

SW
195–255°
Metal or ceramic

E
75–105°
Wood or glass

W
255–285°
Metal or ceramic

NE
15–75°
Metal or ceramic

NW
285–345°
Metal or ceramic

N
345–15°
Wood, metal or glass

Dispersing energy with wind chimes

Take a compass, stand near the centre of your home and point the body of the compass towards your front door. Turn the outer dial until zero degrees is aligned with the needle. Now look at the reading on the dial next to the centre line of the body of the compass (see page 145). Look at the chart on the left to decide which type of wind chimes to use.

kitchen & diner

This is where you store, prepare and cook your food which will absorb some of the chi energy already in the room while you cook. In feng shui it is essential that your kitchen contains healthy chi energy, as you will end up actually consuming some of this energy.

BEFORE

A boiler to the west could have a **destructive influence** on the western energy making it harder to make progress in terms of your finances and relationships.

There is a risk that a sink to the west can **drain** the energy associated with your ability to focus on your **financial income** and romance.

Sitting with your back to the door makes it **harder to feel secure** and there is a greater risk of being **distracted**.

The **corners** from the counter units will direct fast-flowing energy into the room.

Sitting in the path of energy flowing between the doors can make it **harder to relax** and enjoy your food.

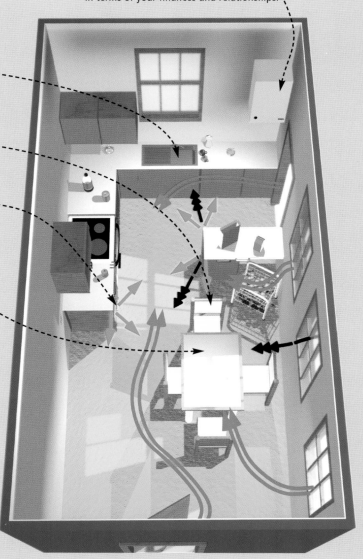

POTENTIAL PROBLEMS
Carry out the following checks in your kitchen:
1. Look under the sink and other areas where there is water to check for any mildew or dampness.
2. Note where there are carpets, soft furnishings or fabrics and check if they retain smells or dampness.
3. Look at what kind of lighting you have. Make an inspection to see how clean your kitchen is.
4. Check behind all kitchen appliances.
5. Check food storage areas and make a note of whether they are clean, orderly and dry.

AFTER

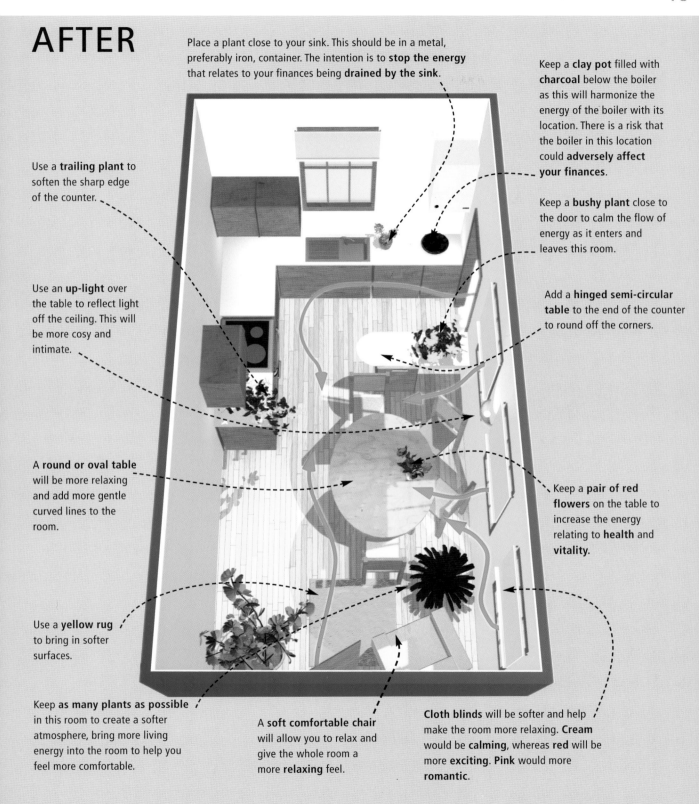

Place a plant close to your sink. This should be in a metal, preferably iron, container. The intention is to **stop the energy** that relates to your finances being **drained by the sink**.

Keep a **clay pot** filled with **charcoal** below the boiler as this will harmonize the energy of the boiler with its location. There is a risk that the boiler in this location could **adversely affect your finances**.

Use a **trailing plant** to soften the sharp edge of the counter.

Keep a **bushy plant** close to the door to calm the flow of energy as it enters and leaves this room.

Use an **up-light** over the table to reflect light off the ceiling. This will be more cosy and intimate.

Add a **hinged semi-circular table** to the end of the counter to round off the corners.

A **round or oval table** will be more relaxing and add more gentle curved lines to the room.

Keep a **pair of red flowers** on the table to increase the energy relating to **health** and **vitality**.

Use a **yellow rug** to bring in softer surfaces.

Keep **as many plants as possible** in this room to create a softer atmosphere, bring more living energy into the room to help you feel more comfortable.

A **soft comfortable chair** will allow you to relax and give the whole room a more **relaxing** feel.

Cloth blinds will be softer and help make the room more relaxing. **Cream** would be **calming**, whereas **red** will be more **exciting**. **Pink** would more **romantic**.

water & power

Although water is a source of healthy chi energy, it will also have a negative influence if the chi energy of the water becomes unhealthy. This makes it important to keep your kitchen clean, dry and free from damp for good health.

Go for gas

The advantage of gas over electricity is that the flame is easier to control. An electric stove radiates electromagnetic fields (EMF), which can effect the chi energy of the food.

It is recommended that you use a stove with a natural flame. Most commonly this would be a gas stove, although, a wood-burning stove also has a similar effect. Rather like a fireplace this type of stove enhances the warm, relaxing atmosphere that can be created in a kitchen.

If you have an electric stove or hob, it would be worthwhile exploring the options for changing to a gas unit. If you live in a remote area you may need to arrange for a tank next to your home to store the gas.

It is also worth considering locating the stove or hob within an island unit in the centre of the kitchen, so that when you are cooking you can face into the room and see the doors and windows. This also makes for a more social setting if your kitchen is part of the dining or living room. You will be able to see and talk to your friends while cooking.

Where this is not possible, consider hanging a mirror behind the stove so that you can see the room behind you. This also creates the impression that the stove is twice its size.

Keep it clean

It is important to keep your kitchen free of dirty or stagnant water. This includes washing-up water left overnight in the sink, leaks and dampness. Even a dripping tap can increase the dampness.

half-day projects

① Create a healthy atmosphere

List all the places in your kitchen that water can stay or places where there is a risk of leaks. Include sinks, taps, dishwashers, washing machines, radiators and pipes.

Make a thorough inspection of all these areas looking for any sign of leaks, **dampness**, rot or **mildew**. This would also be a good time to give everything a clean (see page 43).

Note any areas of concern and arrange for these to be rectified. Any rotten materials will need to be removed and replaced, areas with mildew carefully scrubbed and cleaned and damp areas dried and aired.

② Radiating fire chi through your kitchen

If you wish to change from an electric to a gas appliance begin by **measuring** the existing space in your worktop. Once you have the **dimensions** look around to see what is available. There are many different types to choose from including stainless steel units and enamel hobs and ovens in a range of different colours.

You will need to arrange for a **registered professional** to come and connect your new appliance. Your local gas company, or the company that sold you the item can usually arrange this.

The surfaces in your kitchen will determine how chi energy flows around your kitchen. It is important to use natural materials, as these will enhance the flow of chi energy around a room. Synthetic materials can block and stifle the flow of chi energy.

Hard stone surfaces are easy to clean and dry, and will help chi energy flow freely through your kitchen.

MATERIALS IN THE KITCHEN

YIN

pine

beech

mahogany

brass

copper

aluminium

sandstone

marble

cast iron

stainless steel

granite

YANG

The harder and shinier the material, the faster and more yang the flow of energy will be. Softer surfaces will slow down the energy and create a calmer atmosphere.

As most of the materials will be harder your choice will be confined to wood, metal and stone. Each will have softer or harder versions. For example, brass will be softer than stainless steel and limestone will be softer than granite.

Generally woods will be more yin, metals more central and stone more yang in this selection.

Find out exactly what each surface is made of. Solid wood is always preferable to laminated wood or wood veneer, which is a very thin layer of wood stuck to a board made of wood chips which has been bonded together with resin. Similarly, it is better to avoid materials like MDF (medium-density fibreboard) as they are more like a synthetic material and can give off toxic gases.

two-day project

❶ Creating a yin-yang kitchen

Think about how you would like to **feel** in your kitchen (see pages 18–19). To be more relaxed and make your kitchen more yin use **softer materials**. If you want to make it more dynamic you will need to use more yang, harder materials.

You could change the flooring, worktops and large items of furniture. Also consider replacing small items, such as a **chopping board.** The larger the area the greater the difference it will make to the atmosphere of the kitchen.

Refer to the yin-yang list above, to help you create the atmosphere you want. Get professional **advice** and

quotations to find out which projects will be feasible.

It is important to choose wisely because once a surface has been changed it will become a **permanent feature** which you will have to live with for some time. Do some research into how hard-wearing the surface is and also try out a sample of the surface/material to see if you like it. For example, lay a few new tiles on top of your existing floor in a safe place so that you can see how you feel about them over a few days.

Once you are ready, arrange for the surfaces to be changed by a builder or, if you have the skills, do it yourself.

lighting

Lighting is an important factor in creating the atmosphere of a room and different types of light will set the mood of a space (see pages 36–7).

Direct lighting
Spotlights focus light on your work area while leaving the rest of the room with softer, more diffused light.

Although not as popular today, fluorescent strip lights were commonly used in the kitchen. From a feng shui perspective there are two problems associated with using fluorescent lighting. The first is that it gives off a blue light, which makes a room look colder and institutional, and people's skin tone look pale and unhealthy.

The second problem is that fluorescent lights tend to give off more eletromagnetic fields (EMF) (see pages 26–7). Some people have noticed increased incidences of headaches and loss of concentration when close to this type of lighting.

There is an opportunity to improve the atmosphere in your kitchen by using a range of other types of lighting. Incandescent lighting will generate a warmer orange hue and is suited to general lighting, while halogen lights send out a brighter white light that can be directed to a specific area.

It is best to use a variety of direct and indirect lighting so you can create a softer mood or a more functional arrangement depending on your needs.

half-day project

1 Correct lighting in the kitchen

If you have a fluorescent light think about replacing it. Consider what kind of incandescent light you would like in its place. For instance, choose a light that reflects back onto a white ceiling, spreading the light more softly throughout the kitchen. A light with a **metal reflector** will give a **brighter** light, although over a **smaller** area. If you have a table below the light you can use a fitting that allows you to pull the light down to create a more intimate mood.

Look at the areas where you cook and **prepare** food. Work surfaces, the cooker and the sink will be places that would benefit from **direct lighting**. Check above these areas to see where you can fix **incandescent** or **halogen** spotlights to illuminate these surfaces. Remember not to place these behind you so that you create a **shadow** in front of you.

Once you have designed your lighting plan arrange for a suitable **professional** to carry out your instructions.

KITCHEN COLOURS

The brighter the shade of each colour the more yang and dynamic the atmosphere will be. Choose pale or pastel hues when you want to feel more yin and relaxed in your kitchen.

Direction	Colours
EAST	Green
SOUTH-EAST	Green with the option of blue
SOUTH	Green or yellow combined with light grey
SOUTH-WEST	Pink, light grey, rusty red, silver
WEST	Yellow combined with pink or red
NORTH-WEST	Yellow combined with grey
NORTH	Green, yellow combined with light grey
NORTH-EAST	White or light grey

When choosing colours for your kitchen you will need to be clear about the atmosphere you want to create. In most situations it is helpful to use warm, relaxing colours so that you can enjoy your meals.

In addition, certain colours will complement the direction of the kitchen and will help you to create the most harmonious atmosphere. The kitchen contains fire and water chi energy from the cooker and sink respectively and the colours associated with the directional chi energy can be used to balance these elements (see the five elements on pages 138–41).

The boxed information on this page provides a list of colours appropriate for use in certain directions in order to create the best balance. You do not need to use any of these colours exclusively but should use them in a way that stands out.

Yang colours

Red, orange or yellow will help create a warm, comfortable atmosphere in your kitchen.

Yin colours

Silver and grey are helpful in a western or north-western kitchen, and can be better when combined with orange or yellow.

two-day project

① Decorating

To **redecorate** your kitchen work out in which direction it is situated. Use a compass as described on page 145 or observe the movement of the sun, which is explained on page 9.

Use the information above to get **ideas** for colours. Test a few **samples of paint** and leave them for a few days to see them in **various light conditions**.

In an older home you may need to **strip away old wallpaper** first. If you need to replace wallpaper use a **lining paper** and try to avoid vinyl as it can partially block the natural flow of chi energy.

eating rooms

The atmosphere will have a significant influence on how you feel while you are eating. If it is too stimulating, or yang, you will not feel comfortable and will tend to rush your food

Relaxing light
Candles produce a soft light, which can make an evening meal more intimate and relaxing, alternatively, use indirect lighting, such as an uplight reflected off your ceiling. Shiny cutlery, red napkins and cut glass add sparkle and yang energy when you want to create a more exciting atmosphere.

In the short term this greatly increases the risk of indigestion and in the long term it could lead to digestive disorders. Conversely, if the atmosphere is too relaxed and yin, you risk being in a situation that will not allow you to adopt the right posture for good digestion.

An example of somewhere that is very yang is a fast-food restaurant where bright colours, shiny surfaces and a regimented layout are used. This is ideal for attracting new customers and is equally good at getting them to leave as soon as they have finished eating. Similarly, if your dining room has too many yang features it will not be conducive to the pleasure of eating and you will not want to linger around the table longer than necessary. But by going too far the other way, say, substituting bean bags for chairs, doing away with a table and using plenty of soft surfaces and pastel colours, can make an atmosphere that is just too yin and informal.

Meal times are also social occasions and provide an opportunity for you to spend more time with your family and friends. A round or oval table will help create a more harmonious atmosphere in which everyone can talk to each other. This is particularly important when you have more than six people sitting at a table. It is also advisable to use reasonably upright chairs for eating, as this is better for good digestion. Try to ensure that no one sits with his or her

half-day project

① Healthy eating

Look at your **eating area** and check to see if there are any sharp corners or right angles pointing towards any of the seats. If there are, move the item or soften the edge using a plant (see page 28).

If you like **entertaining** or have a **large family** and there are frequently more than six people eating together, consider buying an oval or round table (see pages 54–5).

Check that your **chairs** enable you to sit in an upright position, so that when you eat you adopt the ideal posture for good digestion and, at the same time, make sure the chairs are **comfortable and relaxing**.

Try using either a linen or cotton tablecloth and large napkins to make the atmosphere more relaxing. Use cream, pink, pale blue or pale green to feel **calmer**. Bright red, bright yellow or orange will be more **stimulating** and may not create a relaxed atmosphere for everyday meals.

Use **candles** in the evening **instead** of **electric lighting**. When you do use electric lights try **directing** the light against a wall or the ceiling (see pages 36–7).

back to a sharp protruding corner or right angle as this can make it more difficult to relax. The direction they face will help them absorb more of that particular chi energy, subtly changing the way they feel. For example, someone facing south will absorb more of the fiery, summer energy associated with this direction helping them to feel slightly more social and outgoing.

Harmonious meals

Place a compass in the middle of the dining table. If it has metal parts you may need to hold the compass above the table to get an accurate reading. Write each direction on a piece of card and place them on the corresponding parts of your table. Remember it is the direction the person faces that counts, so if you want them to face north you should sit them facing the same direction as the needle of the compass. Use the information in this chart to try seating people in the most helpful directions.

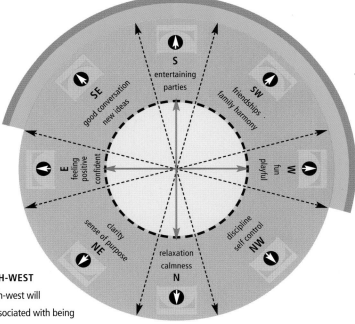

🅐 FACING SOUTH

Someone facing south will feel more social and expressive. It will often be easier for them to attract attention and be noticed. This is helpful for anyone who is too reserved or cautious socially, but not helpful for someone prone to stress.

🅐 FACING SOUTH-WEST

A helpful direction to face when you want to focus on improving the quality of relationships. It helps a person to be practical and down-to-earth during the meal and is considered an ideal position for mothers.

🅐 FACING WEST

Absorbing more western energy makes it easier to feel playful and content, so it is a helpful direction for someone who is too serious or dominating during a meal. This direction is particularly harmonious for children.

🅐 FACING NORTH-WEST

Someone facing north-west will absorb the energy associated with being organized and behaving with dignity. It can also help a person be more of an authority figure. It is considered ideal for fathers but not good for anyone who tends to be controlling.

🅐 FACING NORTH

Sitting facing north is helpful for eating peacefully and feeling relaxed. This is ideal for someone who tends to rush their meals or has a tendency to get irritable or too talkative during dinner.

🅐 FACING NORTH-EAST

Facing north-east can help a person become more outgoing. It is useful for someone who is shy or finds it hard to get into the conversations. This would not be helpful for a child that is prone to tantrums.

🅐 FACING EAST

An east-facing position brings in more enthusiasm and energy, making it ideal for someone who needs confidence and to feel positive. It is considered ideal for children, unless they become too boisterous.

🅐 FACING SOUTH-EAST

Eating facing south-east is helpful if you want to get new ideas and communicate with people. Absorbing more of this energy can make it easier to get on with people and avoid confrontations.

living room

The living room is often the heart of family life, where everyone can spend time together, and where you can entertain friends and relax. It is helpful if the atmosphere of the room allows you to carry out these communal activities successfully.

BEFORE

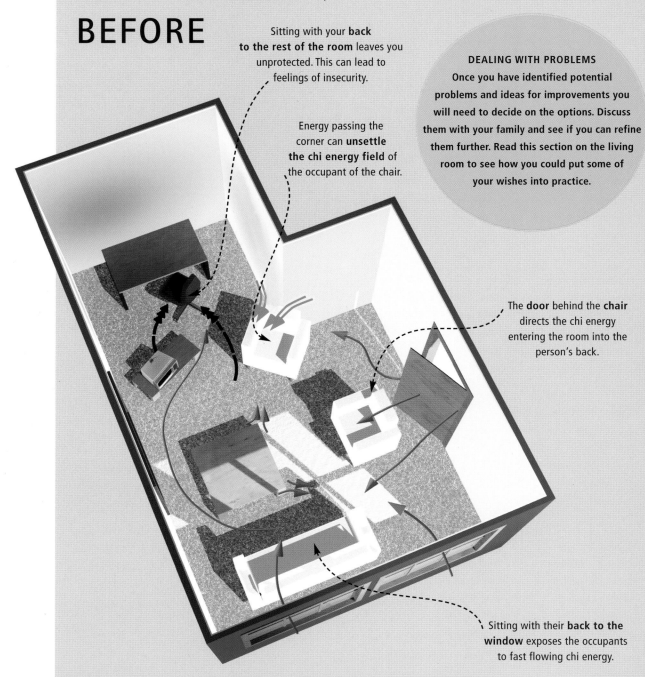

Sitting with your **back to the rest of the room** leaves you unprotected. This can lead to feelings of insecurity.

Energy passing the corner can **unsettle the chi energy field** of the occupant of the chair.

DEALING WITH PROBLEMS
Once you have identified potential problems and ideas for improvements you will need to decide on the options. Discuss them with your family and see if you can refine them further. Read this section on the living room to see how you could put some of your wishes into practice.

The **door** behind the **chair** directs the chi energy entering the room into the person's back.

Sitting with their **back to the window** exposes the occupants to fast flowing chi energy.

AFTER

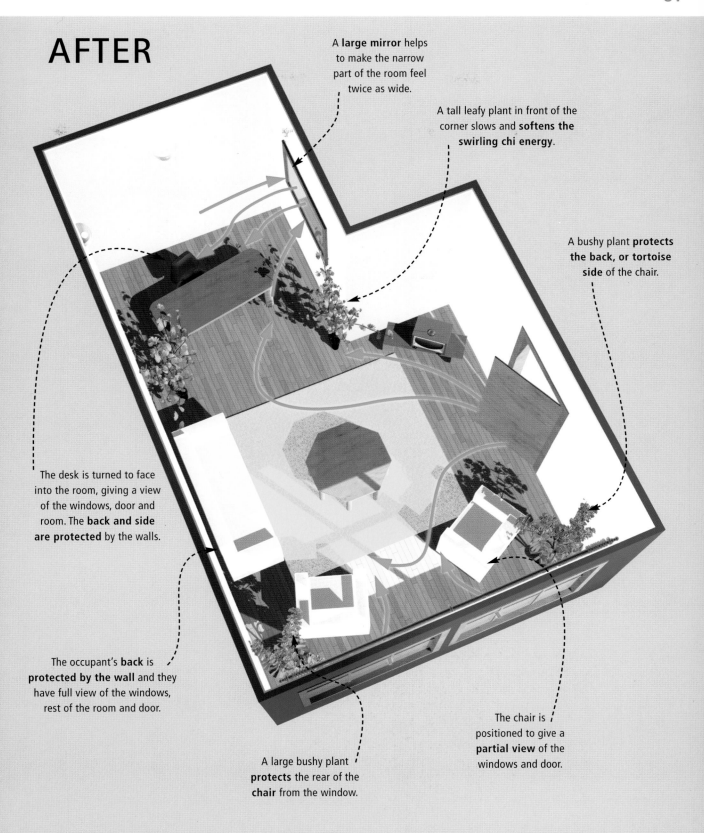

A **large mirror** helps to make the narrow part of the room feel twice as wide.

A tall leafy plant in front of the corner slows and **softens the swirling chi energy.**

A bushy plant **protects the back, or tortoise side** of the chair.

The desk is turned to face into the room, giving a view of the windows, door and room. The **back and side are protected** by the walls.

The occupant's **back** is **protected by the wall** and they have full view of the windows, rest of the room and door.

A large bushy plant **protects** the rear of the **chair** from the window.

The chair is positioned to give a **partial view** of the windows and door.

artworks

You can adjust the atmosphere of your living room by using artworks drawings, paintings, prints and photographs. The imagery of the artwork will help you feel different each time you see it. This in itself can change your chi energy field (see pages 50–1).

FORM		
FORM	**DIRECTIONS**	**FEELINGS**
Tall	*East and south-east*	Getting on with life, doing more, being active
Pointed	*South*	Dramatic, attracting attention, adventurous
Flat	*South-west and north-east*	Stable, steady, cautious
Round	*West and north-west*	Complete, satisfied, inward looking
Wavy	*North*	Flexible, carefree, independent

The form or shape of the features in an artwork or the item itself will create a different effect. The list below shows which energy each will accentuate. The colours in the artworks will also help to change the atmosphere (see pages 38–41). Bright, more yang colours will make the room feel livelier, while artworks with soft colours will help create a calm, more yin mood.

The way artworks affect you is very personal and it is helpful if you keep looking for examples that make you feel good. If you know what sort of atmosphere you want to create in your living room, it will be easier to look in the right direction and find appropriate artworks. The boxed information below gives you some hints on what sort of artworks to use.

Patterns and designs
The mottled irregular pattern breaks up the straight lines in this room creating a more interesting ambience.

① Positioning artworks

Using the lists write down the **kind of artwork** you think would help you most. **Visualize** in your mind what this could look like and where the artwork will be placed. **Determine which direction** this is within your room by using a **compass**. Measure up the **available space**. Look at which **style** and **form** work best in that part of your room.

Make an effort to visit different places to view artworks. Try to find something that will **suit your room** and **match the image** of what will make you feel good.

half-day project

STYLE	
FEELING	**ARTWORK STYLE**
Inspired	Bright colourful modern art, abstract paintings, surrealistic images
Calm	Landscapes, images of water, flowing pictures with subtle colours
Lively	Colourful impressionist paintings, images of sports or movement
Romantic	Statues or paintings of couples in an embrace
Confident	Images of your past successes
Ambitious	Images of things you aspire to own, such as a house, car or yacht

When arranging sofas and chairs you have the opportunity to place yourself and your family in positions that can help you relax, feel more inspired, or be more active.

The directions below refer to the direction you face when sitting in your chair. However the direction is not the only consideration. If several people use this room, the chairs need to be arranged to bring out a good social atmosphere. Generally, having the chairs facing the centre of the room will help achieve this.

It is good practice to sit so your back is protected by a wall, screen or big plant and to have as much of the room as possible open in front of you.

The easiest way to work out which direction you are facing is to sit holding your compass. Decide which of the following directions suit your needs and arrange your furniture so you can face that direction. If this is not possible choose another direction with similar properties and face that direction.

Finding balance
You will need to balance the need to face a beneficial direction with the need to place a chair in a good position within the room.

FACING SOUTH
Good for greater passion, being more expressive and feeling social. If you are entertaining friends it will help you to be noticed more. It is also good for new ideas.

FACING SOUTH-WEST
Associated with adding quality to your life, being realistic and practical. It is helpful if you need to come down to earth and is also beneficial for family harmony and deepening relationships.

FACING WEST
Ideal for romance, pleasure and feeling more content. This is a good direction to sit in at the end of the day if you wish to settle down and is good if you want to be close to someone.

FACING NORTH-WEST
This is the direction to face if you have responsibilities, and to help you take care of your family's needs. It is beneficial if you want to make decisions with greater wisdom, be more organized and feel more in control of your life.

FACING NORTH
The most peaceful direction to face. Sitting in this position is helpful if you wish to feel tranquil, quiet and more meditative.

FACING NORTH-EAST
Beneficial for motivation, a clearer sense of direction, and to become more competitive. Try this if you feel you need a new direction in life.

FACING EAST
Advantageous if you want to become more active, ambitious and busy. It is the ideal direction to sit if you have good ideas but are having trouble putting them into practice.

FACING SOUTH-EAST
This can help lead to harmonious progress in life. It is favourable for creativity and communication – a good direction if you want to have a long talk with someone.

curtains

Curtains provide an excellent way to soften the energy in a room. When closed they replace the hard shiny surface of the glass with soft fabric and can be a colourful feature in a room.

It is important to use a one hundred per cent natural fabric to enhance the flow of chi energy around your window.

There is a wide choice of curtain tracks and poles available, ranging from wood to metal, simple to ornate and hidden to exposed, and there are many ways of hanging and arranging your curtains.

In situations where you want to let in as much light as possible, such as in a north-facing room, make sure that your curtains do not hang over the window. Braid, cord, lace and tassel fringing will help to make your curtains more elaborate and, at the same time, slightly more yin and comfortable. In addition you can use the direction of the window within your room to get ideas for colours.

Curtain style

The fuller the curtains the more comfortable and cosy the atmosphere will seem. Heavy, full-length curtains with lots of gathering and a swathed pelmet will be more yin and calming compared to short curtains with less fullness, made of a lightweight fabric.

half-day project

❶ Choosing suitable curtains
Use the list above to help decide what style of curtain you would like. **Check the direction of the window** by standing in the centre of the room with a compass (see page 145). For ideas on colours see pages 38–41.

Pin fabric samples on the window frame and leave them for a few days before making a choice.

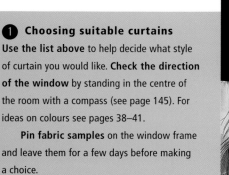

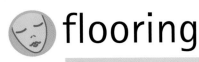

flooring

The floor constitutes a large surface area of the home and by changing the flooring you have the opportunity to change the atmosphere of a room significantly.

TYPES OF FLOORING

YIN

carpets

rush matting

softwood

hardwood

stone

stainless steel

marble

YANG

The easiest way to think about your floor is that **the harder, flatter and shinier the surface the faster the chi energy will flow**. This will make for a more dynamic, exciting and lively atmosphere. A soft, textured or unpolished surface will slow down the movement of chi energy making the room feel more cosy, comfortable and intimate. However, the use of too many thick carpets or rugs can lead to a stale and stagnant environment. They are best suited to bedrooms and should be made from natural materials such as wool or cotton. Choose a natural underlay for your carpet. Synthetic materials, including carpets, will create their own charge of static electricity, which will have a negative influence on the flow of chi energy. Rush-matting and sea-grass flooring will also slow down the flow of chi energy, as they are soft and highly textured. It is important to keep all types of flooring as dust free as possible.

Smooth, polished hardwood flooring will speed up the flow of chi energy, whereas rougher, softwood flooring tends to slow down the flow. The advantage of wood is that it is easy to clean and it creates a light, relaxing atmosphere without the risk of chi energy stagnating.

Stone and marble will help move energy throughout a room and if it is uneven it will tend to scatter the energy to a greater extent. This can be an advantage if you need to reduce the risk of energy stagnating.

FLOORING

This table shows you what type of flooring is best, depending on which part of your home the living room is situated. You will need to determine the direction of your living room (see pages 9 and 145) and then use the chart for ideas on the most harmonious flooring.

Direction	Flooring
East and south-east	Wood, sea-grass
South	Wood, stone, marble, carpet or rugs
South-west, centre, north-east	Stone, marble, carpet or rugs
West and north-west	Stone, marble, carpet or rugs
North	Wood, sea-grass, stone or marble

two-day project

❶ Suitable flooring

Decide on which **kind of flooring** will be of benefit in your living room. If you have carpet you are unhappy with, check to see what type of floor lies beneath by **pulling the carpet back**. You may have a **wooden floor** below that can be made serviceable.

Collect samples of flooring and leave them on your floor to get an idea of what it will feel like. If you are considering a wooden floor try to find a solid wood version.

When you have found the flooring you are happy with, **arrange for it to be laid** by a professional or if you have the skills, lay it yourself.

Rugs

Use rugs on tiled, stone or wooden floors to create more relaxing areas within a room.

colours & patterns

The colours you choose will potentially have the greatest influence on the way you feel when you are in your living room. Feng shui offers three ways to help you decide on the best colours.

Patterns
By placing a patterned rug in this living room you are creating a balance of yin and yang as there is a mixture of both random designs and repeated elements.

Firstly, determine which direction your living room faces, using the methods described on pages 9 or 145. Next, choose your colour scheme with the help of the charts on pages 38–41. These colours will bring out the best of the chi energy in that part of your home, making the room feel in harmony with your natural environment.

Secondly, work out what type of energy was present the year you were born and look up the colours associated with it on pages 148–9. The colours here will work directly on your deepest chi energy field. If you live with someone else find a colour that is in harmony with both of you (see pages 150–1).

Thirdly, think about what aspects of your life you would like to improve using the exercises on pages 14–17. Then look at the colour chart on pages 38–41 to find the colour that brings more of the appropriate energy into the room.

You may find that there is a colour common to all three approaches. Otherwise you will have to decide which has the greatest priority for you.

two-day projects

❶ Colours in the living room

Using the processes described above, **make a list of colours** that would be most helpful to you. Purchase **sample pots** of the colours. You can use brighter shades to create a dynamic, more yang atmosphere or paler hues to generate a calmer, more yin feeling.

Paint **sample patches** on the walls using the various colours and different shades so that you can **observe them over time**. Make the patches **as large as possible** because colours can look very different when they cover a large area. Once you have chosen your colour scheme, **prepare** the room for decoration.

PATTERNS & PAINT EFFECTS
The list below shows you examples of how different effects can make a room more yin and calming or yang and stimulating.

YIN – CALMING	YANG – STIMULATING
Random	Repeating
Wavy	Stripes
Ovals	Circles
Mottled	Regimented
Floral	Diamonds
Rag rolling	Rubber stamping
Brushing/Combing	Stencilling
Sponging	Printing

Patterns and special finishes

Another way of influencing the atmosphere of a room is to use patterns. One way you can achieve this is to use patterned wallpaper or to apply special paint finishes. In terms of yin and yang the simpler and more repetitive the pattern the more yang and stimulating the atmosphere, whereas an irregular pattern, such as that created by rag rolling, will create a more calming and yin environment.

Paint effects

Here the special finish on the walls is tied in with the colour theme in the furniture throughout the room. This leaves a feeling of unity and tranquility despite having used quite a bright colour.

Decorative elements

An alert and more stimulating atmosphere has been achieved here by using several similar patterns throughout the room.

In general a more yang pattern will also make a room feel smaller and is, therefore, better suited to a large room. It will also have a striking and dramatic effect and is most appropriate for rooms that are used for entertaining rather than for general family use.

A textured wallpaper will slow down the flow of chi energy and make the whole room feel relaxing, while a wallpaper with a sheen helps speed up chi energy, creating a more stimulating atmosphere.

❷ Applying wallpaper and special finishes

To prepare for **wallpapering**, use the information on these pages to help you select an **appropriate pattern** or **special effect**. As wallpaper is much harder to change if you are not happy with it you should **be careful** before rushing into a decision. Try to get large samples and **pin them up on your walls** so that you can see which ones you like the most.

Once you are ready, **prepare the walls**. You may need to remove old wallpaper first. This task can be made easier by using a **steam wallpaper stripper**. Fill any cracks or holes with plaster and then put up the wallpaper being careful to avoid **gaps, air bubbles or creases**.

To apply a special paint finish, first you will need to choose the best **colours** (see the project opposite). There are several ways of applying paint to create different finishes but generally, you will need to paint on a base coat and then, using a different shade and technique, such as **coarse brushing, sponging, rag rolling, printing, stencilling or rubber stamping**, add a pattern or design to your walls. If you are not sure of the effect you can always **do a test patch** and then paint over it.

If you do not have the DIY skills for wallpapering or special paint techniques, **hire a professional decorator**.

bedrooms

Restful sleep is essential for good health and general well-being. The main aim when designing a bedroom is to create an atmosphere that will help the occupants wake feeling refreshed, invigorated and energized. The bedroom also has a significant influence on adult relationships, as sex, intimacy and affection often take place in the bedroom.

BEFORE

Sleeping in line with the door directs the chi energy entering the room towards the bed making it **harder to sleep well**. Leaving the door open makes the situation worse.

A **mirror facing the bed** will speed up and reflect chi energy towards the bed increasing the **risk of poor sleep**.

Energy passing the corner begins to swirl directing fast-flowing chi energy towards the bed and increasing the risk of **poor sleep** and, in the long term, **ill health**.

A **lack of curtains** allows chi energy to flow too freely through bedroom.

An opening to the en-suite bathroom increases the risk of **damp chi energy** flowing into the bedroom.

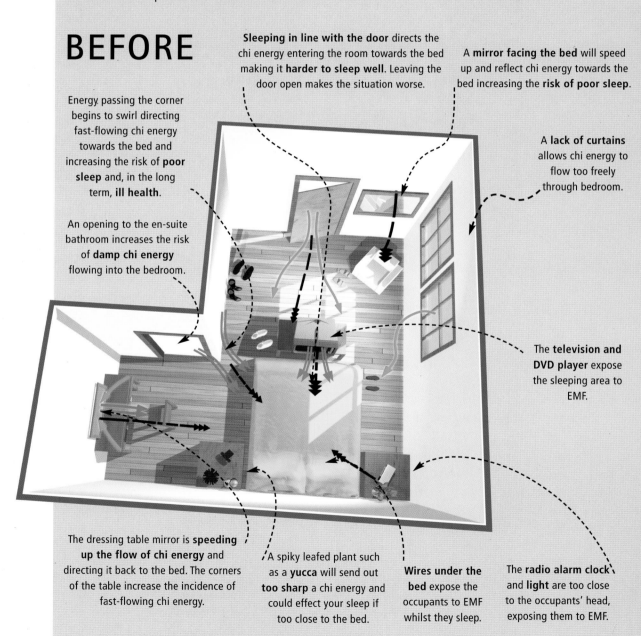

The **television and DVD player** expose the sleeping area to EMF.

The dressing table mirror is **speeding up the flow of chi energy** and directing it back to the bed. The corners of the table increase the incidence of fast-flowing chi energy.

A spiky leafed plant such as a **yucca** will send out **too sharp** a chi energy and could effect your sleep if too close to the bed.

Wires under the bed expose the occupants to EMF whilst they sleep.

The **radio alarm clock** and **light** are too close to the occupants' head, exposing them to EMF.

AFTER

Move the television and DVD player as **far away** as possible to reduce the exposure to EMF.

Use **heavy, full-length curtains** to subdue the flow of chi energy through the windows at night.

Use a screen and plants to slow the energy **between the door and bed**.

Move the mirror so that it no longer faces the bed.

Grow a **tall, bushy plant** in front of the corner to soften the edge and **stop fast-flowing energy** from being directed at the bed.

Attach a door to the en-suite bathroom to reduce the risk of **damp chi energy** flowing into the bedroom.

Add plants to the room to increase the presence of **healthy chi energy**.

Move the wires from **under the bed** to reduce exposure to EMF.

Replace the radio alarm clock with a **mechanical clock** and **move the light away** from the occupants' head.

Use plants with **floppy round leaves** near the bed.

beds & bedding

Beds and bedding have a huge influence on the quality of your sleep as they are within your chi energy field while you are in bed.

Feeling up
A light atmosphere has been created here by using a solid, wooden bed frame and the crisp blue bedlinen and wall paint.

The quality of your sleep will greatly affect your long-term health. It is important to have about six hours of deep undisturbed sleep so that your body can repair and regenerate itself properly. If you cannot achieve this, there is a risk that you will lose vitality, feel irritable, get run down and so become prone to illnesses.

The ideal material for a bed frame is wood, because it does not distort the local magnetic field, whereas a metal frame with iron in it will. Wood is softer than metal and it induces a calm, yin energy on your own chi energy field.

The more solid the bed frame the more yang and stable the energy will be. An ornate bed frame will increase the creative, more yin energy around you while you sleep. A four-poster bed helps contain the energy around you and is particularly useful if you sleep in a large bedroom with high ceilings where the chi energy can move easily and quickly. Drapes around the sides of the bed will be even more effective when it comes to containing the energy.

The height of the bed can also influence your chi energy. It is helpful to maintain a distance of at least 1.8m (2yd) between the top of your bed and the ceiling so that there is plenty of room for your chi energy to move freely during the night. The higher the bed the more you may be stimulated intellectually and the lower it is the more practical you should feel.

half-day project

❶ Better bedding
Examine all your bedding to see what it is made of. Include the filling of duvets and mattresses. Look to see what your bed frame is made from. Separate the **natural and synthetic** bedding into two piles and **throw away the synthetic**.

If you are thinking of changing your bed or suffer from **insomnia** and your existing bed is **metal**, consider purchasing a **wooden** framed bed. Measure the height of your ceiling and subtract 1.8m (2yd) to determine the maximum height of your bed. Use the information above to decide whether you would like a **higher or lower bed.**

Try out **different mattresses** and **futons** in stores to see if you can find a natural item that you feel comfortable with. You will need to turn your **mattress or futon** over and around regularly, so allow enough room at either side and around the foot of your bed to make this possible.

Set up your new bed using the information on this and the next page. Use the pile of **natural bedding** to make up your bed. When buying new bedding, check to see what it is made of and **think about the colours and style** that would suit you best.

Mattresses

Always choose a mattress that is made of natural materials. Cloth, wool, straw and hair are preferable to foam and other man-made materials. Synthetic materials carry a static charge and, as this will be within your chi energy field, it will have a direct effect on the way you feel. It can eventually make you feel low in physical and emotional energy.

Cotton futons are ideal in terms of their passive influence on the movement of energy. They are essentially four to eight layers of thick cotton batting bound by a strong cotton cover. In Japan, they are placed on top of bamboo tatami mats. In the West, most people use wooden slatted bases to raise them off the floor so that they can air properly. Futons can often help sufferers of back problems because of their firmness.

Pocket sprung mattresses contain metal springs, which distort the local magnetic field. This alters the energy movement in a way that can become chaotic. Waterbeds produce more watery chi energy, which is too damp for good health.

THINGS TO AVOID:

Steel and iron bed frames, electric blankets, synthetic materials.

Bedding

Non-static materials, such as pure cotton or linen are the best fabrics to have next to your skin. Synthetic fabrics build up a static charge, which will effect the flow of energy.

Cotton and linen allow your skin to breathe, which is important as you can secrete up to 1litre (1¾pt) of fluid at night through your skin while sleeping. Silk can be very sexy and exciting. Lacy or embroidered bedding is more yin and can make your bed feel more cosy.

The colour of your bedclothes will alter the energy of your bedroom during the day. For greater romance you could try using bedding with some pink or red in it. Cream or black can help if you to feel more sexual.

Avoid using an electric blanket as it will expose you to EMF and will distort the natural magnetic field.

position of the bed

The location of your bed in terms of the direction the top of your head points and your relationship to the rest of the room will have one of the greatest influences on your chi energy field. So, if you want to experience far-reaching changes in your life, make sure that you sleep with your head facing the direction best for you.

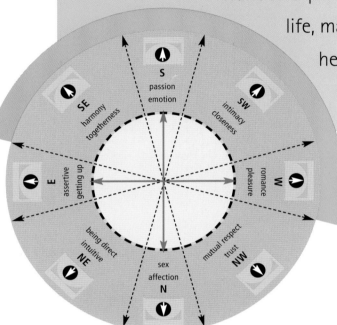

The information below will help you to decide which direction the top of your head should face when lying in your bed.

You may need to experiment by having your bed at an angle to the walls to test the direction that is best for you. If you find your life improves you can re-arrange your room around the new position you have chosen.

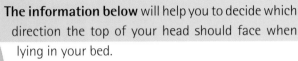 FACING SOUTH

Its high energy and hot, fiery nature makes this direction helpful if you want to feel more passionate, expressive and social. However, it is not normally recommended for anyone who has trouble sleeping, gets stressed easily or is argumentative. It can be a mentally stimulating energy that can help to sharpen your mind.

FACING SOUTH-WEST

This is a good direction to point if you want to feel more settled. Beneficial south-western energy focuses on improving the quality of your life in terms of a better relationship, a happier family life and greater satisfaction at work. It is also helpful for good sleep, practicality and being realistic.

FACING WEST

Western chi energy combines the benefits of good sleep with feelings of contentment. It helps in terms of your finances and romance. At times the feelings of contentment can also lead to laziness, and reduced motivation, making it more suitable for someone who has already become established in his or her career.

FACING NORTH-WEST

North-west is a helpful direction if you need a long, deep, sleep. It also brings with it the energy associated with leadership, responsibility and feeling in control. It could be too serious for a young person.

FACING NORTH

North is a very peaceful direction to point which makes it ideal for insomnia sufferers, however, it can make your whole life too quiet. This direction will enhance feelings of peace and tranquillity, and bring you closer to the spiritual world. It can also help you to feel more intimate, affectionate and sexual but, generally, it is not ideal for a young person.

FACING NORTH-EAST

This energy can be too hard, and piercing for good sleep and could have the effect of making you feel on edge. It may also increase the incidence of nightmares. The advantage is that it improves your motivation, competitiveness and decisiveness. It can help if you want to get a clearer sense of direction in life.

Protruding corners or right angles pointing at the bed

Energy moving around a protruding corner or right angle will begin to swirl. Sleeping in a whirlpool of energy, can make you disorientated and confused.

We spend more time in bed than anywhere else and, consequently, it is where we tend to absorb the most environmental chi energy. When we sleep we are especially passive and receptive to outside forces. In oriental medicine the spiral in your hair, found near your crown, is believed to be the point where most of the chi energy enters your body. The direction the top of your head faces will influence the kind of energy you will absorb. For these reasons the position of your bed provides a wonderful opportunity to enhance your own chi energy field.

Synthetic materials

These materials carry their own static charge of electricity, which can interfere with your own natural movement of electromagnetic energy. Natural materials such as cotton, linen, silk, or wool will tend to avoid this problem. The closer the fabrics are to your skin, the more influential they are.

⬛ FACING EAST

Eastern energy is ideal for young people. It relates to the beginning of the day and helps induce the feeling that everything is in front of you. Good for ambition, getting things done and for being kept busy. It is helpful for building up your life and starting new projects. As the energy of the east is most active at the beginning of the day, it also helps in terms of waking up with enthusiasm.

⬛ FACING SOUTH-EAST

Good for communication, relationships, imagination and increased creativity, this energy can help you form new ideas, be persistent and work towards your long-term goals. It is associated with your future prosperity and growth.

reducing emf & sharp corners

An electromagnetic field (EMF), produced by anything that uses or transports mains electricity, that passes near your bed is potentially

harmful as you will be immersed in its field for longer periods of time (see pages 26–7). The best remedy is to move the source as far from your bed as possible.

Softening sharp edges is crucial to peaceful sleep. Protruding corners, sharp edges or right angles pointing at your bed are potentially harmful because you spend long periods of time in bed and you are more vulnerable to any negative influences while you sleep.

Eliminate sharp edges

Lie on your bed and look around the room to see if any protruding corners or sharp edges point towards any part of your bed. Include walls, wardrobes, cupboards and chests of drawers. Take into account any shelves or cupboards above your bed. Soften the edges with plants or fabric.

SOURCES OF EMF IN THE BEDROOM: bedside lights, radio alarm clocks, televisions, DVD players, video players, hi-fi equipment, wires, electric blankets and electric heaters.

Reducing EMF

Try using candles and mechanical clocks instead of lights and electric clocks

half-day project

① Eliminating EMF

Switch on all the **electrical equipment** in your bedroom and, as a rough guide, **take a compass** and slowly move it over your bed watching the needle to see if it remains **steady** or **swings to either side**. The more it swings the more likely it is that there is EMF or something magnetic close to your bed.

Start by moving electrical items **away from your bed**. If space is limited even a small distance has the **potential to make significant reduction** in the effect of EMF.

Look around your bed to see if there are any **wires running close to your bed** or underneath it. Check behind the

headboard and the wall either side of the bed to see if there are any electrical sockets. If your bedroom has a carpet you may need to look under it to **check for wires running below the carpet**.

Try to use sockets located further away from the bed and re-route the wires to those sockets, keeping them well away from the bed. You may need to use extension leads or even get an electrician to move sockets.

You can further reduce the presence of EMF by unplugging all your electrical sockets before you go to sleep.

lighting

As most of the time you spend in your bedroom will be during the night when there is no natural light, other forms of lighting have a greater influence on this room than others. Use lighting in the bedroom for functional purposes, enabling you to see clearly, and also to create a relaxed and romantic mood.

In general, it is best to keep bedroom lighting as soft as possible. For this reason avoid using small fluorescent energy saving items as they generate a blue colder light.

It would help to make as much of your lighting as indirect, as possible. Lights that reflect off a wall or ceiling will be gentler on your eyes and more calming. Where you need more light use free-standing spotlights, wall-mounted lights or ceiling lights that can achieve this effect.

Lamps

If you have table lamps, use low-wattage bulbs and thick shades to create a more subtle source of lighting.

Colours of the shade

Choose according to the kind of mood you want to create: pink for calm and pleasure, purple to be more passionate and yellow to be more settled.

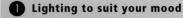

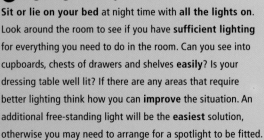

half-day project

① Lighting to suit your mood

Sit or lie on your bed at night time with **all the lights on**. Look around the room to see if you have **sufficient lighting** for everything you need to do in the room. Can you see into cupboards, chests of drawers and shelves **easily**? Is your dressing table well lit? If there are any areas that require better lighting think how you can **improve** the situation. An additional free-standing light will be the **easiest** solution, otherwise you may need to arrange for a spotlight to be fitted.

Turn on each light individually and see what kind of **atmosphere** it produces. See how you feel with each option.

Does any make you feel sleepy, relaxed or romantic? If you are not happy with the options **try the following**.

Place a pair of candles in the south-western part of your bedroom. If this is not possible try the east, south-east, south or north-east. Make sure they are in a **safe** place well away from anything combustible in case you fall asleep with them lit. **Light the candles** when you want to calm down, feel romantic or be sexual. **Scented candles** will further enhance the atmosphere.

pictures & plants

The bedroom is a good place to focus on romantic relationships. Because it is a private place, you and your partner are likely to be more intimate with one another here than elsewhere in your home. The western and south-western parts of a bedroom are ideal for any objects that can improve relationships, as these are the areas where the energy associated with romance and relationships is found.

Pictures

Hang a romantic picture in the south-western or western part of the room. Photographs of you and your partner in intimate poses or having fun are helpful here.

The imagery you choose will be personal to you and you may need to think carefully about what will make you and your lover put energy into the quality of your relationship.

Plants will create a healthy environment in your bedroom as they bring living chi energy into the space and help keep the room dry. Plants are also ideal for absorbing sounds and, therefore, help to keep the room quiet for good sleep. For more information on the way plants can change an atmosphere, see pages 46–7.

Flowers are an excellent way of bringing extra colour into your bedroom as they radiate living energy. You can change the atmosphere easily, according to your mood – brighten it up or calm it down depending on your choice of flowers (see pages 32–3). The scent from flowers will help make your bedroom feel fresh and pleasant to be in.

Romance and passion

If you want to make your bedroom a place where you could feel more passionate use bright purple flowers. Pink will help you feel more romantic, while blue can help you feel more positive.

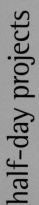

half-day projects

❶ Romantic imagery

The following are suggestions which may help you to focus on **improving your relationship**. Use a compass (see page 145), or the method described on page 9 to locate the south-western and western parts of your bedroom. Read through the text above and try out those that **appeal** to you. Ask your partner do the same and incorporate his or her ideas.

Place a pair of **red or pink flowers in a silver-coloured metal vase** in the western part of your bedroom.

Put a **statue of a couple in a passionate embrace** in the south-west. Use **aromatherapy oils** to create a relaxing scented atmosphere. Pour a few drops into a candle burner.

❷ Plants and imagery

Look at the **natural light conditions** in your bedroom to see what plants you could introduce. Avoid having plants with pointed leaves, such as **yuccas or cacti**, near your bed as the energy will be too yang and, therefore, not so relaxing.

Position the plants in your bedroom with care. Make sure you look after them properly. **Dying plants could introduce an unhealthy energy** into your bedroom.

Decide what would help you feel good in your bedroom. Choose the appropriate **flowers and colours** and use them to decorate your room. Change the water every day to keep it fresh and discard the flowers as soon as they begin to wilt.

The storage facilities in your bedroom – cupboards, wardrobes, chests of drawers – will determine how easy it is to keep clean and uncluttered. The better organized your storage space the more likely you are to use it.

Usually things go wrong when there are too many clothes for the amount of storage space available. You will also need to get the right balance of hanging space, draws and shelving. Free-standing storage units are ideal as you can move them around your bedroom if you want to change the position of your bed.

HOW TO BE CLUTTER-FREE
A dressing room next to your bedroom can provide the ideal solution for storing clothes. This room can contain open hanging space and shelves making it easy to see everything and use it. The advantage is that it opens up the bedroom and makes it easier to keep clutter out of the sleeping area.

Storage
Multi-purpose storage units
are useful if you are short of space.

Flexible storage units
These will allow you to change them as your needs develop. Open units make it easier to see everything but increase the need to be tidy.

half-day project

① Organize your clutter
Remove all of your clothes from your bedroom. Use the information on page 42 to help you sort through everything putting the clothing that you use infrequently **to one side**. If possible, see if there are other places in your home where you can store these, such as a **loft, garage or a cupboard under the stairs**.

　Group the remaining clothes into piles that are best suited to a hanging space, shelving or drawers. Replace the items so that each has **plenty of space**, is easily accessible and there is some **extra space for new purchases**. You

should now be able to see if you need extra space and if so what kind of storage space you need.

　Look for the **appropriate storage unit**. This should ideally be made from solid wood, have rounded edges and be in a style that will help you feel good in your bedroom.

children's rooms

For most parents, the ideal atmosphere in a child's room is one in which he or she enjoys a full night's sleep. However, in feng shui you also need to make sure that the chi energy in this room is supportive of the growth and development of the child.

BEFORE

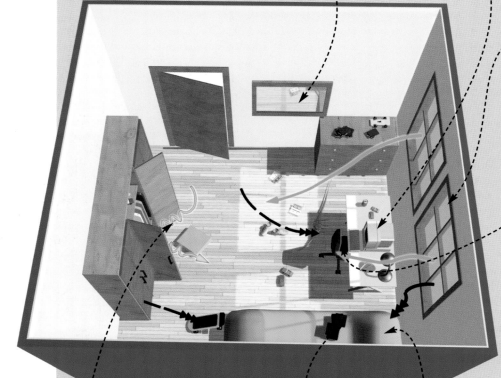

A **mirror facing the bed** will speed up and reflect chi energy towards the bed, increasing the risk of **poor sleep**.

The **computer and desk light** exposes the sleeping area to **EMF**.

A **lack of curtains** allows chi energy to **flow too freely** through the bedroom.

Sitting with your **back to the door** and the rest of the room can be unsettling and make it difficult to **concentrate** on **homework**.

Energy passing the **sharp edges** begins to swirl, directing **fast-flowing chi energy** towards the bed, increasing the risk of poor sleep and, in the long term, **ill-health**.

Wires **under** the **bed** expose the occupant to **EMF**.

Sleeping with your head **close to the window** directs the **chi energy** entering the room towards you making it **difficult to sleep well**.

AFTER

Add plants to increase the presence of healthy chi energy. This is particularly helpful near a computer.

Sitting **facing into the room** with a view of the door and windows is a more powerful position.

Move the mirror so that it does not face the bed.

Move the computer as far away from the bed as possible to reduce the exposure to **EMF**.

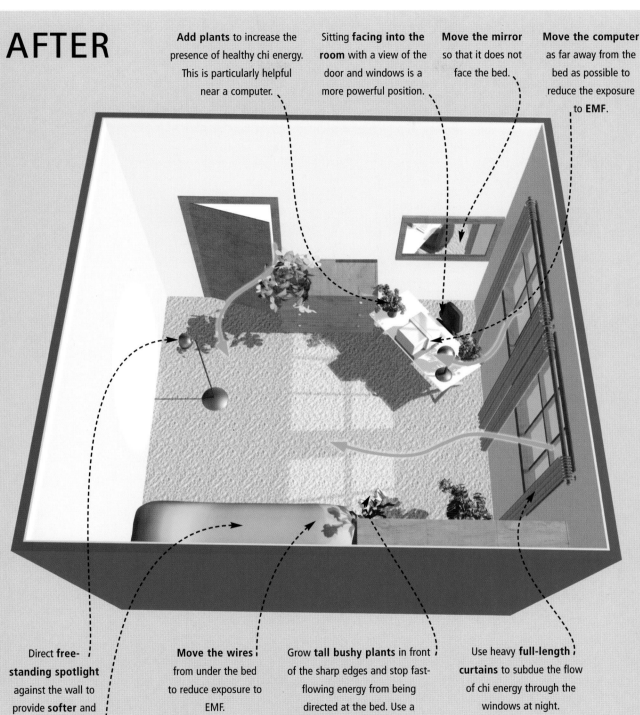

Direct **free-standing spotlight** against the wall to provide **softer** and more relaxing lighting.

Move the wires from under the bed to reduce exposure to EMF.

Grow **tall bushy plants** in front of the sharp edges and stop fast-flowing energy from being directed at the bed. Use a **hanging plant** on the corner of the chest of drawers.

Use heavy **full-length curtains** to subdue the flow of chi energy through the windows at night.

Sleep **further** from the window to feel more settled. In this position it is important to **keep the door closed** at night.

a natural environment

The more natural the atmosphere in your children's rooms, the easier it will be for them to feel relaxed there. This can lead to better sleep and better behaviour. Avoid artificial materials as there is a rule that they may give off subtle fumes and build up a charge of static electricity which could compromise your child's health in the long term.

It is helpful to create an open space in your children's room so chi energy can move freely and they have room to play.

If you are short of space you could replace the bed with a futon, which can be rolled up during the daytime to create a larger play area.

If your children have a lot of electrical toys, you might want to store them outside the bedroom to reduce EMF.

Use natural materials

Avoid furniture made from MDF (medium-density fibreboard) or veneered wood as these could add toxic fumes to the room. Try to always use solid wood, as this is a much better conductor of chi energy.

half-day project

❶ Natural materials

Check what type of materials are used in the **soft furnishings** in your child's bedroom. Include **bedding, curtains, carpet, rugs and cushions**. If these contain synthetic fibres think about replacing them with something made from pure cotton or linen.

Also **check through their clothing** to see what it is made of. Ideally, substitute pure cotton, linen or wool for clothes made from synthetic fabrics. The closer an item of clothing is to your **child's skin**, the greater its influence on their chi energy field. Most important are **under clothes, pyjamas and sheets**.

Grow several **healthy plants** in the room. It is beneficial to use a variety of plants, however, it would help to use plants with **floppy leaves close to the bed**, or throughout the room if your child finds it difficult to relax.

If it is appropriate, try using candles or **safety/night lights** instead of electric lights at night. See if you can **re-route wires** so they are well away from your **children's beds**.

Each time you buy something for your children's room remember to check the material the items are made of.

furniture

The location of your children's beds within their bedroom can influence their sleeping patterns. One of the greatest influences will be the direction the top of their head points as this will determine what type of energy they absorb during the night. It will also have an influence during the day.

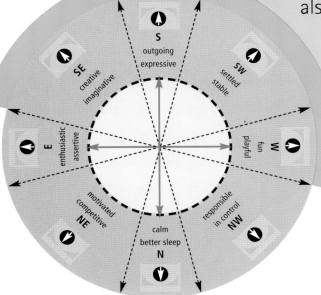

Each direction is associated with a family member (see pages 146–7) and for children it is better to avoid those that are associated with mothers and fathers.

NORTH-WEST Father

The chi energy of the north-west is associated with leadership, organizational skills and feeling in control. These are not normally appropriate for a young child who will tend to become difficult to influence and more serious with this kind of chi energy.

NORTH Middle son

North is a very quiet direction and it can help a child who finds it difficult to sleep. It can also suit a newborn baby. However, only use this direction for a child's bed temporarily, as the chi energy of the north is too still for a growing child.

NORTH-EAST Youngest son

This direction is too hard and piercing for good sleep. It could even make your child more prone to tantrums. This is an energy that would be helpful if you think your child, could be more motivated and competitive.

EAST Eldest son

East is considered an ideal direction for young people. It carries the energy of growth, making it helpful for a child at the beginning of his or her life. As the energy of the east is most active at the start of the day, it also helps a young person to wake up feeling enthusiastic.

SOUTH-EAST Eldest daughter

Turning the bed so that your child's head points towards the south-east will help him or her feel more imaginative and creative. If facing east is too energizing for your child try this direction as the chi energy will be gentler.

SOUTH Middle daughter

Due to its high energy and hot, fiery nature, sleeping with the top of his or her head pointing south could result in poor sleep for your child. However, the advantage of this direction is that it helps develop quick thinking and a spontaneous spirit.

SOUTH-WEST Mother

Sleeping with your head pointing south-west is a settled position, which can encourage good sleep. However, the chi energy of the south-west is too mature to be harmonious for a young child, but will encourage practicality and a cautious, caring nature.

WEST Youngest daughter

Pointing west combines the benefits of good sleep, with a playful atmosphere. It is more settled and may benefit a child who has difficulty in sleeping well. This can encourage feelings of contentment.

a dual-purpose room

Apart from sleep this room may also be used as a playroom. A dual-purpose room introduces the challenge of creating a fun atmosphere during the day and a peaceful one at night.

It is important to watch out for your child's bedroom becoming overwhelmed by plastic toys, as this will help to create a rather artifical environment for them to play and sleep in. If the room becomes messy or cluttered it can result in children not wanting to spend time there and losing respect for their environment.

It is possible to use paints and wall coverings to create a playful atmosphere for during the day. Stencilling is a useful way to make a child's room feel more stimulating. The colours and patterns can stand out from the plain surfaces and add a more vibrant atmosphere to the room.

Try to get your children more involved in setting up the room and even to help you redecorate. Use colours, fabrics, plants, lighting and natural materials to soften the atmosphere so that it can transform into a peaceful room to sleep in.

Paint effects and stencilling

You can stencil part of the walls or pieces of furniture, such as a chest of drawers, or the edge of a table.

❶ Appropriate stencilling

Choose the place or piece of furniture you want to **stencil**. Decide on a colour scheme that will create the most **helpful atmosphere** for your child (see page 38-41). Look at **different designs** for your stencil. **Jagged designs will be more yang** and help make the room feel livelier, whereas **curved or wavy patterns will create a calmer, more yin atmosphere**.

There is a wide choice of stencils and imagery available that will appeal to a young child and stimulate his or her imagination. For example, silhouettes of the **moon and stars**, **flowers**, **animals** or **cars and trains**.

You can either use a stencil brush, a small sponge or spray paint to apply the stencil, depending on the kind of effect you are looking for.

Similarly, you can use **ordinary emulsion paint** or **specialist stencil paint**. Follow the manufacturer's instructions and apply the paint to the surface you wish to stencil.

half-day project

storage for children

 It is essential to provide accessible and functional storage in children's rooms to help them keep their rooms tidy. Encourage your children to be tidy and to regularly throw away, or give to charity, unwanted toys.

There should be slightly more storage than the amount of things which need to be put away. Otherwise, you will need to sort through everything and either get rid of things that are no longer needed, or put items that are rarely used into deeper storage, such as a garage, loft or cellar. Open storage, such as shelving, has the advantage of enabling your children to see everything. Boxes or baskets make it much easier to store toys that are made up of many pieces, for example, building blocks, farmyard animals, railway sets or construction kits. It is a good idea if your children play with these sorts of toys on a large cotton sheet. When they have finished they can fold all the pieces up inside the sheet and then put the whole thing into the appropriate box or basket. Boxes and baskets are also easier to move around from one room to another. Try to encourage your children to be organized by maybe playing with just one toy at a time. Once they have finished they should put that toy away and move on to the next one. You can also put paints, crayons and toy cars into containers.

Size matters
To make the storage easy to use, take into account the age and height of your children. While they are young, low shelves, boxes on the floor, chests and chests of drawers are best.

half-day project

❶ Suitable storage
Take everything out of storage and start to **group** things according to **how accessible they need to be**. Think about the kind of storage that would be best for each item – toys, books, paints or games.

If necessary, **purchase the appropriate boxes**, baskets, sheets, **containers and shelves** so that everything has a place.

Put everything away, showing your children how they can do it. Slowly **train your children** to use the new system.

Easy to use storage
Whatever storage you use, it needs to be easy for children to put everything back in its place.

 103

home offices/studies

The home office is becoming increasingly important as more and more people have the opportunity to work from home. Computers, the Internet, e-mail, telephones, fax machines, photocopiers and scanners mean that any home office can operate globally.

BEFORE

In this position you **face a wall** and have your **back to the door.** You also have a poor view through the windows.

The desk is **too small**.

The computer is **too close** to the chair.

Situated here, the **printer is too close** to where you sit.

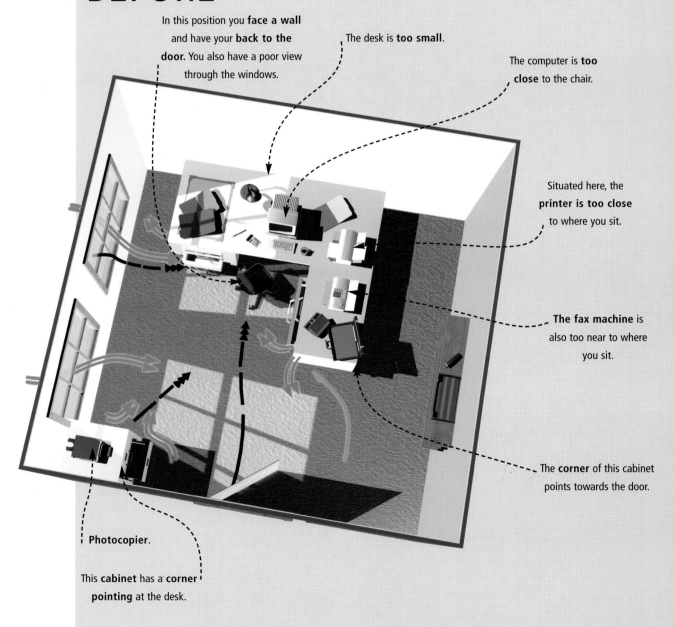

The fax machine is also too near to where you sit.

The **corner** of this cabinet points towards the door.

Photocopier.

This **cabinet** has a **corner pointing** at the desk.

AFTER

Move the fax machine and photocopier as far away from your seat as possible.

Use **hanging plants** over the corners of the cabinets and near the electrical equipment.

Try a **larger desk with curved edges** to reduce fast-flowing chi and allow greater flexibility in the direction you face.

Move the printer further away from where you sit.

Keep a **good distance** between your computer and yourself. Try using a **laptop** if you want to save space and also have the option of working in other parts of the home.

mirrors

Generally, people tend to work in one of the smaller rooms in their home. Unfortunately, there is a risk that chi energy can become too confined in small spaces. Mirrors are a useful way of making the study feel larger than it is. Also they will help to move the energy faster around the room making it a livelier and more yang place to work.

A long, narrow room will feel twice as wide with mirrors along one side. To balance the proportions of an L-shaped room, put up a mirror on one of the walls that form the inside of the L shape.

Mirrors speed up the flow of chi energy in a room making it dynamic and more yang. Hang a large mirror wherever it feels right or where you need more light.

A mirror will help you see the room behind you if you work facing a wall. Hang a mirror in front of you so that you can see as much of the room behind you as possible. Ideally this would include the door to your study and window.

Advantages of mirrors

Mirrors reflect natural light helping to brighten up a dark room. Hang a mirror on a wall that is at 90 degrees and adjacent to the window so that it reflects light into the room.

half-day project

❶ Stimulating mirrors

Sit in your study and decide whether you would benefit from a mirror. If you want the room to feel **livelier** and **more yang** use the information above to find the **ideal location for a mirror**.

Measure the available space and find an appropriate mirror to hang there. The **larger the mirror the more effective** it will be. Hang the mirror and make an assessment as to how you feel in the room.

GUIDELINES:
1. **Do not hang mirrors directly facing a door, window or another mirror.**
2. **Use one large mirror rather than several small mirrors and avoid mirror tiles as they disjoint and fragment the image.**
3. **The mirror should not be hung so the top of your head is cut off.**
4. **Always keep mirrors clean.**

The most immediate influence on you while you work is your desk. This is because it effects your own chi energy, which not only defines how you work but also the way you feel while you work.

OFFICE CHAIRS

As so much time is spent sitting, it is essential that an office chair is comfortable. One of the main causes of backache is bad posture. If the base of the spine is not angled correctly, muscles along the back and neck, have to compensate and as these muscles become tired and sore. If they are subjected to this same regime on a regular basis there is a risk of long-term pain. To reduce this risk use a chair with a seat that tilts. By adjusting the angle of the seat it is possible to maintain the optimum angle for your lumber vertebrae, so that your back, shoulders and neck are positioned over the base of your spine. In addition, the back of the chair needs to be adjustable as does the height. In most cases it is helpful to have a chair on casters.

The material the desk is made of, its shape and size, and the way objects are arranged on the desktop will all have an influence on the way you work. In general, an oval, softwood desk or one with rounded edges in, say, pine, will be more relaxing and best-suited for creative work. A rectangular, dark, hardwood desk in, say, mahogany, would be better for more formal situations.

A large desk with plenty of clear space on which to work will boost confidence and help you to feel equipped to take on more work without getting stressed. In the long term it may help you to become more ambitious.

A tidy desk

Keep your desktop clear of clutter and any drawers or storage spaces well organized to help you to work efficiently.

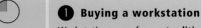
half-day projects

❶ Buying a workstation

Workstations vary from a **traditional, rectangular desk** to a **modern, specially shaped unit** designed to incorporate a computer, with the option of **adding on extensions**. When there is sufficient space, make the work surfaces as **generous as possible**. Curved worktops create a more natural appearance and reduce the risk of fast-flowing chi.

A **round desk will also avoid cutting chi** and make a relatively small room feel more comfortable. Too many **sharp edges will make a study seem less comfortable**, and you may find it difficult to spend long periods of time there.

A solid wooden desk will stimulate a natural flow of chi energy. Desks that are made of some form of **chipboard** – wood chips or wood particles bonded together with adhesives – or **MDF** (medium-density fibreboard) tend to **block the flow of chi energy** in a similar way to that of **plastic**. These materials are usually covered with a thin veneer of real wood.

A **glass-topped desk** will **speed up the flow of chi energy** across the desktop and make it a **spontaneous**, more yang place to work. This type of surface is helpful if you wish to work at your desk for long periods of time.

organizing your desk

The surface of your desk or workstation will make a difference to the way you feel about working there. If it gets cluttered with paperwork you will find it difficult to be organized and effective. It is, therefore, important to have readily accessible and easy to use storage facilities. Today, maintaining a tidy, uncluttered desktop should not be a problem as computers enable us to work with much less paper.

Take all the items off the top of your desk so that you have a clear surface. Decide on whether or not it is essential to have each item on your desk. One way of doing this is to put everything into a box next to your desk and over a period of time see which things you really need. Some items, which you do not want to throw out but do not need to be on your desk could be put into storage. Try to keep as much as you can in desk drawers so that your desktop is clear.

Reduce EMF on your desk

To help reduce your exposure to electromagnetic fields (EMF) position yourself as far away from electrical equipment as possible and keep a plant on your desk next to your computer. This could be a peace lily or spider plant.

half-day project

❶ Clearing surfaces

Use the **principle of the four animals** (see pages 136–7), to help you decide where to put things. **Place an imaginary layout of the four animals over your desk** so that the phoenix is furthest away and **place objects** in the areas that **most suit the chi energy** of that particular direction.

For example, the **right-hand side** of your desk is **associated with the tiger** and western chi energy, which, in turn, relates to financial income, so you could **keep loose change**, cheques paid to you, or **something made of gold or silver** in this direction.

The area at the **front**, furthest away from where you sit, **is the phoenix** and is associated with the south, which, in turn,

relates to public recognition. This part of the desk would be an ideal place for any **awards** that you have received.

The **left-hand side** of your desk is **associated with the dragon** and eastern chi energy. Here you could put something that **reminds you** of what you want to **achieve** with your **career** or business.

The area immediately **in front** of you relates to the **tortoise** and the north, which, in turn, is associated with personal development through courses and career experience. You could keep a list of ways in which you would like to see yourself grow and develop in this area.

The direction you face aligns you within a particular energy which can make a significant difference to the way you work. You can also choose a direction according to the kind of work that you do.

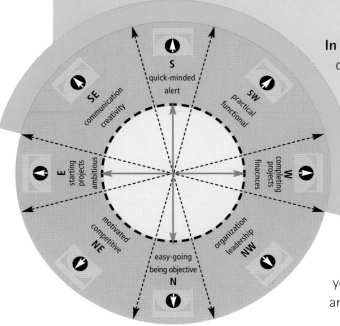

In addition, the position of the desk in relation to doors and windows will have a significant influence on the way you feel in your office or study. In the case of a door it will also effect the way in which you are perceived by other people should you have visitors to your study. Ideally, the door should be in front of your desk, which can be at an angle, as long as the door is not to the side or behind the desk.

An L-shaped, kidney-shaped or oval desk or workstation gives you the option of facing different directions for various tasks. For example, you could face east while working on your computer and south-east to do more creative work.

FACING SOUTH

Promotes quick thinking, the ability to be noticed and expressiveness.
Favourable for activities relating to sales, PR, marketing and entertainment.

FACING SOUTH-WEST

Promotes qualitative characteristics, consolidation and practicality.
Favourable for activities relating to human resources, customer services, team-building and buildings.

FACING WEST

Promotes financial awareness, the ability to complete tasks and contentment.
Favourable for activities relating to finance, accounts and investments.

FACING NORTH-WEST

Promotes organizational skills, leadership qualities and responsibility.
Favourable for activities relating to management, administration and forward planning.

FACING NORTH

Promotes objectivity, calmness and flexibility.
Favourable for activities relating to self-development, training and cash flow.

FACING NORTH-EAST

Promotes hard work, motivation and a competitive attitude.
Favourable for activities relating to competition, purchasing, trading and buildings.

FACING EAST

Promotes activity, ambition and confidence.
Favourable for activities relating to new projects, computers and information technology.

FACING SOUTH-EAST

Promotes creativity, communication and persistence.
Favourable for activities relating to communication, marketing, distribution, travel and creativity.

bathrooms

The bathroom can have a big influence on your chi energy. It is where you wash yourself and eliminate bodily waste. You are also washing away unwanted chi energy by releasing emotions and old ideas. For example, you may feel emotionally refreshed after a shower.

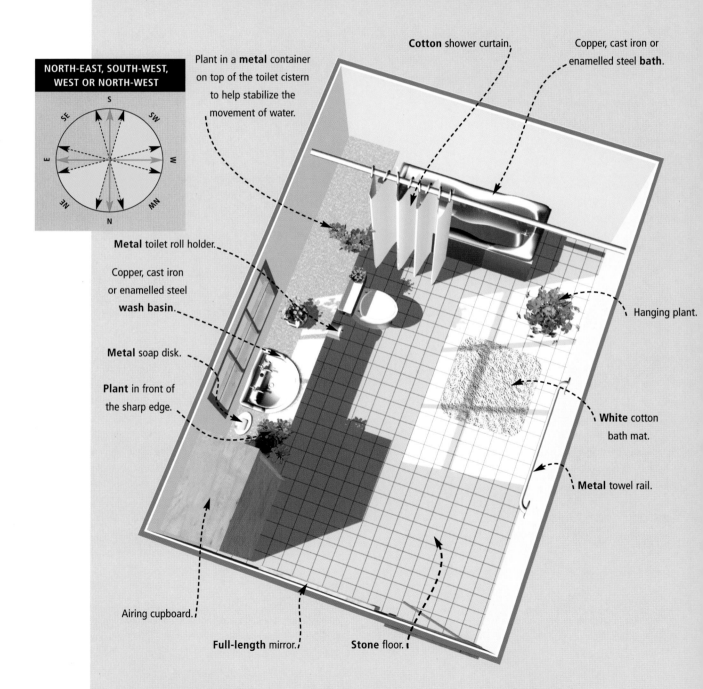

NORTH-EAST, SOUTH-WEST, WEST OR NORTH-WEST

Plant in a **metal** container on top of the toilet cistern to help stabilize the movement of water.

Cotton shower curtain.

Copper, cast iron or enamelled steel **bath**.

Metal toilet roll holder.

Copper, cast iron or enamelled steel **wash basin**.

Metal soap disk.

Plant in front of the sharp edge.

Hanging plant.

White cotton bath mat.

Metal towel rail.

Airing cupboard.

Full-length mirror.

Stone floor.

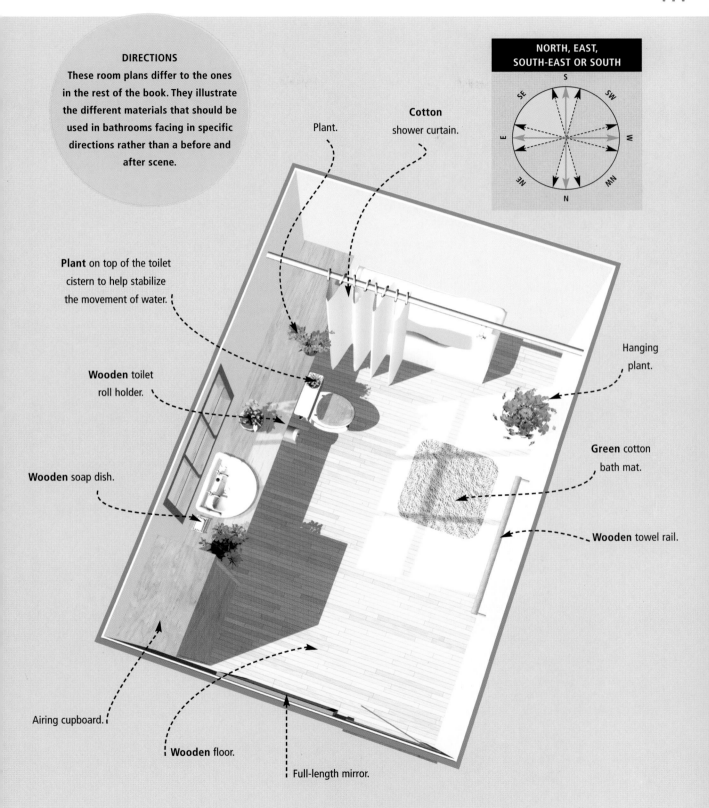

DIRECTIONS
These room plans differ to the ones in the rest of the book. They illustrate the different materials that should be used in bathrooms facing in specific directions rather than a before and after scene.

NORTH, EAST, SOUTH-EAST OR SOUTH

Plant.

Cotton shower curtain.

Plant on top of the toilet cistern to help stabilize the movement of water.

Hanging plant.

Wooden toilet roll holder.

Green cotton bath mat.

Wooden soap dish.

Wooden towel rail.

Airing cupboard.

Wooden floor.

Full-length mirror.

plants

Plants are the best way of ensuring that the chi energy of your bathroom does not stagnate. They bring in their own living energy, which keeps the room feeling fresh and alive.

In addition, they absorb moisture from the air, greatly improving the atmosphere of the room and reducing the risk of dampness. This is one of the key factors in keeping your bathroom healthy. Ideally, to be able to grow plants in your bathroom you need a window. But these days it is common now to site bathrooms in the centre of homes, particularly in apartments so you may be limited growing plants that will survive without natural daylight.

Keeping dry
A large, open bathroom will be easier to keep healthy and chi energy will flow freely. Combined with sunlight and plants such a bathroom will maintain helpful chi energy.

half-day project

❶ Plants for vitality

Any **plants that like humidity** will be ideal for your **bathroom,** as they will soak up the **steam** when you have a bath or shower.

Consider where you could put plants in your bathroom. If you need to **put up shelves,** measure the space available, purchase appropriate materials and fix them securely in the most appropriate position. Look at the information on pages 46–7 for **ideas on the best materials** to use, not only for shelves but also for **plant containers.**

Assess how much **light** the plants will receive and then purchase the appropriate plants for that environment. Re-pot

the plants into your **new containers** and place them in your bathroom. Look after your plants carefully and keep them **healthy**.

When you shower or have a bath the steam creates **condensation** on most bathroom surfaces. Over time this can lead to **mildew and rotting**; the chi energy from this is considered particularly **unhealthy**. To avoid this and the build up of old chi energy it is good practice to **keep the bathroom uncluttered,** aired and as dry as possible. The more plants you have the better the atmosphere will be.

 # windows

The need to keep the atmosphere in the bathroom fresh and clean is very important, therefore, the free circulation of chi energy through the window is essential. A bright sunny room will create a lively, dry atmosphere. The sunlight charges up the chi energy of the room, which helps stimulate a flow of energy through the room reducing the risk of stagnation.

Large windows
The bigger the window and the more light that can flow through it, the less likely it is for energy to become unhealthy.

For this reason it is not recommended that you have curtains in your bathroom. In general, wooden slatted blinds are ideal, especially if your bathroom is to the north, east, south-east or south of the centre of your home. In the five elements (see pages 138–43), wood absorbs the energy of the water. You can use wooden or metal blinds if your bathroom faces the other directions. Curtains are acceptable when you have the luxury of a very large bathroom.

Using screens
Enclosing the bath with screens when it is by a window makes it easier for you to relax for a long time in your bath. You should move the screens when you have finished.

half-day project

① Blinds for privacy

First **measure the size** of your bathroom window. It is helpful to **make a sketch** and note the essential measurements. **Take this with you** when you purchase your blinds.

Look at **different styles of wooden blinds**. The most common are horizontal slatted (**Venetian**) blinds. You will probably have to order these blinds to fit, although some manufacturers produce them in standard window sizes. These **can be adjusted** to allow light in without direct sunlight.

Wooden blinds come in either a natural wood finish or painted in different colours. Alternatively, you can use blinds made of **thin wooden or bamboo strips** that roll or fold up. (It is also possible to find **stiffened fabric vertical blinds**, which are useful if you want your bathroom to feel taller.)

Make sure the blinds are fitted in such a way that they **can be pulled up to expose the whole window**, if you so desire, allowing the **maximum amount of natural light** to enter. Also ensure that you can open the window and expose the bathroom to **plenty of fresh air**.

 colours

The decor in your bathroom needs to be approached differently to other rooms. The main objective is to harmonize the water chi energy with the ambient energy of the position the room has in your home.

Colourful extras
In addition to paint you can use plants, lighting and accessories to add colour. Here the candles create a softer, orange light. Wood harmonizes the fire energy of the candles with the water.

The following provides the ideal colours for each location of your bathroom:

NORTH
To soak up the abundance of water chi energy created by a bathroom in the north, you should use more tree chi energy in the form of green.

NORTH-EAST, CENTRE AND SOUTH-WEST
The soil, five element chi energy of the north-east has a destructive effect on water, which disturbs the atmosphere of the bathroom, leading to the creation of a potentially unhealthy chi energy. A strong presence of metal chi energy will help create greater harmony. To achieve this use the following colours: off-white, grey, pink and silver, which are associated with metal chi energy.

EAST AND SOUTH-EAST
The water chi energy is in harmony with the tree chi energy of the east and south-east so the colours green or blue would be suitable.

SOUTH
Water in the form of a bathroom to the south of the centre of your home has a destructive effect on the fire chi energy of the south. This could lead to a lack of passion, opportunities to make a name for yourself and social life. Tree chi energy will harmonize these energies and this would be helped by using the colour green.

WEST AND NORTH-WEST
The metal chi energy of the west and north-west is drained by the water chi energy of the bathroom. This could, in turn, have a draining effect on your ability to focus on your financial income. To boost the metal chi energy use the colours associated with it, which are off white, grey, pink and silver.

 two-day project

1 Decorating your bathroom
Use a compass (see page 145 or the method described on page 9) to **determine in which direction** your bathroom is located. Use the **information above** to help you decide on the **colour** for your bathroom. Try some **test patches** on the walls so you can see which feels best to you. Remember to use a paint that is **suitable for a bathroom**.

Prepare the walls for decoration. Scrape off any cracked or peeling paint. If there are any signs of damp you may need to let the plaster dry out and treat it before continuing. **Apply the paint** and see how your bathroom feels.

Hard, flat and shiny materials allow energy to move faster. As the bathroom is likely to be relatively small and, as it is also prone to stagnation due to dampness in the atmosphere, it is generally better to use hard, more yang surfaces.

If your bathroom is in the **northern, eastern, south-eastern or southern** parts of your home, wood will help to harmonize the chi energies. If your bathroom is in the **south-western, north-eastern, western or north-western** parts of your home, stone or metal will help harmonize the chi energies.

The floor will usually be the largest surface area and, therefore, have the greatest influence on the flow of chi energy through your bathroom; however, you can also apply the following feng shui principle to any other surface in your bathroom.

The direction of your bathroom within your home will make certain materials better suited to harmonizing the essentially water chi energy of the bathroom with the ambient energy of that part of your home.

MATERIALS

The following lists different types of materials and their effect on the flow of chi energy:

Wood will have a neutral effect in your bathroom and can help it feel warm and comfortable. Softwoods, such as pine, will be more yin and relaxing than hardwoods, such as mahogany, which is more yang and dynamic.

Marble has the effect of allowing energy to move much faster. This can create a more exciting environment, and also one that helps prevent stagnation.

Stone and ceramic tiles have similar properties to marble, but if they are uneven they will tend to scatter the energy more. This can be an advantage if you need to reduce the risk of energy stagnating through the whole room. This is particularly desirable if the bathroom does not have exposure to natural light.

Synthetic materials, including carpets, can create their own charge of static electricity, which may have a negative influence on the flow of energy through your bathroom. These need to be avoided.

Fabrics tend to slow the movement of energy and will make a room more relaxing, however they should be used in the form of things that you can take out of the bathroom to wash and dry. This could include a shower curtain, bath mat and towels.

---

half-day project

❶ Bathroom materials

Stand in the centre of your home and use a compass (see page 145 or the method described on page 9) to determine in which position your bathroom is located within your home.

Use the information above to decide what type of materials your bathroom would benefit from.

If you want to change your **bathroom floor**, measure up the space, make a plan of your floor area and look at the different types of flooring available. **Bring home different samples** and position them in your bathroom so you can get a better idea of which you would feel most comfortable with.

Flooring
Before deciding on flooring for the bathroom bring home samples and try them out to see if they create the right atmosphere.

conservatories

A conservatory has a unique atmosphere as it is both a part of your home and part of the garden. It is a very natural environment and, if you are adding a conservatory to your home, it is helpful to be aware of this throughout every stage of its design and specification. Wherever possible use natural materials and allow plenty of space for plants.

A calm retreat
The lush planting and natural materials used to create this conservatory will have a wonderful natural atmosphere in which you can relax and find peace.

Most conservatories will be designed to catch as much sunlight as possible and usually face a sunny direction. It is helpful if your conservatory catches the sunlight during most of the day as you will be able to use it for greater periods of time. Nevertheless, they can become very hot so it is helpful to site at least some part of the conservatory in the shade.

The materials you use will influence the atmosphere of the conservatory. If your conservatory faces east, south-east or south use wood wherever possible, whereas metal and stone would be better if it faces south-west or west.

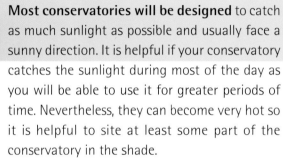

half-day project

❶ Seating arrangements
It is **advisable** to do this exercise **before** the design of a new conservatory is **finalized**, as it may bring to light **problems with the proposed plans**.

Draw up a floor plan of your conservatory or proposed conservatory, using a convenient scale such as 1m:4cm (1yd:2in). **Draw and cut out chairs** and other furniture to the same scale. It may help to cut out other items, such as plants, so that you can see how you will use the whole space. **Look at ways of positioning the seating** so that you are facing the most helpful directions (see page 79).

An inspiring experience
The clean lines and quiet planting give this conservatory an open, more lively atmosphere.

When you add a conservatory to your home you will change the shape of the floor plan of your home. The ideal-shaped floor plan is as square as possible so that each of the eight directions are well represented. In some floor plans the proportions are such that only a few of the eight directions are present.

This is typical of a narrow or L-shaped home. It is, therefore, helpful to add the conservatory in a way that balances out the shape of the floor plan. Try not to add the conservatory in a way that makes the situation worse.

Conservatory seating

Having a conservatory provides you with an opportunity to spend time in a more natural environment, especially if you live in a climate where the weather is not suitable for spending long periods of time outdoors.

Conservatories can be used for a range of functions including eating, working and socializing. The seating can be arranged so as to make the experience of being there as comfortable as possible, whatever the occasion. You may find that grouping the seats together and using plants around them to contain the chi energy creates a very relaxing atmosphere.

WHAT IS THE BEST POSITION FOR YOUR CONSERVATORY?

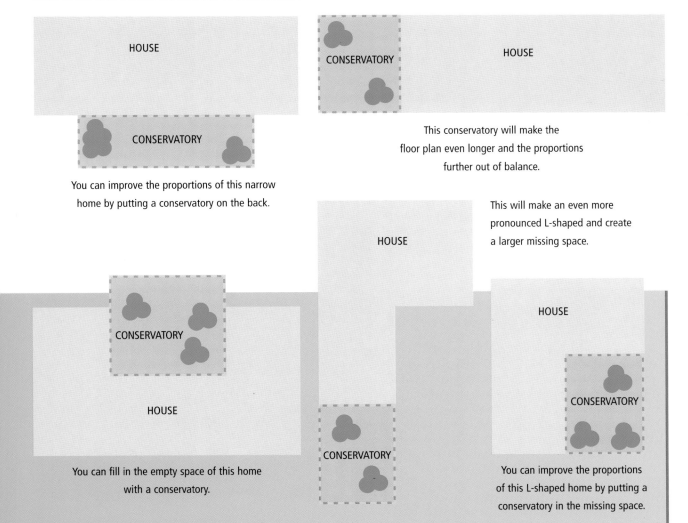

You can improve the proportions of this narrow home by putting a conservatory on the back.

This conservatory will make the floor plan even longer and the proportions further out of balance.

You can fill in the empty space of this home with a conservatory.

This will make an even more pronounced L-shaped and create a larger missing space.

You can improve the proportions of this L-shaped home by putting a conservatory in the missing space.

plants

A conservatory allows you to bring nature indoors so you can sit in the warm and enjoy the natural chi energy of plants.

Planting variety

Introduce a wide range of plants, which can be placed in a variety of situations. For example, an indoor rockery, water feature and large tropical plants will provide interesting and unique features.

SUITABLE PLANTS

When you are planning where the various components of your conservatory will go, you can either use the compass method or the principle of the four animals to determine the most harmonious situations.

To use the compass method see page 145, or use the method on page 9. Draw a simple plan of your conservatory and make a note of the different directions on the plan. Refer to the chart below and look at how you can best fit in a water feature, rockery and plants.

ITEM	HARMONIOUS DIRECTIONS
Water feature	East or south-east
Rockery	Centre, south-west, north-east, west, north-west or north
Tall plants	North-west, north or north-east

To use the four animal method (see page 136) you can assume that the rear of the conservatory where it joins your home relates to the tortoise and that the front is associated with the phoenix. You will then need to try and keep the front of your conservatory as open as possible while protecting the area behind any seats with large plants. Make sketches of different layouts before implementing them in your conservatory.

 half-day project

❶ Choosing plants and containers

Depending on the **position of your conservatory**, you will want to choose either harmonizing or calming planting. Decide where to put **key features** such as seating, **rockeries and water features** before deciding on planting and the **size and shape** of individual plants.

Utility rooms, garages or lofts can easily become home to all kinds of junk. Many people use them as a holding area for things that they cannot decide what to do with.

It makes sense to keep these possessions in such places because they are away from the areas of activity within the home. However, over time the amount of possessions you hoard can build up to a level which will have a negative effect on your whole home.

To see how this might effect you, find out which direction your utility room, garage, or loft is from the centre of your home and then check on pages 146–7 to see what aspects of your life the direction is associated with.

Clearing clutter

Clutter, even when in your garage, loft or utility room, can leave a negative atmosphere around the home. Investing in a storage unit can have multiple benefits to your life; not only will you be organizing your clutter into a tidy area that will make chores around the home easier, but you could also use the oportunity to throw or give away any items that are not needed anymore.

two-day project

① Cleaning the atmosphere

Take everything out of your garage, loft or if appropriate utility room. **Throw or give away** anything that you no longer need or want to keep. If you have not used something for many years and it does **not have any strong sentimental value** it may be the time to **let it go**. Take the opportunity to give the area a **thorough clean out** and **refresh** the energy.

Once you have taken out the objects you no longer need, separate the items for **long-term storage** from those that you will need access to. Try to **organize the space** so that it is neat and tidy. For example, put items for long-term storage into **boxes** and **label them clearly**. Stack the boxes so that it is easy to read the labels.

Do some research into **different types of storage systems**. Certain items need to be easily accessible. Shelves are useful as it is **easier to see** where everything is. However, you will need to design them so that they hold your containers **safely**.

back gardens

A garden allows you to have a change of environment, which will refresh and change your chi. If you have the space it would be helpful to create different areas with their own distinct atmospheres.

YIN PATH LAYOUT

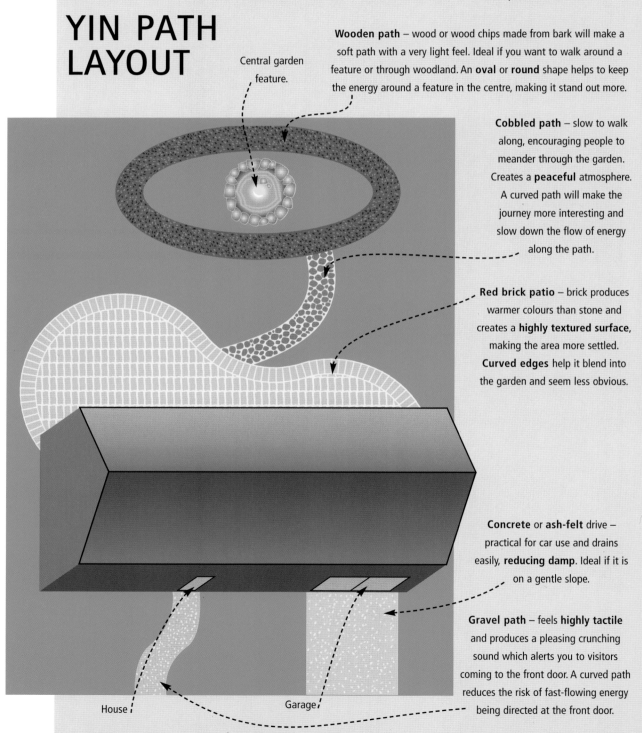

Central garden feature.

Wooden path – wood or wood chips made from bark will make a soft path with a very light feel. Ideal if you want to walk around a feature or through woodland. An **oval** or **round** shape helps to keep the energy around a feature in the centre, making it stand out more.

Cobbled path – slow to walk along, encouraging people to meander through the garden. Creates a **peaceful** atmosphere. A curved path will make the journey more interesting and slow down the flow of energy along the path.

Red brick patio – brick produces warmer colours than stone and creates a **highly textured surface**, making the area more settled. **Curved edges** help it blend into the garden and seem less obvious.

Concrete or **ash-felt** drive – practical for car use and drains easily, **reducing damp**. Ideal if it is on a gentle slope.

Gravel path – feels **highly tactile** and produces a pleasing crunching sound which alerts you to visitors coming to the front door. A curved path reduces the risk of fast-flowing energy being directed at the front door.

House

Garage

YANG PATH LAYOUT

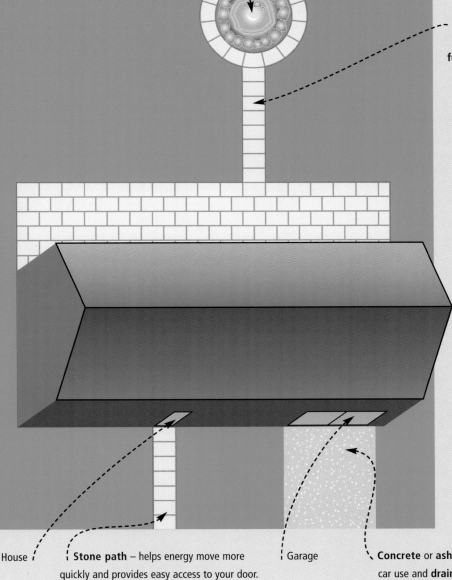

Central garden feature.

Circular stone path – strongly contains the energy around the feature and helps to make it stand out.

Straight stone path – creates a direct link, making your garden **functional** but less interesting. Adds clean lines and separates the path from nature, helping to make the path stand out. Using the same material throughout links the different parts of your garden together, but lacks creativity.

House

Stone path – helps energy move more quickly and provides easy access to your door. **Easy to keep clean**. Directs energy straight at the front door and not suitable near a busy road.

Garage

Concrete or **ash-felt** drive – practical for car use and **drains easily** reducing damp. Ideal if it is on a gentle slope.

installing a birdbath

A birdbath is a simple way of introducing a water feature in the garden. It needs no plumbing and no electricity. All you need to do is find the best place for it and put it in position.

Still water
A container of still water will add to the tranquility of a garden space.

Like all water features the birdbath would be best sited to the east and south-east. If this is not possible, keep a good distance between your home and the birdbath. You will need to make sure that the water in the birdbath is clean and renewed regularly.

The sight of birds in your garden can be very satisfying so position the birdbath in an area that is clearly visible from your windows.

FEATURES IN THE GARDEN

Statues Metal statues will concentrate and focus energy and are best in the south-western, central, north-eastern, western, north-western and northern parts of the garden.

Stone statues will settle the atmosphere and are harmonious in the southern, south-western, central, north-eastern, western and north-western parts of the garden.

Wood or wicker statues help to create a lighter atmosphere and are ideal to the north, east, south-east and south.

Water features These add a living energy to a space. It is most important that the water is fresh and unpolluted. Ideal directions for a water feature are east or south-east from your home. If you cannot position it in one of these directions keep the water well away from your home. Moving water in the form of a fountain or waterfall will generate livelier, active energy. Still water, such as a pond, has a calming relaxing effect. In the case of a pond it is important to introduce plenty of natural wildlife to avoid stagnation.

Stones Rockeries and statues create a solid secure atmosphere and can be used to good effect in the north-east, west, north-west, south-west and centre of your gardens.

Trees Tall trees, such as a silver birch, are best sited to the north and north-west. In these positions they will not cast a shadow over the garden and they will be in harmony with the natural energy of that part of the garden.

Paths The material the path is made of will define the flow of chi energy. For example, a path made of smooth, flat paving stones, encourages a faster flow of chi energy. A rough path made from gravel, loose stones or wood chips slows down the flow of chi energy, helping you to relax.

half-day project

❶ Siting a birdbath

Take a compass reading to see which part of the garden is to the east and south-east. Alternatively, **watch the sun rise** over the horizon to see which direction east is. As the sun rises in the sky it will be in the south-east.

Look to see if these parts of the garden are suitable for a **birdbath**. If not, you will need to find another location, but make sure it is **not too close to your home**.

Go and **look at different types of birdbaths** and find one that appeals to you.

Prepare the site by **making it level** and ensuring that the birdbath has a **firm foundation**.

Put the birdbath in its place and fill it with water.

Moving water
Flowing water will stay fresh and add vitality to a space.

paths

MATERIAL FOR PATHS

YIN

bark mulch

wood decking

railway sleepers

gravel

bricks

rough paving stones

smooth paving stones

YANG

Paths will effect the appearance of your garden as well as the feeling you will experience of when you walk through it. When planning the layout, you will need to decide how you would like to experience your garden. Think about which areas in which you would like to relax and move slowly and the parts which need to be more functional.

When you choose the material for a path you will need to think what it would be like to walk along each surface. Having a variety of surfaces will make your garden feel more interesting. In addition, a path made from a hard, flat surface, such as paving stones, will encourage energy to move much faster. If the path is straight the energy will be faster still.

Materials for stone paths

Grey cobblestones will create a solid, yang feel compared to yellow-coloured gravel. Cream stone will help create a lighter, yin atmosphere when compared to dark grey and blue slates.

Shapes of paths

A curved path encourages chi energy to circulate through the garden and, similarly, slows down the progress of chi energy.

two-day project

❶ Planning your path

Make a plan of your garden and mark the areas that you would like to use for different purposes. An interesting way of doing this is to describe how you would like to **feel** in each place. This will then be your guide for the **design of each part** of the garden.

Think how you would like to **link up the different parts** of your garden. Look at the list for different ideas for materials.

Using your drawing, **mark out the path** in your garden using sticks. Leave them for a few days so that you can make **adjustments** until you are happy with the plan.

Lay the paths and see how it feels to use them.

water features

Water has a special significance in feng shui as it is a vital ingredient for human life. About 70 per cent of a person's body weight is made up of water.

Water holds a great attraction for many people. Often holidays, picnics or sports involve going somewhere where there is water, whether it be oceans, rivers, lakes, canals, waterfalls or swimming pools.

Water that forms a part of your local landscape will have an effect on the chi energy of your home, and when the conditions are favourable it has the ability to increase vitality. In feng shui, metal energy represents money, while water energy represents the movement of money. To create an outdoor water feature with positive chi energy you need to consider the way the water flows, and the location of the water from the centre of your home.

The water should be clean, fresh and unpolluted. Water that becomes stagnant creates unhealthy, stale chi energy, which, if close enough to your home, can adversely effect the chi energy there. Dirty polluted water diminishes the water's ability to increase your vitality.

Moving water will create more yang chi energy than still water. For example, a waterfall will have an active, more yang influence than a pond. At the same time the downward movement of a water feature will have a more grounding effect, as opposed to a bubbling spring which will be more uplifting.

Fast-flowing water that moves in a straight line will have a more yang influence than slow-moving water that meanders through gentle curves. Ponds and bogs can have the most yin influence, but are also most likely to become

Yang influences

Various aspects of a garden pond will create a more yang influence on your garden and home, such as downward moving water in a waterfall.

two-day project

① Water features

Use the information above to decide on the **type of water feature** you want and where to put it. Check the **prospective site** in your garden. If you want to combine it with other features such as a **rockery** you will need to **plan the whole area**.

You will probably need a **water supply**, as the water will evaporate. Many water features use a **header tank** with a valve that turns off the water when it reaches the **appropriate level**. The tank, which is usually located below the ground, then **keeps the water feature topped up** with water.

Prepare the ground for your water feature and **install it** as recommended. **Finish with plants** and any other features. You will need to make sure that the water remains **fresh and clean**.

If you already have, or want to build, a water feature in a direction other than east or south-east, there are remedies to make the water harmonious within the energy of other directions. This is based on the five element theory explained on page 138–43. You will first need to work out the direction of the water feature from the centre of your home (see page 145).

South and north Place objects that represent tree chi energy between the water and your home. For example, you could grow tall plants, such as bamboo, in this position. Alternatively, place wooden garden furniture or plant trees between the water and your home.

South-west, north-east, west and north-west Add objects that represent metal chi energy between the water and your home. For example, metal garden furniture, plants in cast iron containers or you could construct a rockery between your home and the water.

stagnant. Here it is important that there is a wide variety of thriving wildlife to avoid stagnation.

Faster, yang moving water will tend to speed up the flow of chi energy in your home making it feel more fresh, clean, and alive. Slower, yin moving water will lead to a gentler, peaceful flow of chi energy.

Water that flows towards the main entrance of your home has a greater ability to bring chi energy indoors, while water flowing away from the entrance could diminish the chi energy inside your home. It could even lead to the feeling that money is flowing away from you.

The direction in which the water lies from the centre of your home will also have an influence, particularly if it is within the shadow of your home during the winter months. It is most beneficial to have water located to the east or south-east of the centre of your home where the water will help build up the tree chi energy of these directions.

Harmonizing water
The plants that are placed around your water feature will affect its harmonizing qualities.

statues & rockeries

Metal objects and stones will help contain and settle the energy in your garden. They can become points of focus and strong features. These materials are most harmonious to the south-west, west, north-west, north or north-east of your home especially if they are close to it. A wooden statue is harmonious in the north, east, south-east or south.

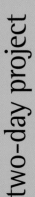

A rockery is often a lower feature than a statue and, therefore, creates a more stable feeling, whereas a statue will often command a greater presence and be a more striking feature. The ideal site for a rockery is to the north-east. However, you could also choose the south-west, west, north-west or north which would also be harmonious.

The way a statue influences the flow of chi energy is primarily determined by its shape and the material it is made of. In addition, many forms of statuary are symbolic and this can influence your own flow of chi energy. For example, a statue of a couple in a loving embrace will help encourage feelings of romance.

When planning a garden you can use statues to emphasize an area. For example, a statue in the middle of a circle will draw attention to that area. A statue can also complete a view, and one at the end of a path will define what the path leads to. You can also use a statue to create a surprise. For instance, you could partially hide one among plants, or a statue could suddenly come into view as you round a corner.

A balanced rockery
Mixing large and small stones combine yin and yang to make an interesting contrast.

two-day project

① Building a rockery
To build a rockery, **begin by establishing the site**. The ideal site for a rockery is to the north-east, but the south-west, west, north-west or north are also **harmonious**. Think about how you want the rockery to look. **Look in gardening books** or magazines for inspiration. Prepare the site and build your rockery.

Colour contrasts
You can create exciting colour combinations in the garden by surrounding a rockery with steel grey chipped slate and luscious green foliage.

Planting a rockery

Soft plants provide the ideal contrast to the hard rocks creating a harmony of
extremes. This more open and clean design creates a dynamic, yang space.

THE CHI ENERGY OF STATUES

To increase the romance in your life,
place a romantic, metal statue on a round
base in the western part of your garden.
The statue should have red in its colouring,
or you can surround it with red flowers,

**To strengthen the chi energy associated
with progressing your career,** try putting
a tall, wooden statue surrounded by green
plants in the eastern part of your home or
garden.

**To enhance the chi energy that can lead
to greater family harmony,** install a low
clay or plaster statue, with yellow-leaved
plants or flowers around it, in the south-
western part of your garden.

For greater peace and tranquillity, a
glass statue with a flowing shape would be
ideal in the northern part of your garden.
An ice statue would have a similar effect.

**To increase the fire chi energy
associated with fame,** public recognition
and passion, position a star-shaped or
pyramid statue in the southern part of your
garden. Purple flowers around the statue
will enhance this further.

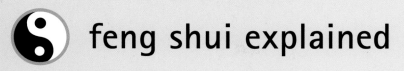 feng shui explained

history of feng shui

Feng shui, meaning wind and water, is the art of designing a home for the success of the occupants. The origins of feng shui are said to have begun about 4000 BC along the banks of the River Lo in northern China where ancient civilizations had built up.

The history and different styles of feng shui

A man named Fu Hsi had become well-known for building up the river banks to avoid the flooding that had been a regular occurrence. When Fu Hsi was later meditating on the banks of the River Lo he noticed a tortoise crawl out of the water. On its back he saw a pattern of water drops that formed the basis of the magic square. This became one of the fundamental principles of feng shui.

Different styles of feng shui

Feng shui has gone through many changes and different systems have developed. This is not surprising since the art of feng shui has spanned such a long time and has been used over such a large part of the world. To a beginner this can be a source of confusion, particularly if you have inadvertently studied more than one style, as at times they can appear contradictory. At various stages in the history of feng shui radical changes have taken place, such as changing the position of the trigrams producing the earlier heaven sequence and the later heaven sequence. The application of the basic principles of feng shui are not set in stone but have been developed in different ways by various people over thousands of years.

The styles popular in the west are the Japanese Compass, Eight House, Flying Star, Form and Three Gate systems. The Japanese Compass, Eight Houses and Flying Star methods all use a compass as the basis for deciding how the energy in each part of a building will influence its occupants. In these methods, the earth's magnetic field, the sun's solar energy, and the influence of the planets are all thought to have the greatest effect on the way energy flows through a building. The Form School does not use a compass but uses the surrounding landscape and the feng shui animals to orientate the different chi energies. The Three Gate system is a more recent adaptation where the entrance to a home or room is used to orientate the eight energies. The Flying Star, Eight House and Form School are often combined together and the practitioner will use different aspects of each to make a recommendation.

All the different schools of feng shui share the basic principles of how energy moves, yin and yang, the five elements and the eight trigrams. The difference is in how these principles are applied in real life. The Japanese Compass method is the style used in this book.

CHINESE CALENDAR

The ancient Chinese calendar was a solar calendar that had a ten day week made up of yin and yang pairs of the five elements. The calendar was orientated around the winter and summer solstice and the equinoxes. It was based on a close knowledge of the various phases of the sun, moon and other planets. The awareness of astronomy is impressive, considering that this calendar was developed several thousand years ago. The Chinese changed to a lunar calendar, which is still used to this day.

chi energy

Chi energy is a subtle electromagnetic energy that flows through everything. It flows around our bodies carrying our thoughts, ideas and emotions, so that every cell in our body is fed with blood-transporting oxygen and nutrients.

When your thoughts or feelings change your chi energy changes. This is why having negative emotions can, in the long-term, result in a health problem. If you have visual images in your home that make you feel happy or inspire you with positive thoughts, your chi energy will change, and it is this chi energy that will circulate around your body.

At the same time, whatever effects your chi energy will also change the way you think and feel. If you are feeling depressed, which suggests that your chi energy is too slow and dispersed, and you are then immersed in some opposite, extreme chi energy, such as, violent storm, it will be very difficult to maintain your depressed state. This is because your own chi energy will speed up in response. Similarly, when you feel angry, which is a sign that your chi energy is too intense and concentrated, you will let go much more quickly if you breathe slowly and deeply while stretching and letting your chi energy slow down and expand..

Your chi energy field does not stay inside your skin and will typically extend between 10cm (4in) and 1m (1yd) around your body. This makes it easily influenced by the chi energy around you. The atmosphere in a room can, therefore, help you think or feel differently. One of the great benefits of feng shui is that you can set up a room to help you think or feel the way you want to. More than this, you can also set up a room so that your thoughts and emotions are those that will most help you succeed in life.

Some of your own chi energy mixes and changes with the chi energy around you. As the chi energy around you also contains chi energy that carries

information from far away a wide range of information from the whole universe is constantly influencing you. This includes the weather, the phase of the moon, season and position of the sun. Through statistical information we now know that all these things effect our behaviour and emotions. Feng shui also takes account of the position of the planets and the movement of the earth in relation to the galaxy.

CHI ENERGY IN YOUR BODY

Your personal chi energy will move through your body along pathways. The largest of these is in front of your spine and it is where the seven chakras of energy are located. Chi energy then moves around your body along these runs, known as meridians, eventually feeding every cell. If you are intellectually stimulated, more of your chi energy will move up around your head, whereas, at times when you are physically active, there will be a greater concentration lower down your torso. When you are relaxed, outgoing and social it is easier for your chi energy to expand horizontally, while being independent or spiritual will make your chi energy field expand vertically. Drawing your chi energy field in, making it closer to you, will make it easier to be determined and avoid other people's influences. Projecting your chi energy field will make it easier to express yourself.

- crown
- mid-brain (pituitary)
- throat
- heart
- stomach (solar plexus)
- hara (navel)
- reproductive organs (coccyx)

yin & yang principles

The concept of yin and yang is a powerful tool which will enable you to make vital connections between yourself and your environment. If you are experiencing a problem, ascertain whether it is because you are too yin or yang. Once you know if you need to be more yin or yang to feel better or be more successful you can use this guide to change the chi energy in your body.

The lists below will help you to determine your current state. These detail common emotional and physical ailments associated with being too yin or too yang. Next, look at the ideas for making your home more yin or yang and try to introduce more elements to counteract your own state. So if you often feel depressed, which is a yin condition, you should try making your home more yang (see pages 134–5).

NEGATIVE

EMOTIONS

Too yin
Depressed
Insecure
Lonely
Worried
Pessimistic
Helpless
Feel a victim
Complaining

Too yang
Aggressive
Violent
Tense
Frustrated
Angry
Impatient
Ruthless
Less emotional

PHYSICAL ATTRIBUTES

Too yin
Lethargic
Feel cold
Frequent infectious illnesses
Diarrhoea
Swellings and excess liquid
Damp skin
Headaches at front of head

Too yang
Stiffness
Constipation
High blood pressure
Dry mouth
Dry skin
Headaches at back of head
Frequent minor accidents

POSITIVE

EMOTIONS

More yin
Relaxed
Calm
Imaginative
Creative
Artistic
Sensitive
Caring
Receptive

More yang
Enthusiastic
Alert
Quick
Focused
Precise
Accurate
Confident
Determined

PHYSICAL ATTRIBUTES

More yin
Supple
Relaxed
Loose
Flexible

More yang
Strength
Stamina
Endurance
Quick reactions

Everything is either more yin or more yang

Everything in our universe can be classified as more yin or yang than something else. Yin and yang are relative terms that are used to compare one thing with another. For example, resting is a more yin thing to do than working. At the same time resting is more yang than sleeping. Yin and yang can be applied to structural things such as a home, food, or a person's body. It can also describe non-physical states including emotions, images and processes.

Everything seeks a state of balance

Although everything is either more yin or yang, as a whole, they seek to find some kind of balance. Individually nothing is in perfect balance, or can be in perfect balance, as everything will always be either more yin or yang. Therefore, something that is more yin is able to reach a more balanced state with something that is more yang. Often we drift to one side of the middle, and more balanced, path. For a while we become more yin and then find we have to adapt and so make changes that make us more yang. It is a constant balancing act that helps us adapt and respond to the world around us.

Yin and yang attract each other

Anything that is more yin will automatically attract something that is more yang. The greater the difference, the greater the attraction. The principle is similar to the poles of a magnet: plus and minus attract each other. Therefore, as you become more yin you will find that you attract more yang things into your life and vice versa. For example, if you eat something more yang, such as a dry salty snack, you will begin to crave liquids, which are more yin.

Nothing is solely yin or yang

Everything has some yin and some yang in it, but there is always more of one or the other to start with. But rather than thinking of yin and yang in terms of black and white, it is more accurate to think of it in terms of different shades of grey as there is more or less of each element dominating. Because everything contains its opposite, it means that everything has two sides to it. For example, winning the lottery may enable you to buy everything you ever wanted, but it could also result in the loss of your family and real friends. At the opposite end of the spectrum, losing your job may cause worry and financial hardship, but it could also lead to a far better career in the long term. There is always something positive in a negative situation, just as there is something negative in a positive situation.

Everything changes

Everything is always moving from being more yang to yin or from being more yin to yang. For example, a person might be more yang – irritable, frustrated and pushy, but as time goes by he or she may become more yin – relaxed, peaceful and calm. The opposite is also true, someone who is more yin depressed, listless and quiet could be in the process of becoming more yang – active, dynamic and quick. It is more important to see where you are going than worrying about where you are in the present.

As we all strive for greater control in our lives, the concept of yin and yang can help us to see where we are out of balance, and help us understand how to fix it. Whatever happens to us has both yin and yang elements and this allows us to perceive positive benefits in painful experiences and pitfalls in rewarding ones. Because everything is always changing we have the opportunity to change ourselves and our experience of the world using the principles of yin and yang.

yin & yang **household items**

Just as the sun's movement through the sky alters our individual flow of chi energy, the sun will also influence the flow of chi energy throughout your home.

As the sun rises, the eastern and southern parts of your home will be vitalized by its energy. The sun's movement from morning to midday is more yang, so every day the eastern and southern parts of your home will be energized by a more yang chi energy. In the southern hemisphere this will be the eastern to northern parts.

After midday, as the sun descends, the western to northern parts of your home will be energized by more yin chi energy. In the southern hemisphere this will be the western to southern parts.

The sunny side of your home is better suited to activities that require you to be more yang and the shady side will help you with activities that require you to be more yin. If you think that you are already too yin or yang then spending more time in a place that has the opposite type of chi energy will help you to feel more balanced. For example, if you have difficulty in relaxing, you can assume that you are too yang. To feel more balanced you should spend more time in the yin side of your home and, by sleeping there, you will take in more peaceful yin chi energy.

If you feel low you are too yin. Being active in the sunny side of your home will help you take in more yang chi energy.

To become more yin try the following in your home:

- Add soft furnishings, such as comfortable chairs and sofas
- Fit full-length curtains made from a natural material, such as cotton or linen
- Use rugs or carpets made from natural fibres, such as pure wool
- Try large cushions including floor or beanbags
- Use tablecloths, cotton napkins and cloths on polished surfaces
- Avoid bright colours and use pale or pastel colours instead
- Use pale green, blue, cream, pink or black in colour schemes
- Indirect lighting that is reflected off the wall or ceiling will be softer and more relaxing
- Use dimmer switches so that you can soften the lighting
- Use candles instead of electric lighting, when appropriate
- Table lamps with fabric shades
- Keep all doors closed to slow down the flow of chi energy
- Play music that helps you relax, so as to fill a room or space with yin sound waves
- A slow-moving water feature, such as water trickling over a stone will be very relaxing
- Try sleeping with the top of your head pointing to the north, west, south-west or south-east
- Curved or wavy patterns and objects help disperse chi energy
- Mottled patterns, irregular lines, rag rolling, coarse brushing or plaster finishes are more yin
- Soften sharp edges or corners with plants or fabrics
- Grow plenty of plants with large, floppy leaves
- Arrange your furniture so that you break up any straight lines
- Slow down energy in corridors, or where doors are in line, with bushy plants

To become more yang try the following in your home:

- Add metal objects, especially if they are shiny
- Use polished surfaces, such as a wooden table or floor
- Mirrors reflect chi back into a room so it moves faster
- Choose wooden blinds instead of curtains

- Wooden, tiled or stone floors create a harder chi energy that can flow faster
- Reduce clutter to avoid chi energy stagnating
- Open spaces help chi energy to flow freely
- Use bright colours such as red, orange and yellow
- White walls and ceilings will reflect all the available chi energy back into the room
- Rhythmic music generates more yang, active sound waves
- Grow plants with pointed or spiky leaves
- Use bright lights such as halogen lights or spotlights
- Spotlight features in a room to add more energy to a space
- Try a formal, more structured layout of furniture
- Minimalist spaces allow chi energy to move more quickly, helping you to be active
- Large blocks of a single colour create a more yang space
- Sleep with the top of your head pointing east, south, north-west or north-east
- Add a fast-moving water feature, such as a fountain or waterfall
- Keep windows open and uncovered to allow more chi energy to both enter and leave a room
- Colourful flowers (red, purple or yellow) add yang chi energy
- Real fires will add more yang fiery chi energy

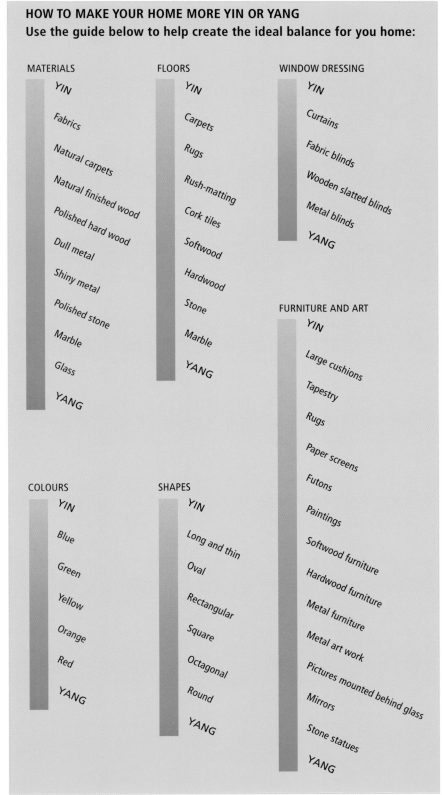

HOW TO MAKE YOUR HOME MORE YIN OR YANG
Use the guide below to help create the ideal balance for you home:

MATERIALS
YIN
Fabrics
Natural carpets
Natural finished wood
Polished hard wood
Dull metal
Shiny metal
Polished stone
Marble
Glass
YANG

FLOORS
YIN
Carpets
Rugs
Rush-matting
Cork tiles
Softwood
Hardwood
Stone
Marble
YANG

WINDOW DRESSING
YIN
Curtains
Fabric blinds
Wooden slatted blinds
Metal blinds
YANG

COLOURS
YIN
Blue
Green
Yellow
Orange
Red
YANG

SHAPES
YIN
Long and thin
Oval
Rectangular
Square
Octagonal
Round
YANG

FURNITURE AND ART
YIN
Large cushions
Tapestry
Rugs
Paper screens
Futons
Paintings
Softwood furniture
Hardwood furniture
Metal furniture
Metal art work
Pictures mounted behind glass
Mirrors
Stone statues
YANG

the feng shui **animals**

The animals are used to help understand the flow of chi energy around us. The idea is that each person carries a pattern of energy in their chi energy field that can be represented by five animals.

Two of them, the dragon and the phoenix, are mythical, but the others are real animals: the tiger, the tortoise and the snake. The energies themselves have similar characteristics to those of the east, south, west and north which are used in the compass. However, in this context, they are not fixed by any direction and can rotate according to the position of the person or the layout of the room. It is only when you are facing south or have a south-facing room that the energies converge.

To align the animals it is easiest to think in terms of the tortoise and the phoenix. The tortoise, with its hard shell, represents the back of something. It is often associated with a part of the home or garden that can provide protection, such as a solid wall, hill, mountain or trees. The phoenix is a legendary bird ready to fly off ahead of you and represents your front. In your home it would be an area into which chi energy can expand – an entrance, window or large vista.

You can imagine them in the form of a big armchair. The back of the chair represents the tortoise and the open front the phoenix. The left armrest takes the form of the dragon, the right the tiger and the seat itself the snake.

This method is very useful when deciding where to sit in a room. Look at your options so as to find the tortoise. This will usually be a solid wall or a heavy piece of furniture. Next look for the phoenix, which could be a large window, the door to the room or a fireplace.

Try to sit so that you have both the protecting energy of the tortoise to your rear and one of the features of the phoenix in front of you. The sides can then be partially open. For example, a light or candle to your left would be supported by the eastern energy of the dragon and a table to your left would represent the energy of the tiger.

This approach is particularly useful in restaurants or meetings where you can make a quick analysis of your options and then choose the one that helps you best align with the animals. For example, choose a seat in a restaurant where you have your back to the wall and can see as much of the restaurant as possible. This will help you feel more secure and settled.

CHARACTERISTICS OF THE ANIMALS				
animal	direction	element	season	time
dragon	East	tree	spring	morning
phoenix	South	fire	summer	midday
tiger	West	metal	autumn	afternoon
tortoise	North	water	winter	night
snake	Centre	soil	all	all

Each animal has a mythical personality that can enhance your understanding of the energies around you.

snake

Situated in the centre, the snake's role is to help co-ordinate the other animals. Alert and focused it takes in information from the other creatures and provides direction.

tortoise

The strength of the tortoise's shell makes this animal representative of security and protection. It is the energy that provides long-term stability and is also associated with longevity.

tiger

The tiger's aggression and strength represents a more defensive energy that is concerned with our basic material needs. It has the power to defend and attack when our well-being is threatened. This energy is more focused on keeping the things we have.

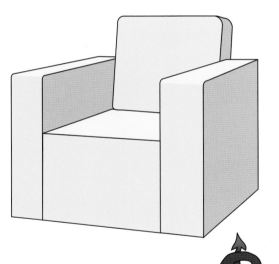

phoenix

The phoenix flies far ahead looking for our sense of purpose and life's vision. It is a quick and excitable energy that provides the emotional desire to do things. This bright and colourful bird is highly visible and projects our energy into our surroundings.

dragon

This far-sighted creature helps us to create our goals in life. It represents the future and can provide us with the ambition and desire to move forward. It is a decisive energy that provides a sense of urgency and enthusiasm.

the **five elements**

The five elements – tree, fire, soil, metal, water – break chi energy down into five different types. These are related to the time of the day and the season. Imagine the atmosphere at certain times of year and day to get a feel for each element. The five elements are unique in the way they relate to each other.

Each element will nourish and feed the next in a clockwise direction. As it does this it looses some of its own chi energy. However, this is replenished by its own preceding chi energy.

If one of the five element chi energies becomes deficient, the preceding chi energy will jump across and have a destructive influence on the following element. So if tree chi energy is deficient, water will have a destructive influence on fire chi energy. This series of relationships is often assessed to see whether there are conflicts of energies within your home that are causing problems in your life.

Become familiar with each of the five elements so you can recognize them in their different forms in your home. Using the box opposite, look around each room in your home and pick colours, materials or features that represent each of the elements. For example, you might have wooden furniture, electric light, yellow

---

THE FIVE DIRECTIONS
EACH ELEMENT RELATES TO THE OTHER FOUR
– IN A CLOCKWISE DIRECTION

1 The preceding element supports it and enhances the chi energy.

2 The following element drains and calms the chi energy.

3 The element before the preceding element has a destructive influence on the chi energy.

4 The element after the following element is destroyed by this chi energy.

The processes of one and two are considered to be harmonious whereas the processes of three and four are turbulent.

walls, a stone floor, and a water feature representing tree, fire, soil, metal and water respectively.

• The elements define how chi energy moves through your home. For example, a tall plant will increase the upward flow of chi energy. This would be useful under a heavy beam where the energy one can feel seems oppressive.

• One element will be dominant in each part of your home according to its direction. This matches the movement of the sun where it rises (upwards) in the east, fully radiates in the south (outwards), descends in the south-west (downwards), diminishes in the west (inwards) and is unseen in the north (flowing).

• Each element has a colour(s) that will bring more of the associated element into your room.

• Every shape or pattern represents an element. These can be represented by patterns on fabrics and wallpaper, the shape of furniture and artworks. To increase or reduce the impact of an element, take a look at your home to see if there is anything you need to change.

• Each element is associated with particular materials and by using these materials you will bring more of that element into the room.

• The five element features are a powerful way to change the energy of a room without redecorating.

CHARACTERISTICS OF THE ANIMALS

	tree	fire	soil	metal	water
element					
movement of chi energy	Upwards	Outwards	Downwards	Inwards	Flowing
direction	East	South	Centre & South-west	West	North
colour	Green	Red & purple	Yellow & brown	White, pink & grey	Black
shape	Tall & rectangular	Serrated, spikes & triangular	Low, flat, & rectangular	Round, arched & oval	Irregular, wavy and curved
material	Wood, bamboo, paper	Plastic (but kept to a minimum in feng shui)	Clay, ceramic, cotton wool, soft stone, bricks	Metals, hard stone	Glass
powerful features	Tall plants	Lights, candles, fireplace	Charcoal in clay containers	Metal objects & mechanical clocks	Water features

YOUR OWN ENERGY

Each of the five elements has a range of emotions that are connected with it. If you feel particularly affected by one of the emotions below check which of the five elements it relates to. This would indicate that there is too much of that particular element around you or that it is part of a destructive relationship. To help reduce this energy, strengthen the chi energy of the following element in the cycle. To harmonize it with the other chi energies, as well as avoid a destructive relationship, strengthen the preceding element. So if you feel depressed you would enhance your surroundings with more soil and water chi energy.

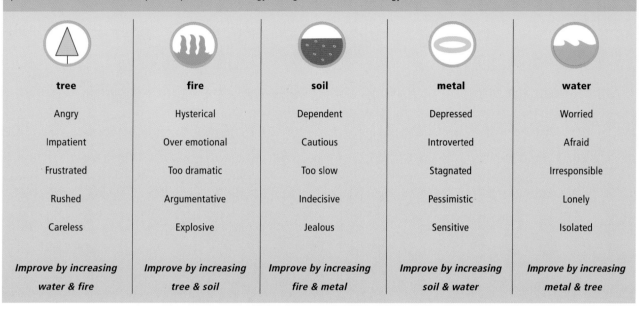

tree	fire	soil	metal	water
Angry	Hysterical	Dependent	Depressed	Worried
Impatient	Over emotional	Cautious	Introverted	Afraid
Frustrated	Too dramatic	Too slow	Stagnated	Irresponsible
Rushed	Argumentative	Indecisive	Pessimistic	Lonely
Careless	Explosive	Jealous	Sensitive	Isolated
Improve by increasing water & fire	*Improve by increasing tree & soil*	*Improve by increasing fire & metal*	*Improve by increasing soil & water*	*Improve by increasing metal & tree*

Once you have taken a good look at your life and home and have decided which of the five elements you want more of in your home, look through the list below for options on how you can achieve this. For example, you can add flowers, art, sculptures, water features and plants to introduce more of any element into a room.

Using the five elements

Use the charts on this page and pages 138–9 to decide what element you need more of in your home. If you are experiencing particularly angry and frustrated emotions it may help to add a water feature either indoors or out.

There are two instances in which you can use the five elements for problem solving. The first is to identify something you would like to change about yourself and the second is to diagnose a problem with the chi energy in your home.

Another, simpler approach is to go around each room and see if you can identify at least one item from each of the five elements in each room. Ideally, there would be some kind of balance of each element. The colours associated with the five elements are different to those of the nine ki and eight directions used in this book. Take a look at the chart below and refer to pages 138–9 for ideas about how to add more of an element.

ASSOCIATIONS WITH THE FIVE ELEMENTS				
tree	**fire**	**soil**	**metal**	**water**
Wooden objects or surfaces, such as wooden flooring, counter tops or furniture	Candles or a real fire when lit	Clay, soft stone or other soft materials from the earth, such as pottery, terracotta tiles or limestone	Metal surfaces including stainless steel, iron, brass, copper or aluminium	Water features, although these should be to the east or south-east of a room
The colour green	Bright lights when lit		The colours white, pink, grey or silver	
Tall shapes, such as a coat stand	Sunlight	The colours yellow, brown or beige	Round, spherical or dome-shaped patterns or objects	The colour glossy black or a translucent glossy cream
Plants, especially tall plants	The colour bright red or purple	Low, spreading plants in clay container.	Plants with round leaves	Mirrors or glass-fronted pictures
Vertical lines, for example a striped wallpaper	Pointed, star-shaped, triangular, pyramid shaped or zigzag patterns or objects	Horizontal shapes or lines	Hard stones such as slate, granite or marble	Glass table tops
Uplights	Plants with pointed leaves	Low, wide furniture, such as a chest, coffee table or futon base	Metal furniture, especially if it is round	Wavy lines, mottled patterns, curved furniture or an irregular layout
		Fabrics, such as rugs, carpets, curtains or soft furnishings		Plants that grow along a structure such as vines or ivy

the **five elements** of your home

Chi energy is most likely to become disrupted in your home when water or fire is placed in an area where there is a potentially disruptive relationship with the balancing energy.

For example, a bathroom in the southern part of your home will mix water and fire together, which in the absence of tree energy will be destructive.

Use wood to balance fire and water

Wooden blinds or shutters, wood panelling or a wooden screen are all supported with other wood accessories to balance the opposing forces of fire and water chi energy.

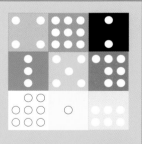

FU HSI'S DISCOVERY

This pattern of numbers, know as the Magic Square, forms the basis of Nine Ki astrology and Feng Shui. It was discovered thousands of years ago by the Chinese Emperor Fu Hsi, legendary originator of China's great philosophical text the I Ching, or Book of Changes.

Bathrooms, toilets and utility rooms

Any kind of household equipment that uses water, such as a washing machine, sink, bath or lavatory, will mix water chi energy with the chi energy of the part of your home it is located in. These can be harmonized by using the five element theory (see Glossary, page 154). The principle is to add more of the chi energy in between the two potentially destructive elements. For example, fire and water is made harmonious by tree energy.

NORTH

Additional water in a direction that is already associated with water chi energy risks an excess of water chi energy, which may make you feel anxious, lonely or isolated. This will need to be balanced by more tree chi energy, in the form of plants, wooden surfaces and the colour green.

NORTH-EAST, SOUTH-WEST OR CENTRE

The soil chi energy can have a destructive influence on water chi energy causing a loss of vitality, poor health and a reduced sex drive. Harmonize the water and soil chi energies with more metal chi energy. This can be achieved with more metal surfaces, round shapes, tiles and the colours silver or grey.

EAST AND SOUTH-EAST

Water chi energy supports tree chi energy so this is compatible. However, it is good practice to put more tree chi energy here in the form of plants, to reduce the risk of tree chi energy draining away.

SOUTH

The water energy will potentially destroy the fire chi energy of the south making it harder to be sociable, passionate or expressive, unless there is sufficient tree chi energy. Add plenty of plants, wooden surfaces or objects and the colour green.

WEST AND NORTH-WEST

The water chi energy can have a draining influence on the metal chi energy of this direction, risking a lack of financial awareness, pleasure or romance. To reduce this risk, reinforce the metal chi energy with more metal surfaces, round shapes, tiles and the colours silver or grey.

Kitchens, fireplaces and central heating unit

Similarly, the same five element principles can be applied to any form of fire. This would apply to a stove, gas hob, oven, fireplace, gas heater or candles.

NORTH

The water energy of the north will have a destructive influence on the fire, unless there is sufficient tree chi energy, risking reduced passion, expressiveness and ability to make new friends. Plants, wooden surfaces and the colour green will restore the balance.

NORTH-EAST, SOUTH-WEST OR CENTRE

The fire chi energy will support the soil chi energy of these directions making this a harmonious relationship.

EAST AND SOUTH-EAST

Fire chi energy will be supported by the tree chi energy of these directions. To further strengthen tree chi energy you can bring in more plants, wooden surfaces and the colour green.

SOUTH

This can create an excess of fire chi energy in one place, risking greater hysteria, being over emotional or argumentative. Reduce this with more soil chi energy using clay, terracotta or the colours yellow, beige or brown.

WEST AND NORTH-WEST

Fire chi energy can have a destructive influence on the metal chi energy of these directions, making it harder to feel content, romantic, playful, enjoy the pleasures of life or think of ways to make money. To remedy this, place artist's charcoal in a clay container close to the source of fire. Best colours here would be yellow, black or brown.

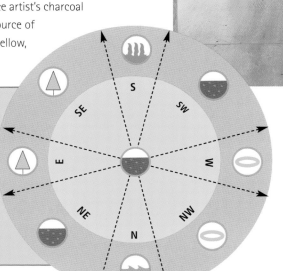

Each direction has its own five element chi energy. These are: **N** Water • **NE** Soil • **E** Tree • **SE** Tree • **S** Fire • **SW** Soil • **W** Metal • **NW** Metal • **Centre** Soil

Balancing fire and tree energies
The dominant stove is a powerful fire element that is supported by tree energy in the form of wooden floors, a basket of logs and a calming brown sofa.

using a **compass** & **house plans**

Items required

• **Compass** • **tape measure** • **360° protractor** • **ruler** • **pencil** • **paper**

The compass needs to have an outer dial that can be rotated to take bearings, and a means of aligning the body of your compass with your home. These are available in shops that specialize in camping and hiking equipment. A protractor is a round Perspex disk with 360 degrees marked on it, commonly available from stationary retailers.

MAKING A FLOOR PLAN OF YOUR HOME

'Your home' refers to the space you own, rent, or occupy. In the case of an apartment concentrate solely on the parts that are yours.

1. Using a long retractable steel measure, note the length and width of each floor of your home, then of each room, and of staircases and corridors.

2. Convert the measurements to a convenient scale, for example 1m = 1cm. So if your room measures 5.2 x 3.5m, the rectangle on the plan would have to measure 5.2 x 3.5cm.

3. Transfer the measurements to the plan in the appropriate positions. Add to the plan all windows, doors and fitted store cupboards, wardrobes and kitchen units. Indicate on the plan the way the doors open into the rooms.

4. Mark on the plan all details relevant in Feng Shui terms. Mark the fixed features in one colour, the movable ones in another, and the problem features in a third colour.

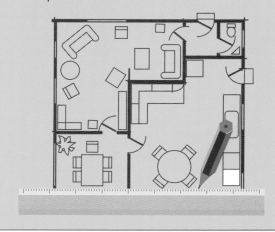

Finding the eight directions of your home

Find a part of your home where you can obtain a consistent compass reading by walking around your home keeping the body of your compass pointing in the same direction. Things made of iron or steel or electrical appliances will alter the magnetic field. Steel beams, pipes or water tanks, can be concealed in a building and may distort your compass readings. Follow the steps below to make an accurate compass reading and find the eight directions of your home:

1. Lay the drawing of the floor plan so that it is in line with your home in the area where you are sure to obtain a consistent compass reading.

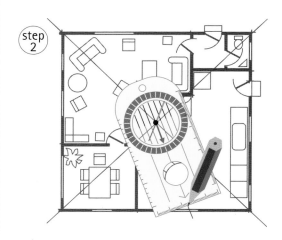

2. Now place your compass on the plan, so that the centre of your compass is over the centre of the drawing of your home (see illustration on page 144).

3. With a pencil make a mark on your drawing in the direction the needle points. Draw a line from the centre of your floor plan through the mark. This line will be pointing towards magnetic north.

4. Photocopy the eight directions in the box on the right on to a transparency and put over the floor plan of your home so that the centre of your transparency is over the centre of your floor plan. Turn the transparency until the line pointing north on the transparency lines up with the line pointing north on your floor plan (see illustration below).

5. To draw the eight directions on to your floor plan, mark the ends of the lines from the transparency on to the floor plan. Remove the transparency and draw lines through your marks and the centre of your floor plan. For greater clarity, draw these lines with a coloured pencil.

Once you lay the transparency over your floor plan you will be able to use it to gain useful information about your home. The following provides simple examples:

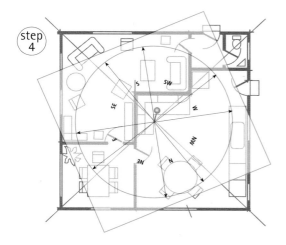

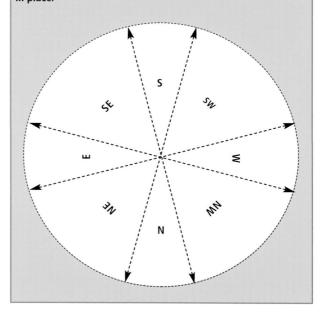

FENG SHUI COMPASS

Photocopy this page onto a sheet of transparency (this is commonly available from photocopy shops). Place the sheet over your plan with the centre of the circle over the centre of your home and turn it so that the north arrow corresponds with north on your plan. You may find it easier to push a pin through the centre of the transparency and plan to keep them in place.

• Look at your floor plan through the transparency and see which of the eight directions covers the greatest area and which the least. The direction that covers the least could be deficient in your home. For example, if there is little of the east on your floor plan you could find it harder to feel ambitious, be enthusiastic and start new projects. If this is the case, you could install a water feature, add some plants, use the colour green and more wood in this part of your home, in order to increase the deficient eastern energy. See the ideas on the transparency.

• Check in which direction your bathroom, lavatories, utility rooms, sinks, stove, heating unit and fireplace are located. Use the information on pages 142–3 to implement remedies.

the **properties** of each **direction**

There are eight different types of chi energy, each being connected with one of the eight directions in your home. Each direction is associated with a time of day, a season, one of the five elements and a trigram.

The trigrams are a series of three parallel lines, which are either solid or broken. The solid lines are yang and the broken lines yin. The trigrams are linked to a family member and those that share one of the five elements have their own unique symbol from nature. These all combine to give each energy a particular character, which can each be helpful for certain aspects of your life. The list below and to the right provides the basic information for each direction. Some of the colours in this nine ki system (see pages 148–9) are different to the ones used in the five elements.

CHI ENERGY OF EACH DIRECTION

EAST

Helpful for being enthusiastic, confident, assertive and, conversely, for feeling frustrated and angry. Increases the desire to start new projects, be alert, focus on details, get things right, analyze, be precise and concentrate. The symbol of thunder gives this energy a loud, forceful edge, which is helpful for going out and making things happen.

SOUTH-EAST

Helpful for being persistent, sensitive and feeling positive, but can make you feel irritable and impatient. Increases the desire to be creative, imaginative, generate new ideas, seek harmony, communicate and spread ideas. The symbol of wind makes it ideal for spreading ideas in a similar way to how the wind spreads seeds.

SOUTH

Good for being passionate, excited, generous, flamboyant and dramatic but, at the same time, proud, hysterical and self-centred. Increases the desire to be expressive, sociable, spontaneous, outgoing, get noticed, lead fashions and be quick minded. This fiery chi energy is bright, colourful and radiates energy.

SOUTH-WEST

Good for being caring, patient and sympathetic, and conversely, dependent and jealous. Increases the desire to be practical, down to earth, consolidate, add quality, form long-term relationships and be secure. The late summer represents the time of year when fruit and vegetables have stopped growing and are ripening. It is, therefore, the ideal energy for improving the quality of whatever you do.

WEST

Good for being romantic, content and playful, and conversely, being depressed and pessimistic. Increases the desire to enjoy the pleasures of life, be wealthy, form new relationships, be stylish and complete projects.

NORTH-WEST

Helpful for being in charge, dignified, responsible but, at the same time, authoritarian and arrogant. The desire to feel in control, organize, plan ahead, find and be a mentor, be respected and have integrity.

NORTH

Helpful for being sexual, spiritual and independent, and conversely, isolated and aloof. Increases the desire to be flexible, find peace, study, develop oneself, improve health, be objective and be different.

NORTH-EAST

Helpful for being motivated, driven and outgoing but, conversely, greedy and shrewd. Increases the desire to seize opportunities, win, compete, learn, be decisive, clear-minded and adventurous.

CENTRE

This energy links all the eight directions. It does not have a specific trigram, time or season, but can be said to represent them all. As such it is an energy that can help you become the centre of attention and attract people to you. It is the most powerful of all the chi energies and is, therefore, treated with respect.

ASSOCIATIONS OF EACH DIRECTION

EAST
Trigram **Yin / Yin / Yang**
Five Element **Tree**
Symbol **Thunder**
Family Member **Eldest son**
Nine ki number **3**

Colour **A bright green, similar to a new leaf**
Time **Morning**
Season **Spring**

SOUTH-WEST
Trigram **Yin / Yin / Yin**
Five Element **Soil**
Symbol **Earth**
Family Member **Mother**
Nine ki number **2**

Colour **Matt-black or brown, similar to charcoal or rich soil**
Time **Afternoon**
Season **Summer changing to autumn**

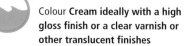
NORTH
Trigram **Yin / Yang / Yin**
Five Element **Water**
Symbol **Water**
Family Member **Middle son**
Nine ki number **1**

Colour **Cream ideally with a high gloss finish or a clear varnish or other translucent finishes**
Time **Night**
Season **Midwinter**

SOUTH-EAST
Trigram **Yang / Yang / Yin**
Five Element **Tree**
Symbol **Wind**
Family Member **Eldest daughter**
Nine ki number **4**
Colour **A dark green like that of a mature leaf and a sky-blue**
Time **Mid-morning**
Season **Spring changing to summer**

WEST
Trigram **Yin / Yang / Yang**
Five Element **Metal**
Symbol **Lake**
Family **Youngest daughter**
Nine ki number **7**
Colour **This is the colour of the sunset, including a rusty red, maroon and pink**
Time **Early evening**
Season **Autumn**

NORTH-EAST
Trigram **Yang / Yin / Yin**
Five Element **Soil**
Symbol **Mountain**
Family Member **Youngest son**
Nine ki number **8**
Colour **A brilliant white rather like a snow peaked mountain**
Time **Early morning**
Season **Winter changing to spring**

SOUTH
Trigram **Yang / Yin / Yang**
Five Element **Fire**
Symbol **Fire**
Family Member **Middle daughter**
Nine ki number **9**
Colour **A fiery, bright reddish purple**
Time **Midday**
Season **Midsummer**

NORTH-WEST
Trigram **Yang / Yang / Yang**
Five Element **Metal**
Symbol **Heaven**
Family Member **Father**
Nine ki number **6**
Colour **Silver grey or off white. This should represent the colour of metal**
Time **Late evening**
Season **Autumn changing to winter**

CENTRE
Trigram **None**
Five Element **Soil**
Symbol **None**
Family Member **None**
Nine ki number **5**
Colour **Yellow, or orange**
Time **None**
Season **None**

nine ki astrology

Everything in the universe has both time and space. Neither can exist without the other. Being in the right place at the right time has launched many people's successful careers.

It is, therefore, important not only to look at the feng shui of the space that you live or work in, but also the feng shui astrology of when you make changes to your life. There are two types of astrology commonly used in feng shui, the one used here is the nine ki system and the other is the four pillars. The principles for the nine ki system are essentially the same as for this style of feng shui.

Your nine ki number

In this section you will learn how to work out your own nine ki year number. Use this to provide more information about your relationships and how to work out what phase you are in each year. This will help you to identify when it is the best time to do something. Sometimes you may find that although you are keen to change something about yourself or your life it just does not happen. The reason may be the nine ki phase you are in. If this is the case, it will often be easier to relax and make a concerted effort when you are in a better phase. The idea is to achieve more with less effort. If you can have the forces of nature working for you rather than against you everything becomes easier.

At the time you were born and you became separate from your mother's chi energy you developed your own pattern of personal chi energy. This chi energy stays with you for life and influences the way you feel during each subsequent year. Using the nine ki system, it is possible to predict the way you will feel in the coming years and to use this information to help you achieve your goals in life at a time when you are most likely to succeed.

To calculate your own nine ki year number write down the year you were born. Add the last two digits together. If the result is another two digit number (that is, 11 to 18) add the two digits again. You will now have a number between one and nine. Subtract this number from ten if you were born during 1900 to 1999, or nine if you were born from 2000.

examples

Born in **1961**   6+1=7   10-7=3   **Nine ki number three**
Born in **1989**   8+9=17   1+7=8   10-8=2   **Nine ki number two**
Born in **2001**   0+1=1   9-1=8   **Nine ki number eight**

The beginning of the nine ki year is on the third, fourth or fifth of February, so if you were born during January or the first three days of February you will need to base

Nine ki numbers

This table lists the nine ki numbers, their elements and associated colours. The top colour is your supporting colour, the middle your strengthening colour and the lowest your calming colour.

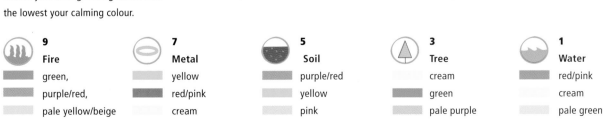

8
Fire
purple/red
white
pink

6
Metal
yellow
silver/grey
cream

4
Tree
cream
blue/green
pale purple

2
Soil
purple/red
black
pink

9
Fire
green,
purple/red,
pale yellow/beige

7
Metal
yellow
red/pink
cream

5
Soil
purple/red
yellow
pink

3
Tree
cream
green
pale purple

1
Water
red/pink
cream
pale green

your calculations on the previous year. For example, if you were born on the first of February 1971 you would use the previous year 1970 and your nine ki year number would be three. If you are born on the third, fourth or fifth of February you will need to consult the nine ki chart below.

It is also common to reverse the number for women so that while the ambient chi energy descends by one each year, females energy increases by one. In the system used in this book, it is assumed that the ambient energy when you where born will influence males and females similarly as in most forms of astrology.

HOW TO USE THE TABLE:

Find the year you are interested in and look at the date and time the year changed. If you were born after the date and time your nine ki year number is shown at the top of the column. If you were born before the date and time your nine ki number will be the same as the previous year which is at the top of the column to the left.

Nine Ki Number	9	8	7	6	5	4	3	2	1
Symbol	fire	mountain	lake	heaven		wind	thunder	earth	water
Element	fire	soil	metal	metal	soil	tree	tree	soil	water
Year	1910	1911	1912	1913	1914	1915	1916	1917	1918
Beginning date	4 Feb	5 Feb	5 Feb	4 Feb	4 Feb	5 Feb	5 Feb	4 Feb	4 Feb
Time (GMT)	23:41	05:33	11:11	17:01	22:53	04:34	10:31	16:18	22:06
	1919	1920	1921	1922	1923	1924	1925	1926	1927
	5 Feb	5 Feb	5 Feb	4 Feb	5 Feb	5 Feb	4 Feb	4 Feb	5 Feb
	04:00	09:43	15.34	21:28	03:13	09:06	14:58	20:49	02:46
	1928	1929	1930	1931	1932	1933	1934	1935	1936
	5 Feb	4 Feb	4 Feb	5 Feb	5 Feb	4 Feb	4 Feb	5 Feb	5 Feb
	08:31	14:19	20:11	01:53	07:42	13:28	19:13	01:03	06:47
	1937	1938	1939	1940	1941	1942	1943	1944	1945
	4 Feb	4 Feb	5 Feb	5 Feb	4 Feb	4 Feb	4 Feb	5 Feb	5 Feb
	12.36	18:32	00:20	06:15	12:07	17:57	23:51	05:39	11:26
	1946	1947	1948	1949	1950	1951	1952	1953	1954
	4 Feb	4 Feb	5 Feb	4 Feb	4 Feb	4 Feb	5 Feb	4 Feb	4 Feb
	17:18	23:03	04:50	10:40	16:29	22:29	04:07	09:52	15:42
	1955	1956	1957	1958	1959	1960	1961	1962	1963
	4 Feb	5 Feb	4 Feb	4 Feb	4 Feb	5 Feb	4 Feb	4 Feb	4 Feb
	21:29	03:15	09:07	14:57	20:47	02:38	08:29	14:24	20:17
	1964	1965	1966	1967	1968	1969	1970	1971	1972
	5 Feb	4 Feb	4 Feb	4 Feb	5 Feb	4 Feb	4 Feb	4 Feb	5 Feb
	02:08	07:57	13:46	19:32	01:19	07:04	12:50	18:37	00:23
	1973	1974	1975	1976	1977	1978	1979	1980	1981
	4 Feb	4 Feb	4 Feb	4 Feb	4 Feb	4 Feb	4 Feb	4 Feb	4 Feb
	06:13	12.08	17:56	23:48	05:38	11:28	17:21	23:10	04:59
	1982	1983	1984	1985	1986	1987	1988	1989	1990
	4 Feb	4 Feb	4 Feb	4 Feb	4 Feb	4 Feb	4 Feb	4 Feb	4 Feb
	10:53	16.83	22:27	04:18	10:05	15:57	21:42	05:28	09:20
	1991	1992	1993	1994	1995	1996	1997	1998	1999
	4 Feb	4 Feb	4 Feb	4 Feb	4 Feb	4 Feb	4 Feb	4 Feb	4 Feb
	15.04	20:51	02:42	08:27	14:18	20:10	02:00	08:01	13:51
	2000	2001	2002	2003	2004	2005	2006	2007	2008
	4 Feb	4 Feb	4 Feb	4 Feb	4 Feb	4 Feb	4 Feb	4 Feb	4 Feb
	19:39	01:35	07:20	13:08	18:57	00:38	06:31	12:16	17:59
	2009	2010	2011	2012	2013	2014	2015	2016	2017
	3 Feb	4 Feb	4 Feb	4 Feb	3 Feb	4 Feb	4 Feb	4 Feb	3 Feb
	23:55	05:40	11:31	17:28	23:05	05:05	10:55	16:40	22:37

relationships

You can use your nine ki numbers to try to predict how you will feel in a particular relationship. One way to approach it is to look at which of the five elements is associated with each number and see how they relate to each other.

• A relationship between people with the same ki energy helps them to understand each other better and potentially reach a closer relationship. However, there is a risk that the relationship could become stagnant, if they know each other too well.

• A relationship between people whose elements are next to each other in the five element cycle is potentially harmonious and supportive. People often naturally find that they are attracted to people who either support or calm their energy.

• Two people with elements that are opposite each other on the five element cycle will find each other different and exciting. In these relationships there can be great attraction, although it is difficult for each person to understand the other.

WATER & WATER
In this relationship, as both have the same kind of energy they will identify with each other but being independent they should respect each other's desire to spend time alone. More metal energy in the form of the colour pink or sleeping with their heads pointing west or north-west will help bring these two people closer together.

WATER & TREE
This is a harmonious relationship where the person with water energy is supportive of the person with tree energy. The nature of water energy is to be independent while tree energy is busy and career orientated. A water energy person who feels tired should try wearing pink, red or grey and sleeping with the top of his or her head pointing west or north-west.

WATER & FIRE
The social outgoing nature of fire energy is at odds with the more independent spiritual water energy. One way to make this relationship more harmonious is to introduce more tree energy, creating a new compatible relationship between water, tree and fire. They could try sleeping with the top of their heads pointing east or south-east, growing more indoor plants and using more green.

WATER & SOIL
The soil energy person is more careful, stifling the water energy person's independent spirit. The water energy person's desire to go with the flow could make the other feel insecure. Greater metal energy in the form of material wealth, sleeping with the tops of their heads pointing west or north-west, as well as more pink, silver or grey would help make this relationship more harmonious.

WATER & METAL
The metal energy person is solid and supportive of the water energy person's energy. A metal energy person tends to enjoy the love and affection that the water person can offer. For greater metal energy they should try sleeping with the tops of their heads pointing west or north-west, as well as more pink, silver or grey will help reduce the risk of the metal energy person feeling drained.

TREE & TREE
Tree energy people will have good understanding of each other and will both be able to pursue their careers actively. It will be a more career-orientated relationship, and the risk is that it could lack passion, intimacy and affection. They may lack patience with one another and should try adding more quiet water chi energy, using a cream colour and a water feature in the east or south-east.

TREE & FIRE

The tree energy person will be supportive of the fire energy person and both will enjoy an active, outgoing life. The tree energy person will stimulate the fire energy person in terms of being ambitious and building up his or her career, while the fire energy person will be able to make social connections and organize an active social life. They should try sleeping with the tops of their heads pointing east or south-east, growing plants and using the colour green.

TREE & SOIL

Tree energy will tend to overwhelm the soil energy. The person with tree energy will be enthusiastic to get on with life and could become impatient and frustrated with the soil energy person's more careful approach. Under these circumstances the soil energy person can feel harried. If both of them are particularly sociable, it will add more fire energy, improving the situation. They should try placing candles in the south and using more purple to boost fire energy.

TREE & METAL

The risk is that the metal energy will stifle the enthusiasm of the tree energy. A metal energy person can be too organized and methodical for the go-ahead, more reckless style of the tree energy person. An active sex life will bring in more water energy as will sleeping with the tops of their heads pointing north.

FIRE & FIRE

Both people will be emotional, passionate and enjoy a social life. However, any arguments could be intense and explosive and lead to frequent separations. These upsets should blow over, although the relationship will be fiery. If this is the case, soil energy will have a calming influence. This can be increased if they were to sleep with the top of their heads pointing south-west or using more yellow in the home.

FIRE & SOIL

This is a harmonious relationship. The fire energy person adds sparkle, spontaneity and passion into the soil energy person's life, while the soil energy person helps calm the more fiery, over emotional side of the fire energy person.

They both bring a warm-hearted, caring approach to the relationship. The fire energy person will be good at building up a circle of friends while the soil energy person will maintain long-term friendships.

FIRE & METAL

The fiery, passionate, spontaneous fire energy person may find the metal energy person too reserved and organized, while he or she will tend to be too flamboyant and impossible to pin down. For this relationship to succeed they will need more soil energy in the form of building a home and family together. They should try sleeping with the tops of their heads pointing south-west and using more yellow in the home.

SOIL & SOIL

These people share many values in life and have the ability to understand each other well. The risk with this relationship is that they could get bored with each other and feel the need to find more exciting company. They should try adding more fire in the form of a reddish purple colour, candles in the south and an active social life.

SOIL & METAL

This is a harmonious relationship where the metal energy person appreciates the caring nature of the soil energy person. They both like to plan and take a long-term approach to life and should grow closer together. If the soil energy person feels drained it may help if both people absorb more soil energy by sleeping with the tops of their heads pointing south-west and using more yellow in the home.

METAL & METAL

This can be a harmonious relationship with common interests in material wealth, style and having fun. However, more soil energy will help make this a more intimate, long-term relationship. People in this type of relationship should try sleeping with their heads pointing south-west or west and using more yellow in the home.

timing

In nine ki astrology the prevailing ki energy at the time of an important event in your life will stay with you for many years. For example, if you were to start a romantic relationship at a favourable time it will increase the chance of it getting off to a good start. The initial patterns that become established at the beginning of a relationship can become the rock on which you get through difficulties in later years.

Conversely, if you start a relationship when you or your partner is going through a difficult time, you may set up more destructive patterns of behaviour that become recurring themes as the relationship progresses.

Similarly, if you begin a new business venture at a favourable time and enjoy success it is easy to ride through any difficulties later because of the momentum of your earlier successes. If you start a business at a time when you are vulnerable you may

The following chart provides information on the kind of emotions/ attitudes that you might experience, together with activities that might come easily to you during each phase. Also listed are the nine phases of a relationship and a business cycle.

DIRECTION	EMOTIONS/ATTITUDES	PHASES OF A RELATIONSHIP	BUSINESS CYCLE
EAST tree	Enthusiastic, ambitious, active, confident and focused. Starting new projects. Building up your career.	You will be more active and positive with your lover, but may be more irritable, short tempered and less inclined to listen.	Good for starting projects.
SOUTH-EAST tree	Creative, imaginative, persistent and communicative. Travel, writing, music, art.	You will tend to seek greater harmony in your relationship, avoiding confrontation. Could be more persistent and find it is easier to feel positive about your relationship.	Good for expansion and marketing will help develop. internationally. Good for travel and distribution.
CENTRE soil	Powerful, changeable, forceful and attracting attention. New opportunities. Interesting offers.	You will enjoy being the centre of attention. You may be more indecisive with regards to your feelings towards your lover and could be tempted by others.	A period of change which can help become adaptable. Good for attracting interesting opportunities.
NORTH-WEST metal	Dignified, self disciplined, wisdom, organized and in control. Leadership. Finding a mentor.	You will developing mutual respect, as well as setting your relationship on a more serious and permanent footing. You could become too domineering.	Stronger leadership helps the development of long-term-plans. Easier to gain trust and respect.

never build up the confidence, self belief and momentum to carry you through any problems that might occur. For this reason, those events that have a profound influence on you are the ones that need the greatest consideration in nine ki astrology.

First locate the year you are interested in on the chart on page 154 and then find your nine ki year number in that column. For instance, if you want to know which phase you will be in during 2005 look at the column with the 2005 at the top.

Next find your own nine ki number in the year column. Look across the row until you find the direction that applies to your number. For example, if your nine ki year number is seven your number will be in the row that corresponds to north-east in 2005. Therefore, if your nine ki number is seven in the year 2005, you will be influenced by the chi energy of the north-east.

This chart works on a nine year cycle so it is easy to expand the charts into the future as far as you wish to keep track of your nine ki number for specific phases. You will notice 2002 to 2010 follow this nine year cycle completely and the numbers will then start to repeat themselves in 2011. On a piece of paper you can add further columns and continue into the future by **decreasing** the number in each column by one. Once you get to one begin again at nine.

Similarly, you can extend the chart to the left and look at past years going back as far as you wish. This is useful if you want to work out what phase you were in at a particular time in the past, perhaps in reference to an important event in your life. This time, **increase** the numbers in the columns by one everytime you go

DIRECTION	EMOTIONS/ATTITUDES	PHASES OF A RELATIONSHIP	BUSINESS CYCLE
WEST metal	Content, seeking pleasure, romantic and fun-loving. Greater financial awareness.	You will be contented, seeking pleasure, romantic and fun-loving. You will develop a new relationship.	Easier to ncrease profitability and raise finance. Good for completing projects.
NORTH-EAST soil	Motivated, quick, decisive, competitive and clear thinking. Winning things. Sports. Quick profits. Investments.	You will be in a playful, boisterous phase in which you do a lot together. You may feel more like fighting with your lover and are better able to stand your ground.	Ideal to be more competitive and quicker to react to opportunities.
SOUTH fire	Expressive, emotional, generous, social, noticeable. Winning awards. Being noticed. Building a reputation.	You are in a more passionate, warm and generous phase. You may feel argumentative and could react strongly if your pride is hurt.- Big bust-ups followed by emotional reunions are likely.	Better able to increase sales through positive PR. Easier to be noticed.
NORTH water	Independent, peaceful, spiritual, flexible and objective. A new approach to life. Studies. Healing. Conception.	This is an ideal time for sex, affection and exploring each others deeper side. You could become more aloof and drift away from your lover. Ideal time for conception.	Good for concentrating on internal systems becoming more flexible. Easier to be objective.
SOUTH-WEST soil	Practical, realistic, intimate, caring and sympathetic. Motherhood. Relationships. Adding quality to life.	You will feel cosy, comfortable and intimate with your lover. You may prefer to stay in together, but could lose the excitement and spontaneity in your relationship.	Develop more harmonious relationshps with its employees and clients. Improve quality of business.

It is most useful to use the nine ki system to plan ahead, using a five-year plan with a list of things you would like to achieve. When you do this you can set out your goals and see which years would be best to act on them. For example, if you want to start a new relationship see if you will be in the south-east, south-west or west in the coming years.

back a year. For example, in 2001 your number in the east will be 6 and in 2000 it will be 7, and so on.

The chart on pages 152–3 shows you how each phase can influence your energy and, therefore, your emotions, thoughts and behaviour. Each phase is associated with one of the five elements and your own nine ki year number is also associated with an element. In the phases when your five element is harmonious with the element of the year you should feel more comfortable and life will flow a little easier. Conversely, when you are in a phase where your element is not harmonious with the element of the year, you may find you feel ill-at-ease or less able to embrace the energy of that phase.

YEAR CHART										
	2002	**2003**	**2004**	**2005**	**2006**	**2007**	**2008**	**2009**	**2010**	**2011**
EAST	5	4	3	2	1	9	8	7	6	5
SOUTH-EAST	6	5	4	3	2	1	9	8	7	6
CENTRE	7	6	5	4	3	2	1	9	8	7
NORTH-WEST	8	7	6	5	4	3	2	1	9	8
WEST	9	8	7	6	5	4	3	2	1	9
NORTH-WEST	1	9	8	7	6	5	4	3	2	1
SOUTH	2	1	9	8	7	6	5	4	3	2
NORTH	3	2	1	9	8	7	6	5	4	3
SOUTH-WEST	4	3	2	1	9	8	7	6	5	4

glossary

ABDOMEN
Front of your body between your ribs and pubic bone. The centre of this area is known as the hara in Japan and considered to be the area where you store chi energy.

ANIMALS
The five animals used in feng shui – dragon, phoenix, tiger, tortoise and snake – are used to describe your outer chi energy field.

CHAKRAS
These are seven areas – crown, mid-brain, throat, heart, stomach, abdomen/hara and reproductive organs – where there is a greater concentration and movement of chi energy.

CHI ENERGY
A subtle electromagnetic energy that flows through the universe eventually connecting everything. In humans it carries our thoughts, ideas and emotions.

CONVEX
A fish eye shape. It can apply to a mirror, metal plate or glass.

CUTTING CHI (OR FAST-FLOWING CHI)
Fast-flowing chi energy, also known as sha chi, that can have the affect of cutting through other slow moving chi energy.

EIGHT DIRECTIONS
The four cardinal points of the compass – east, south, west and north – with the directions in-between – south-east, south-west, north-west and north-east – make up the eight directions that are used in the Japanese Compass system. Each direction carries a certain kind of energy.

EMF
EMF stands for electromagnetic fields, which are the magnetic fields created by an electric current. These distort the earth's magnetic field and when close to a person, submerge them in a stronger artificial field. There are concerns that this could increase the risk of cancer.

FIVE ELEMENTS
Five natural elements – wood/tree, fire, soil/earth, metal and water–- are used to describe five types of chi energy that are based on the seasons and times of day.

FLUORESCENT LIGHTS
An electric current is passed through a glass tube containing a low pressure vapour to produce ultraviolet radiation, which is converted into a visible light by a coating on the tube. These are also used for extra economy bulbs.

HALOGEN LIGHTS
A light where the filament is surrounded by a halogen vapour. It is often used with a transformer to produce a low-voltage light.

HARMONIOUS
In the context of feng shui, harmonious means that the different chi energies mix easily and enhance each other.

I CHING
An ancient Chinese book that will provide advice based on a process of divination that produces a hexigram – based on two trigrams.

KIRILIAN PHOTOGRAPHY
A form of photography invented by the Russian scientist Kirilian that captures a field of energy around any living thing on film.

MAGIC SQUARE
Fu Hsi's magic square consists of the numbers one to nine arranged in a square so that whichever way you add any straight line of three numbers they always add up to fifteen.

MAGNETIC NORTH
This is the north that the needle of a compass points to and will be a few degrees different to map north, which is based on the position of the north pole.

MERIDIANS
There are 14 paths of chi energy that flow through the body. Along each meridian are acupressure points, known as tsubos, where the flow of energy can changed more easily.

NINE KI
Ki is the Japanese word for chi energy and nine ki refers to the nine types of energy that make up the magic square. These are used as the basis for astrology in this version of feng shui.

PROTRUDING CORNER
This type of corner is the outside of a right-angle which points into a room, for example, the edge of a wardrobe, as opposed to an internal corner which is the inside of the right angle.

REFRACTING
Changes the course of a wave of energy as it passes from one medium to another. For example, the changing of the direction of light waves as they pass through a crystal.

TRIGAMS
Three horizontal lines drawn above each other. The lines are either broken representing yin, or solid representing yang. Each trigram is associated with one of the eight directions.

YIN AND YANG
Yang represents the sunny side of the mountain while yin represents the shady side of the mountain. The yin-yang symbol shows the yang with a dot of yin in its centre, the yang energy flows into yin. At its fullest point, yin has a dot of yang in its centre. Yin and yang are used to describe chi energy in its various states.

index

index

acknowledgements

Abode 21 left, 113 left, /Andreas von Einsiedel 76, /Trevor Richards 10, /Lucinda Symons 60, /Simon Whitmore 28, 41, 90, 102.

Arcaid/ Richard Bryant/ Architect: Chris Rudolf 96 right, /Richard Bryant/ Architect: Geoffrey Bawa 122 right, /David Churchill 36 left, /Richard Powers 42, 108, /Alan Weintraub/ Architect: Jersey Devil 61 top left.

Bubbles/ Loisjoy Thurston 34.

Carroll & Brown Publishers/ 31 left.

Garden Picture Library/ Eric Crichton 127, /John Glover/ Designer: Paul Dyer 126 right, /Howard Rice 66, /David Russell 62, /Georgia Glynn-Smith/ RHS Chelsea flower show 1997 140, /Friedrich Strauss 116 right, /Ron Sutherland 126 left, /Ron Sutherland/ Designer: Anthony Paul 125.

Octopus Publishing Group Limited/ David Loftus 32, 33 right, 46, 47, /Tom Minnion 48, /Peter Myers 14, 19, 45 right, 52, 87 right, 107, /Ian Wallace 20 left, 21 right, 30, 33 Top, 36 right, /Mark Winwood 24, /Polly Wreford 31 right, 75, /Mel Yates 20 right, 56, 124.

Jerry Harpur/ Designer: Jeff Bale, USA 65, /Cordoba, Spain 61 right, /Designer: Sonny Garcia, San Francisco, USA 118 bottom right, /Designer: Maggie Gundry 116 left, /Designer: Cari Niels, Dallas, USA 64.

Marcus Harpur/ Designer: Bunny Guinness, RHS Chelsea 1998 61 bottom left, /Designer: Chris Grey-Wilson 123 right.

©**Inter IKEA Systems B.V. 2001**/ WWW.IKEA.co.uk 119.

The Interior Archive/ Tim Beddow 43, /Helen Fickling/ landscape design: Gerrit Burger/ Eric Duplan 118 left, /Helen Fickling/ landscape design: Jeff Nichols/ Patrick Watson 57, /Helen Fickling/ landscape design: Patrick Watson 123 left, /Simon McBride/ Garden: Eden,

Corsham 122 left, /Jonathan Pilkington 91 Top, 97 left, /Fritz von der Schulenburg/ Architect: Nico Rensch 27, /Fritz von der Schulenburg/ Designer: Mimmi O'Connell 115 bottom right, /Simon Upton/ Designer: David Hare 49, /Henry Wilson/ Designer: Brett Muldoon 70, /Henry Wilson/ Designer: Denise Lee 77 bottom right, /Peter Woloszynski 63, /Edina van der Wyck 51, /Edina van der Wyck/ Stylist: Atlanta Bartlett 106.

©**Ray Main**/ Mainstream 9, 25, 26 left, 26 right, 35, 37 left, 38, 40, 44, 50, 74 left, 78, 82, 83, 84, 86, 87 left, 91 Bottom, 93 left, 93 right, 94 right, 94 Top, 95 left, 97 right, 103 left, 114 left, /C2 Architects 37 right, /Nash Architects 143, /Designer: Oriana Fielding Banks 95 centre, /Architect: Brian Ma Siy 55, /Designer: Phillipe Starck 54, /Designer: Vincente Wolfe 45 left

Narratives/Jan Baldwin 77 centre, 85, /Jan Baldwin/ Interior Design Anabelle Blake 142, /Jan Baldwin/ Roger Oates Design 71, 113 right.

Red Cover/Christopher Blake 112 right, /Andreas von Einsiedel 112 left, /Jake Fitzjones 74 right, /Ken Hayden 29, 100, /Winfried Heinze 103 right, /Verity Welstead 96 left.

Executive Editor **Anna Southgate**
Editor **Abi Rowsell**
Senior Designer **Rozelle Bentheim**
Designer **Ruth Hope**
Production Controller **Lucy Woodhead**
Picture Researcher **Zoë Holtermann**
Indexer **Hilary Bird**

Icon design **Ruth Hope**
Room plan artworks **Thomas Lisle**
Illustrations **Trevor Bounford**

CONSULTATIONS WITH SIMON G. BROWN

Simon Brown and his colleagues John and Maria Brosnan provide a complete consultation service. Consultations can be arranged to include a site visit or they can all be done by post. These consultations include floor plans with all our feng shui recommendations, a full report including a survey, explanation of the recommendations, feng shui astrology information for this year and the next three years, your best directions for this year and the best dates to implement the recommendations. On going advice by telephone is also included.

COURSES WITH SIMON G. BROWN

Simon provides a variety of courses ranging from one-day introductory courses to a six-day certificate course with homework and an assessment. Please see the website for dates and locations. He also conducts a range of courses for architects and designers.

BOOKS BY SIMON G. BROWN

Simon Brown is a well-known author with his best selling book *Practical Feng Shui* having sold over 500,000 copies.

Practical Feng Shui

Published by Cassell & Co ISBN 0-7063-7634-X

The Principles of Feng Shui

Published by Thorsons an imprint of Harper Collins. ISBN 0-7225-3347-0
Also available as an audio cassette and read by Michael Maloney

Practical Feng Shui For Business

Published by Ward Lock ISBN 0-7063-7768-0

Practical Feng Shui Astrology

Published by Ward Lock ISBN 0-7063-7825-3

Essential Feng Shui

Published by Cassell and Co ISBN 0-7063-7854-7

Feng Shui Food

Written with Steven Saunders and published by Thorsons ISBN 0-7225-3934-7

Practical Feng Shui Solutions

Published by Cassell and Co ISBN 0-304-35476-7

The Practical Art of Face Reading

Published by Carroll & Brown ISBN 1-903258-08-1

Feng Shui

Published by Thorsons ISBN 0-00-719337-9

AKNOWLEDGEMENTS

A great many thanks to all those who have been a big part of my life while writing this book. Especially my gorgeous lover Dragana, mother Patricia, children Christopher, Alexander, Nicholas and Michael; family Adam, Angela, Melanie, Denny, Rosa, Jelena, Mica, Milos and Ankica; dearest friends Jeremy, George, Micheal, Dusica and Enno, Karin, John and Maria, Kim, Henry and Martha, Camilo, Hans and Paola, Shaun, Dave, Roland. Everyone at Norman Motors and all those not on this list. A huge thank you to Alison, Jane and Anna who had the vision and energy to make this book a reality.

CONTACT DETAILS

Simon G. Brown, PO Box 10453, London, NW3 4WD

Tel **020 7431 9897**

Fax **020 7431 9897**

E mail **simon@chienergy.co.uk**

Web site **www.chienergy.co.uk**

INFORMATION ON SIMON BROWN – FENG SHUI CONSULTANT

Simon Brown qualified as a design engineer having two inventions patented in his name. He then began studies in Oriental medicine in 1981 and qualified as a Shiatsu therapist and Macrobiotic consultant. While studying these healing arts he studied feng shui with Japanese masters in the USA. Simon Brown was the director of London's Community Health Foundation for seven years, a charity which ran a wide range of courses specialising in the Oriental healing arts. During this time he was responsible for organising the first major feng shui courses in this country. Simon has, since 1993, made feng shui his full time career. His clients include well-known celebrities such as Boy George and large public companies including The Body Shop and British Airways. He is the author of the UK's best selling **Practical Feng Shui** as well as **The Principles of Feng Shui**. Simon has written numerous articles including those for *Feng Shui For Modern Living*, *Cosmopolitan* and *Vogue* as well as a weekly column for the *Saturday Express*. He has also been involved in many television and radio programmes. Simon is a member of the Feng Shui Society and is currently engaged in setting standards for feng shui education in the UK.